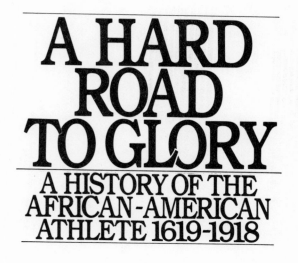

A HARD ROAD TO GLORY

A HISTORY OF THE AFRICAN-AMERICAN ATHLETE 1619-1918

ARTHUR R. ASHE, JR.

A HARD ROAD TO GLORY

A HISTORY OF THE AFRICAN-AMERICAN ATHLETE 1619-1918

WITH THE ASSISTANCE OF
KIP BRANCH, OCANIA CHALK, AND FRANCIS HARRIS

WARNER BOOKS

A Warner Communications Company

An Amistad Book

Warner Books, Inc., 666 Fifth Avenue, New York, NY 10103

 A Warner Communications Company

Printed in the United States of America
First Printing November 1988
10 9 8 7 6 5 4 3 2

Library of Congress Cataloging-in-Publication Data

Ashe, Arthur.
    A hard road to glory : a history of the African-American athlete,
1619-1918 / Arthur R. Ashe, Jr.
    p. cm.
    ISBN 0-446-71006-7
    1. Afro-Americans—Sports—History—20th century.   2. Afro
-American athletes.   I. Title.
GV583.A75 1988   88-20682
796′.08996073—dc19   CIP

Packaged by Rapid Transcript, a division
of March Tenth, Inc.

To my wife, Jeanne, and my daughter, Camera

CONTENTS

FOREWORD *ix*

ACKNOWLEDGMENTS *xiii*

INTRODUCTION *3*

Chapter 1   Boxing *17*

Chapter 2   Horse Racing *43*

Chapter 3   Cycling *54*

Chapter 4   Track and Field *58*

Chapter 5   Baseball *68*

Chapter 6   Football *89*

Chapter 7   Basketball *104*

REFERENCE SECTION *111*

SOURCES *177*

INDEX *187*

Foreword

This book began in a classroom at Florida Memorial College in Miami, Florida, in 1983. I was asked to teach a course, The Black Athlete in Contemporary Society, by Jefferson Rogers of the school's Center for Community Change. When I tried to find a book detailing what has surely been the African-American's most startling saga of successes, I found that the last attempt had been made exactly twenty years before.

I then felt compelled to write this story, for I literally grew up on a sports field. My father was the caretaker of the largest public park for blacks in Richmond, Virginia. Set out in a fanlike pattern at Brookfield Playground was an Olympic-size pool, a basketball court, four tennis courts, three baseball diamonds, and two football fields. Our five-room home was actually on these premises. Little wonder I later became a professional athlete.

My boyhood idol was Jackie Robinson, as was the case with every black kid in America in the late 1940s and early 1950s. But I had no appreciation of what he went through or, more importantly, what others like him had endured. I had never heard of Jack Johnson, Marshall Taylor, Isaac Murphy, or Howard P. Drew—icons in athletics but seldom heralded in the post-World War II period.

These and others have been the most accomplished figures in the African-American subculture. They were vastly better known in their times than people such as Booker T. Washington, William E.B. Du Bois, or Marcus Garvey. They inspired idolatry bordering on deification, and thousands more wanted to follow. Indeed, in the pretelevision days of radio, Joe Louis's bouts occasioned impromptu celebration because, between 1934 and 1949, Louis lost only once.

But if contemporary black athletes' exploits are more well known, few fully appreciate their true Hard Road to Glory. Discrimination, vilification, incarceration, dissipation, ruination, and ultimate despair have dogged the steps of the mightiest of these heroes. And, only a handful in the last 179 years have been able to live out their post-athletic lives in peace and prosperity.

This book traces the development of African-American athletes from their ancestral African homelands in the seventeenth century through the present era. Their exploits are explored in a historical context, as all African-American successes were constrained by discriminatory laws, customs, and traditions.

As I began to complete my research, I realized that the subject was more extensive than I had thought. All of the material would not fit into one volume. Therefore, I have divided the work as follows:

Volume I covers the emergence of sports as adjuncts to daily life from the time of ancient civilizations like Egypt through World War I. Wars tend to compartmentalize eras and this story is no different. Major successes of African-Americans occurred in the ninteenth century, for example, which are simply glossed over in most examinations of the period.

Volume II examines black athletics during that vital twenty-year period between the World Wars. No greater contrast exists than that between the 1920s—the Golden Decade of Sports—and the Depression-plagued 1930s. The infrastructure of American athletics as we know it today was set during these crucial years, and the civil rights apparatus that would lead to integration in the post–World War II era was formalized. Popular African-American literature and its press augmented the already cosmic fame of athletes such as Jesse Owens and Joe Louis, who were the first black athletes to be admired by all Americans.

Volume III is set between World War II and the present. It begins with an unprecedented five-year period—1946 through 1950—in which football, baseball, basketball, tennis, golf, and bowling became integrated. These breakthroughs, coupled with the already heady showings in track and

boxing, provided enough incentive for African-Americans to embark on nothing less than an all-out effort for athletic fame and fortune.

The reference sections in each volume document the major successes of these gladiators. These records are proof positive of effort and dedication on the playing field. More importantly, they are proof of what the African-American can do when allowed to compete equally in a framework governed by a set of rules.

Each volume is divided into individual sport histories Primary source materials were not to be found in the local public library and not even in New York City's Fifth Avenue Public Library. Chroniclers of America's early sports heroes simply left out most of their darker brothers and sisters except when they participated in white-controlled events. Much had to be gleaned, therefore, from the basements, attics, and closets of African-Americans themselves.

Interviews were invaluable in cross-referencing dubious written records. Where discrepancies occurred, I have stated so; but I have tried to reach the most logical conclusion. Some unintentional errors are inevitable. The author welcomes confirmed corrections and additions. If validated, they will be included in the next edition of this work.

Today, thousands of young African-Americans continue to seek their places in the sun through athletics. For some African-Americans the dream has bordered on a pathological obsession. But unless matters change, the majority may end up like their predecessors. Perhaps this history will ease the journey with sober reflections of how difficult and improbable the Hard Road really is. In no way, however, do I care to dissuade any young athlete from dreaming of athletic glory. Surely every American at some time has done so.

A word about nomenclature. Sociologists have referred to nearly all immigrant groups in hyphenated form: Irish-Americans, Italian-Americans, and Jewish-Americans. African-Americans are no different, and this term is correct. Throughout this book, I shall, however, use the modern designation *"black"* to refer to African-Americans. The appellations *Negro* and *colored* may also appear, but usually in quotes and only when I thought such usage may be more appropriate in a particular context.

Acknowledgments

A *Hard Road to Glory* would have been impossible without the help, assistance, contributions, and encouragement of many people. Initial moral support came from Reverend Jefferson Rogers, formerly of Florida Memorial College; Professor Louis "Skip" Gates of Cornell University; Howard Cosell; Marie Brown; my editor, Charles F. Harris; and my literary agent, Fifi Oscard. All made me believe it could be done. An inspiring letter urging me to press on also came from Professor John Hope Franklin of Duke University, who advised that this body of work was needed to fill a gap in African-American history.

My staff has been loyal and faithful to the end these past four years. I have been more than ably assisted by Kip Branch, who has stood by me from the first day; and by Ocania Chalk, whose two previous books on black collegiate athletes and other black athletic pioneers provided so much of the core material for *A Hard Road to Glory*. To my personal assistant, Derilene McCloud, go special thanks for coordinating, typing, filing, phoning, and organizing the information and interviews, as well as keeping my day-to-day affairs in order. Sandra Jamison's skills in library science were invaluable in the beginning. Her successor, Rod Howard, is now a virtual walking encyclopedia of information about black athletes, especially those in college. To Francis Harris, who almost single-handedly constructed the reference sections, I am truly grateful. And to Deborah McRae, who sat through hundreds of hours of typing—her assistance is not forgotten.

Institutions have been very helpful and forthcoming. The people at the New York Public Library Annex went out of their way to search for books. *The New York Times* provided access to back issues. The Norfolk, Virginia, Public Library was kind and considerate. This book could not have been done without the kind help of the Schomburg Library for Research in Black Culture in Harlem, New York. Its photography curator, Deborah Willis Thomas, found many photographs for me, and Ernest Kaiser followed my work with interest.

The Enoch Pratt Free Library in Baltimore, Maryland; the Moorland-Spingarn Library at Howard University in Washington, D.C.; and the Library of Congress not only assisted but were encouraging and courteous. The offices of the Central Intercollegiate Athletic Association, the Southern Intercollegiate Athletic Conference, the Mideastern Athletic Conference, and the Southwest Athletic Conference dug deep to find information on past black college

xiii

sports. The National Collegiate Athletic Association and the National Association for Intercollegiate Athletics were quick with information about past and present athletes. The home offices of major league baseball, the National Basketball Association, the National Football League, and their archivists and Halls of Fame were eager to provide assistance. Joe Corrigan went out of his way to lend a hand.

The staffs at Tuskegee University and Tennessee State University were particularly kind. Wallace Jackson at Alabama A&M was helpful with information on the Southern Intercollegiate Athletic Conference. Alvin Hollins at Florida A&M University was eager to assist. Lynn Abraham of New York City found a rare set of boxing books for me. Lou Robinson of Claremont, California, came through in a pinch with information on black Olympians, and Margaret Gordon of the American Tennis Association offered her assistance.

Many people offered to be interviewed for this project. Two of them, Eyre Saitch, Nell Jackson, Dr. Reginald Weir and Ric Roberts, have since passed on, and I am truly grateful for their recollections. Others who agreed to sit and talk with Kip Branch, Ocania Chalk, or me include William "Pop" Gates, Elgin Baylor, Oscar Robertson, Anita DeFranz, Nikki Franke, Peter Westbrook, Paul Robeson, Jr., Afro-American sportswriter Sam Lacy, A.S. "Doc" young, Frederick "Fritz" Pollard, Jr., Mel Glover, Calvin Peete, Oscar Johnson, Althea Gibson, Mrs. Ted Paige, Charles Sifford, Howard Gentry, Milt Campbell, Otis Troupe, Beau Jack, Coach and Mrs. Jake Gaither, Lynn Swann, Franco Harris, Dr. Richard Long of Atlanta University, Dr. Leonard Jeffries of the City

College of New York, Dr. Elliot Skinner of Columbia University, and Dr. Ben Jochannon.

Dr. Maulana Karenga of Los Angeles and Dr. William J. Baker of the Unversity of Maine offered material and guidance on African sports. Dr. Ofuatey Kodjo of Queens College in New York City helped edit this same information. Norris Horton of the United Golfers Association provided records, and Margaret Lee of the National Bowling Association answered every inquiry with interest. To Nick Seitz of *Golf Digest* and *Tennis*, I offer thanks for his efforts. Professors Barbara Cooke, Patsy B. Perry, Kenneth Chambers, Floyd Ferebee, and Tom Scheft of North Carolina Central University were kind enough to read parts of the manuscript, as did Mr. and Mrs. Donald Baker. Professor Eugene Beecher of Wilson College, an unabashed sports fan, shuttled many clippings our way.

To the dozens of people who heard about my book on Bob Law's *Night Talk* radio show and sent unsolicited but extremely valuable information, I cannot thank you enough. And to the hundreds of unsung African-American athletes who played under conditions of segregation and whose skills and talents were never known to the general public, I salute you and hope this body of work in some measure vindicates and redresses that gross miscarriage of our American ideals.

Finally, to my wife Jeanne Moutoussamy-Ashe, I owe gratitude and tremendous appreciation for her understanding, patience, tolerance, and sacrifice of time so I could complete this book.

Arthur R. Ashe, Jr.
1988

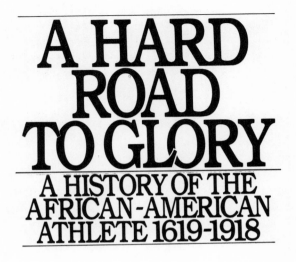

A HARD ROAD TO GLORY

A HISTORY OF THE AFRICAN-AMERICAN ATHLETE 1619-1918

Introduction

Emergence

The black athlete's fame is primarily a product of Western civilization. Western man's penchant for empires and exploration led to such events as the Olympic Games in democratic Greece and the Circus Maximus in the grand design of Rome. As William J. Baker points out, "Competitive sport thrives most in societies where achievement rather than mere birth is the means to success and acclaim."[1] It is probable that if there had been no slave trade—which brought upward of 15 million Africans to American shores—there would be far fewer black athletic heroes anywhere.

Egypt

This story begins, as does the history of all humankind, in the northeastern corner of the African continent. Etched in pottery and art pieces and painted on the tombs of pharaohs and nobles are Egyptian scenes of sports and ball games. In bas-relief and in multicolored hues are depictions of boxing, fencing, swimming, rowing, archery, equestrianism, jumping, running, wrestling, and stick fighting. The tomb of Beni-Hasan is especially graphic.

Religious texts from circa 2200 B.C. mention ball games. The balls used were thought to be divinely directed. Nearly all sports up to and through the American Civil War were limited in some way by prevailing religious thought. State occasions and religious holidays were the times most often mentioned for public displays of athletic prowess. Stick fighting, weight lifting, and wrestling were favored forms of entertainment for visiting dignitaries. During religious festivals, parades preceded the priests from temples like that dedicated to Osiris to areas where ball games were more "acted out" than played out. It was a high honor to be chosen to participate.

Even rulers themselves sometimes even tried their hand in contests. King Amenophis II (1438–12 B.C.) was noted for his athletic skills. According to legend, he was a swift runner, a skilled archer, and a strong rower.[2]

Greece

The ancient Greeks' love of sports bordered on mania. In fact, the Greek word for "athletic contest" is *agon*, from which the word *agony* is derived. Their term for *athlete* translates to "trial" or "contest." In the eighth book of Homer's *Odyssey*, a son of Kind Alcinous taunts Odysseus by imploring, "Come along, sir, have a try at the games yourself, if you have any skill. Sports is the best way to fame for any man alive— what you can do with your arms and legs."

The Greeks believed in maintaining a sound body while cultivating the mind. But the philosopher Aristotle noted that "What is wanted is not the bodily condition of an athlete nor on the other hand a weak and invalid condition, but one that lies between the two." In their open-air gymnasiums, erected for healthful exercise, lectures were given by esteemed orators of the day. Even their mythology reeked of athletic exploits. Zeus was the mightiest god because he defeated Cronus in a test of strength. When competing, young athletes swore by Zeus to obey the rules.

Greece's most memorable bequest was the Olympic Games, the world's first national conclave dedicated to athletic excellence and in honor of the gods. These now famous contests were first held in 776 B.C. in a remote valley near the confluence of the Cladeus and Alpheus Rivers. They lasted five days; the first was given over entirely to religious observances. Hymns were sung, prayers were recited, and oaths were pledged, all in honor of Zeus. The first recorded event was a foot race of about 200 yards. At its height, nearly fifty thousand male spectators (no women were allowed to compete) watched the athletes in running, jumping, chariot racing, boxing, wrestling, and the like. Even junior events were added in 632 B.C.

All these events were individual endeavors, as team sports were considered too genteel. The contestants performed in the nude, although flies and other insects plagued spectators and athletes alike. The highest honors went to the winners of the five-event pentathlon, that included the discus, the javelin, the broad jump, the 200-meter dash, and wrestling. (Even the philosopher Plato got his name from his wrestling coach. His former name was Aristocles.) Although initially only the upper classes participated, this elitism soon gave way to a cadre of professional athletes who were sponsored by patrons and trained all year long.

The Olympics were not the only games dedicated to the gods. A competition for women, the Heraean Games, were held at Olympus in honor of Hera, Zeus's wife-sister. The Pythian Games were staged every fourth year in honor of Apollo. The Isthmian Games in honor of Poseidon were held at Corinth (Plato once participated); another contest, the Nemean Games, also honored Zeus. But only the Olympics bestowed the prized olive wreath on its victors. Perhaps Western civilization might not have taken organized sports so seriously if the cradle of democracy had not embraced it so enthusiastically.

The Romans

The Romans bastardized Greek sports and used them to pacify conquered nations, to amuse the masses, and to entertain their emperors. Many of their performers were slaves who participated in contests "to the death." The Circus Maximus was built to hold 250,000 people; they came to watch chariot races and other bloody pastimes. There were legitimate contests like wrestling, boxing, and running, but the more ghastly "battles royal"—in which a group of gladiators fought until only one remained—were preferred. The Colosseum, which stands in ruins today in central Rome, was the scene of many of these encounters.

Small communities of Christians objected to the bloodletting. Clement of Rome, Ignatius (later sainted), and Tertullian (an African) all condemned the gory shows. Christian opposition in various forms to sports continued into the twentieth century. Sad, too, was the demise of the Olympic Games during the height of the Roman Empire. The last recorded Games were held in A.D. 265. Christian reforms and earthquakes then combined to erase for a time the physical evidence of the grandeur of Mediterranean sport.

The Church's Iron Hand

After the fall of Rome, during the Dark Ages and the Middle Ages, sports took a back seat in importance. European life was circumscribed by the church, which sought to govern the moral code for everything. Village life predominated, and ball games were invented, adopted, and revised according to local custom. The two favored places for play were the local "commons" and the churchyard—in spite of the clergy's opposition.

The Scots played *shinty* and *paille maille*; the Irish their *hurling*; the French their *soule* and *jeu de mail*; the Welsh their *knappon*; the English their *chole*; and the courtiers their *tenez*, or tennis, as it is known today. Even football is mentioned as far back as the 1300s. Bowling games were devised and were favored for gambling. Horseshoes were pitched. The nobility

came up with shuffleboard and later a crude form of billiards. Like it or not, laws or no laws, the populace was going to play games.

Nobles and royalty arranged tournaments (from the French *tournoi*), at which more expensive and elaborate fixtures and sports implements were used. Jousting events were contested by knights on horseback, but they were all but finished by the early 1500s. History records the plight of some famous figures in medieval sport. King Louis X died in 1316 after playing *paume*, a ball game. Charles, Duke of Orleans, played tennis in 1415 while imprisoned by the English after the Battle of Agincourt.

There were royal decrees to regulate sport as well. King Charles V of France complained in the mid-1300s that the peasants were playing games that did nothing to teach the arts of bearing arms. His English counterpart, King Edward III, decreed in 1363 that all able-bodied men must participate in sports that used bows and arrows or pellets and bolts. He also ordered his sheriff to stamp out football, which he considered useless and unlawful. No matter—the peasants played anyway.

By the sixteenth century, this love of sport was institutionalized across Europe. When the first European traders reached Africa, they brought with them a love of games and contests, only to find the Africans themselves just as fond of their own diversions. But there were differences. The European's athletic pursuits were adversely affected by strong, centralized religious objections and royal decrees. The African, on the other hand, considered sports and games necessary for his very physical and psychic survival.

The African Warrior-Athlete

Although the first European slavers in the fifteenth century were from the southern rim of that continent, the northern European exercised greater influence in sports. Nonetheless, when they arrived, they found sports already ritualistically woven into the social fabric of African daily life.

Central Role

Athletic participation was a standard part of every African child's upbringing. The assertion is commonly made that the slaves brought this ability with them to the New World. On the basis of eyewitness accounts and anthropoligical evidence, we can identify several sports that were routinely enjoyed. Africans believed that people were children but once in their short lives and that childhood should be enjoyed.

Races   Africans loved races. The list included running, swimming, climbing, and horse and boat races. Running was a distinct survival skill—hunting parties frequently traveled great distances after game. The Greek historian Herodotus alluded to these runners 1500 years before, saying they were "exceedingly fleet of foot—more so than any people of whom we have information."[3]

The French anthropologist Charles Beart mentioned their swiftness in the early part of this century. There were some extraordinary African runners in Ouagadougou, where he lived in 1934. It was faster for him to send a package to Niamey, almost three hundred miles away, by an African porter than by mail. Swimming was also considered a survival skill. Beart noted that those he observed were as at home in the water as on land. Horse racing had been learned from the Muslim armies that conquered much of the northern latitudes of Africa.

African boat races were witnessed by many European traders. In the 1600s, Jean Barbot of the French Royal Africa Company spoke of the boatmen of Wida (now Ouidah in Benin): "The best canoemen were the Elmea blacks... at Wida by sea and are the fittest and most experienced men to manage and paddle the canoes over the bars and breakings."[4] Two hundred or so years later, a boat race inaugurated intercollegiate competition in America.

Contests   Africans enjoyed contests. Most of them were connected in some way with religious ceremonies, fertility rites, rites of passage, or the entertainment of visitors. Stick fighting was an extremely important skill and was second in popularity to wrestling. Boys and men who tended cattle needed to be adept in it to ward off small animals and rustlers. Prowess with a bow and arrow was prized as a military art and to kill animals for food.

But the most honored contestant was the champion wrestler, who was lauded not only by his village but memorialized in oral histories. There was—and still is—something about this sport form that has enticed every society. In particular, every non–Western civilization has exalted the virtues of wrestling. Frequently, solemn ceremonies preceded these matches, in which they tried to throw their opponents to the ground.

In his acclaimed book *Things Fall Apart*, African novelist Chinua Achebe opens his story with the saga of Okonkwo, who "was well-known throughout the nine villages and beyond." For "as a young man of eighteen he had brought honor to his village by throwing Amalinze the Cat. Amalinze was the great wrestler who for seven years was unbeaten... He was called the Cat because his back would never touch the earth."[5]

Then there were the gymnasts. Suppleness was encouraged in the young and contests were held—sometimes at night under a full moon—to see who could perform the most intricate and complicated feats of physical contortion. The most popular team contest was tug-of-war, in which, while holding fast to a common rope or thick vine, up to two dozen or so equally divided participants tried to pull their opponents across a line in the dirt. It is not too difficult to imagine the hilarity, conviviality, and enjoyment of the spectators as they watched their favorites.

Social Utility

These various sporting events were enjoyed by participants and spectators alike. However, they had significance that went beyond mere enjoyment. They were used consciously to achieve several crucial social purposes.

1. They taught young people general fitness skills. The mimicking of animals in the gymnastic exercises, running, swimming, climbing, and wrestling taught speed, endurance, flexibility, and strength.
2. They taught skills of economic survival. Stick fighting, swimming, running, rowing, fishing, and hunting were necessary talents if villages were to be protected and cared for.
3. They taught civic and cooperative values. Group sports such as tug-of-war instilled solidarity with one another and stressed the absolute necessity of teamwork.
4. They taught military skills. Wrestling, stick fighting, running, throwing spears, riding, and archery were used to train the warrior class (as in the Zulu and Ashanti societies) and standing armies (the Songhai Empire, for example).

Even as late as the end of the nineteenth century, African boys, through sports, were still learning skills hundreds of years old. A Colonel G. Hamilton-Brown described his eyewitness account of young Zulus in 1879. Boys of fourteen or fifteen were "being taught how to use his arms, how to fence with sticks, military drill and dance."[6]

Oh yes—there was always dancing. Most ceremonial athletic contests were accompanied by group dancing—to thank spirits or to ask for favors or good crops or for victory in battle, as examples. Medicine men sometimes divined special omens from the outcomes of athletic games and ordered appropriate dances to suit the occasion. Combining the athletic with the social remained a peculiar facet of African-American life through the twentieth century. It is interesting to note that in the early 1920s the financial success of many black-run basketball, football, and track contests depended on whether a dance was held for the spectators immediately afterward.

These sports skills and societal norms were brought to the New World by enslaved Africans. It made undeniable economic sense to the slave traders to capture the fittest they could find. Once in America, the Africans' love of physical expression combined with a new set of highly organized sports—and little chance for success elsewhere—to produce the greatest athletes the world had yet seen.

African-American Slave Sports

The first waves of African slaves and indentured servants were constrained by the religious beliefs of their European owners and employers. Early white settlers (most of whom were also indentured servants) from rural European villages also loved their sports, but philosophers, clergymen, governors, and kings continued to try to limit these activities. Dutch intellectual Desiderius Erasmus wrote of the villagers' sports-crazy outlook, "We are not concerned with developing athletes, but scholars and men competent to affairs, for whom we desire adequate constitution indeed, but not the physique of a Milo."[7]

The straitlaced John Calvin, who influenced much of religious thought today, warned that "all silly sports be avoided."[8] Martin Luther, however, stressed that "it is the part of a Christian to take care of his body... fulfilling the law of Christ."[9] Later, French philosopher Jean-Jacques Rousseau, who helped formulate the doctrine of the natural rights of man, taught that strong and healthy bodies were to be encouraged.

These mutterings fell on more than a few deaf ears for almost a century. Two books on sports were penned before the importation of the first slaves to America. In 1528 an Italian, Baldassare Castiglione, wrote a handbook, *The Book of the Courtier*, that codified the rules of tennis, archery, fencing, running, and throwing. Three years later, in 1531, Englishman Sir Thomas Elyiot wrote the first book on sports in the English language, *The Book of the Governor*. It, too, was a handbook for the upper classes on running, swimming, hunting, fencing, archery, tennis, and dancing. England entered the slave trade thirty-one years later, in 1562.

A Kinship with the Red Man

In their love of sports blacks had more in common with Native Americans than with their northern European owners. (In 1662 Virginia passed a law making African indentured servants slaves thenceforth. Legal slavery existed in the United States for about two hundred years.) Though both carved out time for leisure, Native Americans were not philosophically or religiously opposed to play for play's sake. They had no puritan work ethic, and they had much free time on their hands. Competition was revered for the same reasons the Africans revered it: to test physical skills, to prepare for war, to defend the village, to teach teamwork, to have some fun—and, oh yes, to gamble.

Native Americans engaged in their own forms of bowling, basketball, field hockey, running (for which the Tarahumara were famous), and lacrosse, which they referred to as "war's little brother." Nations along the East Coast of North America—Iroquois, Chappaqua, Cherokee, Pamunkey, Seminole, and others—intermarried with the African, which further solidified their commonalities. Marriage between Europeans and Africans and/or Natives was soon forbidden, Pocahontas and Captain John Smith notwithstanding. In the mid-1500s Spanish explorer Hernando Cortés found the Aztecs in the Southwest fond of running, wrestling, archery, swimming, canoe racing, lacrosse, and ball games of a quasi-religious nature.

Legal Regulations

Sports so threatened to disrupt daily life among the colonists that laws were passed to regulate them. Virginia Governor Thomas Dale forbade gaming on the Sabbath and put limits on cockfighting, cudgeling, wrestling, football, hurling, skittles, ninepins, foot races, stool-ball, and quoits (horseshoes). But before the first English settlers arrived at Jamestown in 1619, they were given official permission for certain sports activities in King James I's *Declaration on Lawful Sports*. Slaves were to abide by these as well.

King Charles II was an avid sportsman and allowed even more freedom for these pursuits. But colonial governors installed field days (for whites only) to keep sports from getting out of hand. Counties in all the colonies in the seventeenth century posted public notices offering prizes for the best wrestlers, runners, riders, and marksmen.

Slaves began by training gamecocks and horses (before the importation of thoroughbreds) and by working in the "ordinaries," as taverns were called. The State of

Virginia passed a law in 1705 permitting owners to list people as property. Black horse trainers were among the first to be listed. Among themselves and when they had the time before the Revolutionary War, slaves ran and paddled in races, swam, fought mock battles with sticks, wrestled, boxed, and played ball games. Around 1800 a large influx of blacks and mulattos from Haiti and other parts of the Caribbean added more sports choices peculiar to that region.

After the Revolutionary War the northern states began abolishing slavery, although the belief continued that blacks were divinely ordained inferior to whites and that slavery was biblically justified. The vast majority of slaves were concentrated in Virginia and Maryland until 1800, but then cotton helped spread this despicable institution down across the South to Texas. Whites needed continuing justifications for it, and plenty were forthcoming—some of which related to physical abilities.

From a William Hamilton came this quote in 1809: "The proposition has been advanced by men who claim a preeminence in this world, that Africans are inferior to white men in the structure both of body and mind."[10] White men just assumed they were not only smarter than blacks but naturally stronger as well.

The southern states adopted so-called "Black Codes" to regulate social interaction among whites, slaves, and free blacks. Whites and blacks rubbed elbows at cockfights and horse races but seldom at any other sports events. In 1830, North Carolina passed a law stating "that it shall not be lawful for any white person or free Negro, or mulatto, or persons of mixed blood to play at any game of cards, dice, nine-pins, or any game of chance or hazard whether for money, liquor, or property or not, with any slave or slaves."[11]

Historian John Hope Franklin wrote that "Free Negroes were never content with the social intercourse [sports included] that was afforded by their own group and were continuously seeking contact with slaves and white persons."[12] During these antebellum years, Franklin found out, blacks continued to enjoy jumping, wrestling, marbles, trapping game, running, fishing, hunting, and town ball (a form of baseball)—when they could. All these activities, however, were confined to certain times of the year and by legal constraints.

Historian David K. Wiggins wrote that "play was essential to slave children because it was one means through which they learned the values and mores of their parents from one generation to the next."[13] Charlie Davenport, an ex-slave, recalled that "Us tho'ed horse shoes, jumped poles, walked on stilts, an' played marbles."[14] On the game of town ball (or shinny, rounders, or base ball, as the game was variously called then), another ex-slave, Hector Godbald of South Carolina, said, "Shinny was de thing dat I like best; just had stick wid crook in de end of it en see could I knock de ball wid dat."[15] They were not to be denied.

William Johnson's Diary

One free black who left a valuable account of the sporting life of blacks in the years leading up to the Civil War was a barber named William Johnson. He lived in Natchez, Mississippi, and kept a diary of his important affairs. Inadvertently, his writings from 1835 to 1851 constitute the first account by a black man of sports activities among his peers. He described in detail his social milieu about games such as shuffleboard, checkers, quoits, marbles, billiards, and cards. As for true sports, he went to horse races, mule races, and cockfights, and he broad jumped against his sons. And he loved to gamble for liquor and money. Of his luck with a gamecock, he wrote, "I paid five Dollars for him.... I put him down in the yard and the Frizeling chicken whipped him so I find he is not much."[16] Like some other free blacks of means, Johnson was allowed to race his "brag nags," as the slower, non–thoroughbred horses were called. White track owners frequently rented out their courses on weekdays for anyone who could post the right amounts.

Not everyone looked upon these "favors" with approval. Although John Hope Franklin duly noted that holiday times were set aside for black sports activities, Frederick Douglass, known later as the Great Liberator and an ex-slave himself, did not see many good intentions. He thought "those holidays were among the most effective means in the hands of the slaveholders of keeping down the spirit of insurrection among the slaves."[17] But he did note that during such periods "the majority spent the holidays in sports, ball-playing, wrestling, boxing, foot races, dancing and drinking whiskey, and this latter mode was most agreeable to their masters."[18]

Douglass concluded that "everything like rational enjoyment was frowned upon, and only those wild and low sports peculiar to semi-civilized people were encouraged."[19] By "wild and low" he probably meant activities like boxing, cockfighting, and gambling. That he did not mean wrestling is shown in the following quote: "During the holidays young men...could go wooing, the married man to see his wife, the father and mother to see their children, industrious and money-loving could make a few dollars, the great wrestler could win laurels."[20] But up north, blacks encountered a different form of opposition.

More Opposition Before Emancipation

The most well-known black athletes south of the Mason-Dixon Line before the Civil War were jockeys and trainers. North of that line blacks were frustrated in trying to enjoy what were supposed to be public recreational facilities. Sports had become so important in the northern cities that the first newspaper exclusively devoted to the subject, *The Spirit of the Times*, made its debut in 1831. That same year, John Cox Stevens, a wealthy sportsman, opened Elysian Fields in what is now Hoboken, New Jersey. It was the nation's first combination amusement park and sports park. But black patrons were not always accorded friendly welcomes.

In 1834, Robin Carver published *The Book of Sports*, which printed the first rules on various games and sports to date. Walking or pedestrian races were in vogue. Francis Smith, a black walker, was barred from a race in 1835 because he had supposedly entered too late. Except for horse racing, boat racing and pedestrian events were the first sports to lure large numbers of spectators of all races and both sexes.

They especially appealed to the thousands of Irish immigrants who came to America to escape the potato famine in the late 1840s.

By the Civil War, slaves and free blacks were engaging in every sport imaginable. They were already the best jockeys extant. Two of them had fought for the English heavyweight crown. And many more enjoyed their favorite pastimes when they could. Free blacks in particular, noted Rader, "in the urban areas probably were as active in sport as their white counterparts."[21] But the most significant breakthrough was still fifty-odd years away. Not only did emancipation unleash the legal shackles of bondage; it also allowed the black man and woman to form their own sports clubs. This trend, combined with sports at schools, enabled black athletes to compete with anyone who answered their challenge on equal terms.

Sports and the Freedman

With a stroke of his pen, President Abraham Lincoln "freed" the slaves, and 4.5 million ex-bondsmen became United States citizens, albeit with limited opportunities. The best known of these new African-Americans were athletes—jockeys in particular. Harvard University had announced on October 16, 1859, that Abraham Molineaux Hewlett, a mulatto, was appointed its first director of physical culture. Noted *Harvard* magazine, "It is with feelings of pleasure and pride...that 'Conservative Harvard' should be the first of the colleges of this country to incorporate into its course of education an organized system of physical training.... [M]ost fortunately, the services of Professor A. Molineaux Hewlett had been secured. He came with gymnastics experience of four years."[22] He was not the only black instructor.

Young Men's Christian Associations

The Ys, as they were and are still called today, provided the black community with its first generation of trained sports administrators. They were founded in 1844 in England, and the first "colored" branch was established in Washington, D.C., in 1853. Decidedly egalitarian in outlook, the Y's had, within fifteen years, other colored branches, from Charleston, South Carolina, to Boston. One even appointed E.V.C. Eato as its first "colored" representative to their International Convention in 1867. No other body would be as instrumental in the development of sports among blacks as the YMCA.

In some cities in these early years, the local "colored" Y assumed the stature of a private club. Its religious orientation served to dampen criticism—among ethnic immigrants in particular—that the African-American was being given too much. The Ys were in the forefront of what came to be known as the Muscular Christianity Movement, which sought to persuade people that flexing muscles was not anti-Christian. Classes were held in calisthenics, gymnastics, and physical culture.

In 1869, the first student YMCA was formed, at Howard University, the federally funded school established for freedmen in Washington, D.C. This was a momentous event because many other black colleges looked toward YMCA-trained administrators to run their fledgling athletic programs. It also assured the parent YMCA of future leaders. In addition, since most privately funded black schools were religiously affiliated, the YMCA met little opposition.

For the first time ever black women participated in large numbers through the Young Women's Christian Associations. The first "colored" branch for women was founded in 1893 in Dayton, Ohio. Unfortunately, the YMCAs' most influential figure, Luther Gulick, Jr., felt that sports for women "should be restricted...within the school; that they should be used for recreation and pleasure; that the strenuous training of teams tends to be injurious to both body and mind...and athletics do not test womanliness as they test manliness."[23] That statement held back the development of women's sports for a quarter of a century. However, when the National Board of the YMCA was formed in 1907, Mrs. Addie Hunton was appointed Secretary for Colored Student Affairs.

Mrs. Hunton's husband, William, was appointed the first General Secretary of Colored YMCAs in 1888. Eleven years earlier, in 1879, Henry E. Brown had been selected Traveling Secretary for Colored Branches. Brown thus became the nation's first black regional sports administrator. Brown and the Huntons did yeoman work in spreading the good works of the Y. As a clue to the importance of his post, Brown resigned the presidency of Talladega College to assume his position.

The YMCAs became a home away from home for thousands of traveling blacks when dormitories were built. They trained hundreds of athletic coaches, administrators, officials, and athletes. Their play areas became a favorite haunt of generations of black youngsters on Saturday mornings.

School Sports

The first black college opened its doors in 1854. Others soon followed. Their first athletic officials were students, as administrators did not think sports important enough for their own attention. But when sports became significant, the YMCA-trained personnel were ready. Games were initially class affairs, with one year's enrollees competing against another. This scheme worked rather well since nearly all these colleges had three departments: grade school, college preparatory, and college level.

Facilities were wholly lacking in most instances and where they were available, they were made by the students themselves. College presidents were ambivalent about spending official funds on sports for fear of offending their wealthy white patrons or giving the impression of misplacing their priorities. In any event, by 1892 black colleges had begun varsity competition in baseball and football, and students were petitioning for more.

The Tuskegee Institute (now Tuskegee University) was particularly active. In 1890 it hired James B. Washington as its first sports director; he doubled as its bookkeeper. Two years later, the school staged its first track meet, using members of the military cadet battalions. The significance of Tuskegee's and other black schools' initiatives was that they served as the focus of most organized sports activity in the South. The colleges hired trained instructors, who in turn trained local public school instructors, who in their turn taught the black citizenry. No municipal bodies cared to or wanted to spend tax dollars on sports facilities for blacks.

One of the cruelest twists of fate to befall the black athlete came because blacks could not vote in certain places. When the Second Morrill Act was passed by Congress in 1890, funds were allocated to establish Negro land-grant colleges like most of those known as the Big Ten schools today. Like their white land-grant counterparts, some of those funds were for recreational facilities. White southern congressmen, however, arranged for these federally appropriated monies to be funneled through state legislatures. Once there, the funds were diverted for white schools. This practice lasted seventy years in some southern states.

Interscholastic Athletic Associations

Public school sports for blacks fared infinitely better in northern urban cities than in the South. In other parts of the country, public school athletics served as one of the few avenues for status a black boy could have. Writing of his boyhood in Kansas in the 1880s, William Allen White, a white man, said, "The few Negro boys in Eldorado mingled on terms of absolute equality with whites. They held their places according to their skills as fighters, swimmers, runners, ball players, skaters, or school play ground athletes."[24]

In the South, blacks had little hope of getting their fair share, partly because of money and partly because sports were used as a barometer of racial progress. As

Dale Somers noted, "Negro participation in sports was particularly important, for it raised questions about the ability of sports to bridge class lines and racial division."[25] Not only did whites not want to play ball with blacks, they did not want to give the appearance of gradually accepting them as first-class citizens.

Matters were different north of Washington, D.C. In a few cities blacks and whites went to high school together. Most blacks, though, attended all-black institutions, if at all. Interest increased to the point where an organization was formed to foster more growth. The Interscholastic Athletic Association (ISAA) was thus born in 1905 in Washington, D.C. Its founding fathers were Dr. Edwin B. Henderson, W. A. Joiner, G. C. Wilkinson, R. N. Mattingly, and W. A. Decater. Its mandate was simply to provide wholesome scholastic athletic programs in the Washington, D.C.–Baltimore area.

They took their cues from the YMCA and served to augment the meager resources spent on athletics for black school children. The public parks were not much better, for as Rader pointed out, "the playgrounds usually failed to extend their control over spare time activities to those who needed it most—the ethnic youth in the slums."[26] The ISAA was a godsend when needed most. Not long after, churches, clubs, and special interest groups began forming their own leagues and associations to facilitate sports among the young.

The Soldier Athlete

The black soldier is too often neglected in the annals of African-American sports. With the exception of the YMCAs and the public schools, the Army provided more opportunities for the black athlete than any other institution. With a vested interest in the physical well-being and high morale of its soldiers, the Army provided facilities, competition, coaching, and encouragement for its black enlisted men.

Durham and Jones wrote that "The [black] men were carefully picked, held to high standards of physical fitness and mental alertness, and commanded by some of the Army's best white officers."[27] In addition, noted Professor William E. Leckie, "Their stations were among the most lonely and isolated to be found.... Discipline was severe, food usually poor, recreation difficult, and violent death always near at hand."[28]

It is interesting to recall that the first all-black units formed after the Civil War were the Twenty-fourth and Twenty-fifth Infantries. The Twenty-fourth was organized from remnants of all-black groups from Louisiana and Texas. The Twenty-fifth was from New Orleans and made up of some former members of the North Carolina Infantry and the Louisiana Fortieth Infantry. Nearly all were athletes before enlistment. New Orleans could have been designated the black sports capital of the United States just before the Civil War.

Black soldiers reportedly played baseball during the Civil War and continued to enjoy billiards, trick riding, bowling, gymnastics, football, and most of all wrestling. Whenever they could, they arranged games and matches against local clubs and took tremendous pride in their victories. To be forbidden to participate in sports was among the most effective disciplinary measures an officer could take. Such was the black soldier's love of sports.

These athletes became so good, that

later a white officer was moved to write to the *Army and Navy Journal* in 1908, saying, "Surely this is a matter for some thought on the part of those who are responsible to the nation for the maintenance of its prestige and for its defense."[29] This letter was submitted after the Infantry was acclaimed overall winner of an interservice competition in the Philippines.

Club Formation

Black groups participated in the wave of club formations after the Civil War. Most of the early groups were organized by pre–Civil War free blacks. Some were burial societies, to which members paid periodic dues to pay for their funerals. Others were social in nature; these found an added blessing in forming sports teams. The Odd Fellows was perhaps the best known of these initial associations. Their outings filled the "society" sections of black newspapers. Wrote the New Orleans *Louisianian* on July 25, 1874, of one of their gatherings, "The day was spent in agreeable recreation; fishing, bathing, boat sailing, dancing, speech-making incident to the occasion and contesting for prizes."

By the mid-1880s Reconstruction was over, and life for most blacks in the South was akin to that during slavery. The love of sports was, however, as strong as ever. Club members railed at the renewed restrictions on their freedom. They wrote editorials, signed petitions, and protested their re-segregation. Their northern counterparts did not have it much better since social life there was de facto segregated anyway.

Club members also felt maligned by the wave of racial caricaturing of blacks that took place in the 1880s. Blacks were parodied in magazines such as *Harper's*, and cartoons in the white press showed blacks in insulting and foolish predicaments. Clubs of prosperous blacks wanted to distance themselves from such racist stereotypings. They did so, in many instances, by making membership even more exclusive—in essence following the lead of the elite white clubs.

There was one positive and powerful outcome of the clannishness of these groups: their members became the organizers of the associations that led black sports after the turn of the century. The ISAA, the Colored (now Central) Intercollegiate Athletic Association (CIAA), and the Colored YMCAs and YWCAs were all initially run by the sons, grandsons, daughters, and granddaughters of the elite club members of the 1880s.

Up until 1984 few of these black sports and social clubs owned their own facilities. There had not been enough wealthy members to sustain the high, fixed costs. Typically, they used public facilities, and that has been a problem for generations. Chicago first constructed ten parks in 1903 at a cost of $5 million, and other cities soon followed. That helped. More help came from President Theodore Roosevelt, who was an avid sportsman. Roosevelt was quoted as saying, "[S]ports created brawn, the spirit, the self-confidence and the quickness of men."[30] Black club members took him at his word.

The black athlete remained a curiosity, a conversation piece, until 1908. Blacks had always been thought of as innately inferior in mind and body to whites. They were even thought to be part beast. Herbert Spencer made use of the branch of mathematics known as statistics in the latter half of the last century to "prove" that blacks were inferior because their brains were statistically smaller than those of whites. Conventional white thought needed some excuses for why blacks were excelling at sports.

In a prolific twenty-year period between 1892 and 1912, athletes became the best known and most discussed of all African-Americans—yes, even more than Booker T. Washington and W. E. B. DuBois. An editorial in the January 11, 1902, *Baltimore Afro-American Ledger* declared that "Mr [Joe] Gans gets more space in the white papers than all the respectable colored people in the state." Gans, of course, was the world lightweight boxing champion and the first native-born African-American world title-holder. This state of affairs has not changed since.

Notes

1. William J. Baker, *Sports in the Western World*. (Totowa, N.J.: Rowman and Littlefield, 1982), p. 4.
2. Ibid., p. 9.
3. Quoted in *Horizon History of Africa*, vol. 1, p. 184.
4. Quoted in ibid., p. 189.
5. Chinua Achebe, *Things Fall Apart*. (New York: Astoc-Honor, 1959), p. 3.
6. Quoted in *Horizon*, op. cit., vol. 2, p. 427.
7. Quoted in Baker, op. cit., p. 73.
8. Quoted in ibid., p. 74.
9. Quoted in ibid., p. 73.
10. Quoted in Herbert Aptheker, *A Documentary History of the Negro People*

in the United States, vol. 1. (Secaucus, N. J.: Citadel, 1974), p. 52.
11. John Hope Franklin, *The Free Negro in North Carolina, 1790–1860. (N.Y.: W. W. Norton, 1971), p. 187.*
12. Ibid., p. 184.
13. David K. Wiggins, "The Play of Slave Children of the Old South, 1820–1860." *Journal of Sports History* 7 (Summer 1980): 22.
14. Quoted in ibid.
15. Quoted in ibid., p. 27.
16. William H. Johnson, *Autobiography of William Henry Johnson*. (Brooklyn, N.Y.: Haskell, 1970. Repr. of 1900 ed.), p. 74.
17. Frederick Douglass, *Life and Times of Frederick Douglass*. (N.Y.: Macmillan, 1962), p. 147.
18. Ibid., pp. 145–46.
19. Ibid., p. 148.
20. Ibid., p. 147.
21. Rader, p. 93.
22. *Harvard* 6 (Oct. 1859): 38.
23. Benjamin Rader, *American Sports: From the Age of Folk Games to the Age of Spectators*. (Prentice-Hall, 1983), p. 165.
24. Quoted in Katz, *The Black West*. p. 182.
25. Dale Somers, p. 87.
26. Rader, op. cit., p. 16.
27. Philip Durham and Everett L. Jones, *The Negro Cowboys*. (Lincoln: University of Nebraska, 1983), p. 9.
28. Katz, op. cit., p. 204.
29. Letter, *Army and Navy Journal*, February 8, 1908.
30. Quoted in Rader, op. cit., p. 149.

Chapter 1

Boxing

Beginnings

No sport has had as profound an effect on the lives of African-Americans as boxing. Professional bouts have led to racial murders, and injuries to fighters have caused permanent physical and mental harm. Yet the sport retains a viselike grip on the imagination of all of us. There seems to be something primeval about hand-to-hand combat in the ring that makes sober people sit up and pay attention. No athletic event— not the Olympics, the World Series, or the Super Bowl—can match the drama of a world heavyweight title fight between two charismatic boxers.

Boxing now is not the same activity one sees depicted on ancient art pieces. That man began fighting for entertainment early is proved by scenes of boxers on objets d'art of the Egyptian civilization during the time of the pharaohs. The tomb of Beni-Hasan in particular is quite graphic in its wall paintings of boxings. At the time, boxing was a controlled contest in which blood flowed freely and swings were more of the roundhouse variety than jabs or uppercuts. An ancient match would look very crude by today's standards.

The Greeks introduced their own brand of fighting into the Olympic Games, which began in 776 B.C. Boxing started in 632 B.C. and was called *pancration.* It was much gorier than it should have been since no one wore gloves. The Romans followed the Greeks and added what are called battles royal. These spectacles entailed putting several gladiators together in one arena and having them fight it out until only one remained.

There was some opposition to these Roman shows from small Christian sects. Clement of Rome and Ignatius (later sainted) were just two who publicly condemned the bouts to no avail. But after A.D. 400, the gladiatorial bouts stopped. Fighting for sport then fell into a period of disorganization for almost 1,300 years. Then English and French nobles decided that an aristocratic gentleman's education was incomplete unless he could defend himself. What proceeded was a more scientific approach to fighting and the first true break from no-holds-barred brawling.

William Richmond and Tom Molineaux

James Figg capitalized on the English gentry's demand for quality instruction in self-defense. In 1719 he set up his School of Arms and Self-Defense, and he was his nation's first boxing champion. Soon he had a waiting list, and even King George I attended. Interest grew briskly until Jack Broughton—a Figg pupil—formalized the first set of rules for the sport, now known simply as Broughton's Rules.

These guidelines included no hitting below the belt, no hitting an opponent when he was already down, and no holding below the waist, and they standardized the ring. The ring itself—from which the term for boxing matches derived—was round and about twenty-five feet in diameter with a firm dirt floor. A line or mark three feet long was drawn down the middle by the referee to serve as the place the boxers had to return to after a knockdown. Hence the phrases *toe the mark* and *come up to scratch,* in use today. No gloves were used, and blood still flowed—that was what the public wanted. Although boxing was banned in England from 1750 to 1790 because of the number of deaths in the ring, it remained popular nonetheless.

Into this scheme of things came William Richmond of Staten Island, New York, who was born free on August 5, 1763. His mother was an ex-slave belonging to Reverend George E. Charlton, who, after moving to Staten Island from the South, set her free. Growing up along the docks of New York City harbor during the British occupation, Richmond frequently got into bouts with sailors and seldom lost. One day he was noticed by the British Manhattan commander, Hugh Percy, who took an immediate liking to the youngster.

In 1778, Percy was recalled to England. He asked Richmond's mother to let him take her son to England. Richmond's mother reluctantly agreed, and he settled in the English county of Yorkshire to learn cabinet-making. He got into his first fight there by accident. At the horse races near York on August 25, 1791, he was accosted by George "Docky" Moore and subsequently gave him a sound thrashing in a makeshift ring nearby. He immediately received more challenges, since the sport was gaining in popularity. David Mendoza had just been crowned as the first Jewish champion of England in 1792, and his style of fighting was termed "scientific"—meaning he tried to avoid being hit rather than going toe-to-toe with opponents.

By 1800, Richmond was a semi-professional boxer and had an impressive list of wins to his credit. His success attracted wealthy patrons, and he decided to move to London, where he opened a tavern called the Horse and Dolphin on St. Martin's Lane in Leicester Square. After his first publicized loss to George Maddox, he scored enough wins to earn a title berth against the then champion, Tom Cribb. They agreed to fight on October 8, 1805, at Halsham (near Eastbourne) on the village green.

The stakes were high for Cribb in particular: his title, English honor, and the supposed superiority of the white race. For Richmond it was the first time a black American athlete had contested for a national or world title in any sport. The monetary purse was nominal: twenty-five guineas. The atmosphere surrounding the bout was festive. A crowd in the thousands was present, and dukes and other nobles appeared on horseback. No one paid to see fights then; it was first come, first serve for the choice views.

The newspapers had already hired boxing journalists to cover bouts, and their opinions were frequently more credible than those given by referees, who could be bought off at times. The most influential paper was the *London Times.* Its edition of October 9, 1805, reported on the outcome of the bout: "A...battle for twenty-five guineas was fought between Cribb and Richmond 'The Black.' It would [be] insipid for us to enter into particulars respecting the fight, which, if it may be so called, lasted nearly an hour and a half. It was altogether tiresome; the black danced about the ring, fell down, etc., while Cribb, through fear, or some other motive, declined going in, and beating him off hard. It was altogether an unequal match; and an interval of twenty minutes together elapsed without a blow of any consequence being struck. Cribb beat him without hurt. The business of the day was not over until near five o'clock in the evening." The crowd was pleased that, for the second time, a black man had been put in his place.

Cribb formally claimed the heavyweight title in 1807—the same year Britain abolished the slave trade (in law, not in fact)—and then retired. But he was forced to come back and defend English honor in 1810 when one of Richmond's protégés, Tom Molineaux, challenged him. His two bouts against Molineaux were the most famous of the early nineteenth century.

Tom Molineaux came from an unlikely place and an uncommon family. He was born a slave in Georgetown (now part of Washington, D.C.) on March 23, 1874. His father, Zachariah, was a boxer, as were his brothers. His master, Algernon Molineaux, moved with them to a Richmond, Virginia, plantation and frequently arranged for bouts between his slaves and those on neighboring plantations. This was a rather commonplace occurrence, and fortunes were won or lost on the outcomes.

The average price of a healthy, male, field-hand slave around 1800 was roughly a thousand dollars. But the Molineaux boys could command a premium of nearly a hundred percent in a bout if the right deal were struck, and caution was surely taken with them. It just so happened that within a few miles of the Molineaux farm there took place one of the most famous slave revolts on record. Tom Molineaux must have heard about it through the slave grapevine.

Richmond, Virginia, in 1800 had thirty-two thousand slaves and eight thousand whites. On the night of August 31 a very charismatic slave, Gabriel Prosser, and his followers went on a killing spree of revenge and liberation. They murdered as many whites as possible—sparing only Quakers—in hopes that other slaves from nearby plantations would join to take over the city. Prosser's plan was betrayed by other slaves, and he was captured in Henrico County and publicly hanged on October 7. Tom Molineaux was only sixteen years old.

Molineaux's master had won so much on Tom by 1809, that he promised him his freedom if he won one last bout against a slave named Abe. This, too, was not uncommon, as slaves were often set free by benevolent masters for performing some extraordinary service. Molineaux handily defeated Abe, his master won his rather large wager, and Molineaux was set free as promised. With five hundred dollars in his pocket he headed for New York City and soon boarded the H.M.S. *Bristol* for London, England, where he came under the influence of William Richmond.

Under Richmond's tutelage Molineaux began serious training. He won his first bout against Jack Burrows, whose ring name was "The Bristol Unknown." White boxers in England frequently adopted false names so that losses to people like Molineaux would not be so embarrassing. The record books are laden with monikers of fighters who sought to protect their reputations. His next victory, for example, was against "Tom Tough," née Tom Blake.

After six more wins Richmond felt that Molineaux was ready to challenge Cribb to "unretire" and face his pupil. This challenge was printed in the *London Times.* Cribb finally agreed to "meet the Moor." Cribb was three years older than Molineaux and had gained a few extra pounds in his retirement, but the fight was nonetheless set for December 10, 1810, at Copthall Common in Sussex. No fight in memory had attracted so much attention and anticipation. A special attendee was the aging Baron Hugh Percy.

The day of the fight was perfectly miserable. It was raining and cold, and the referee, Ap Rhys Price, had a difficult time getting the ring cleared for the bout. Most reliable reports put at least ten thousand people at ringside. (There were no seats; everyone stood or sat on makeshift benches.) As the fight began, Molineaux quickly established his dominance, but Cribb held his ground. After twenty-seven rounds the bout was still in doubt.

In the twenty-eighth round Molineaux suddenly caught Cribb with a hard right. The Englishman went down, and Price started his count of thirty seconds. (A fighter had thirty seconds to "toe the mark" after a knockdown. A round ended when any fighter went down.) When Cribb failed to "come to scratch," Molineaux and Richmond began a gleeful victory dance. But Joe Ward, Cribb's aide, leaped into the ring in clear violation of the rules and accused Richmond of hiding weights in Molineaux's hands. All the while the timekeeper, Sir Thomas Apreece, kept yelling *"Time! Time!"*

Incredibly, Price waived the rules and allowed Cribb a full two minutes to revive. He went on to win sixteen rounds later over a dejected Molineaux. Richmond was furious but helpless as a blatantly partisan Price bent the rules to defend white English honor. Cribb collected two thousand dollars for his win, and a subscription on the grounds was collected for Molineaux. Richmond immediately demanded a rematch, which was printed in the *Times* on December 25, 1810.

In part, Molineaux wrote, "To Mr. Thomas Cribb...my friends think that had the weather on last Tuesday...not been so unfavorable, I should have won the battle....I therefore, challenge you to a second meeting....I cannot omit the opportunity of expressing a confident hope that the circumstance of my being of a different color to that of a people amongst whom I have sought protection will not in any way operate to my prejudice....Your most humble and obedient servant. T. Molineaux." Molineaux was not an educated man, but this challenge written for him did express his true sentiments and contained a subtle but pointed reference to his previous discriminatory treatment.

Cribb accepted the second challenge, but Molineaux then began taking his return bout too casually. He started drinking heavily and got into an argument with Richmond, which caused their estrangement. When the day of the bout arrived, September 28, 1811, Molineaux reportedly consumed a whole chicken and a quart of ale just before going into the ring. Cribb won in eleven easy rounds.

Molineaux fought three more official bouts and then joined a boxing troupe that traveled through the British Isles. He died penniless, alcoholic, and despondent on August 14, 1818, in Galway, Ireland. He never returned to America and never did see any of his family after his departure from New York.

Richmond continued boxing, giving lessons at his school at Number 6 Whitcomb Street in London, and minding his tavern. He fought his last round at age fifty-two against Tom Shelton. He had a hand in the careers of several other black fighters, including Sam Robinson of New York, "Sutton," Joseph Stephenson of Havre de Grace, Maryland, "Massa Kendricks," "Bristow," and "Johnson." The very first black fighter on record was Joe Lashley, who fought in England in 1791, but it is not known where he was born.

Richmond settled in well in his role as teacher, saying, "[I]f a man of color cannot fight for the English title, then at least I can be a servant [teacher]."[1] He died on December 28, 1829. The *London Times* mentioned that he succumbed to a fit of coughing after spending the evening with Tom Cribb. Richmond and Cribb must have remained friends despite Molineaux's foul treatment.

Pierce Egan, the esteemed chronicler of the sport in his era, had the last and best eulogy for William Richmond: "In the ring, in the point of activity, he stands nearly unrivaled, and is considered to excel every other pugilist in hitting and getting away, and dealing out severe punishment with his left hand." Athlete, merchant, teacher— Richmond was the first in a long line of African-American boxing wonders.

The Anglo-Africans

From the era of the War of 1812 until after the Civil War, boxing had a precarious toehold in America. Religious objections were strong and peaked in the 1840s during the evangelical movement. Bouts were clandestinely held on barges or in private clubs. Slaves continued to box when they got the chance. There was much intraracial opposition. William Johnson, the free black from Natchez, Mississippi, who kept a personal diary from 1835 until 1852, described several public fights between slaves.

But the most cogent thoughts came from the pen of black abolitionist Frederick Douglass. In his autobiography he mentions the holidays at Christmas as a time when "the sober, thinking, industrious ones would employ themselves in manufacturing..."[2] He also believed that southern plantation owners used "those wild and low sports" to keep blacks semicivilized.[3] Perhaps he was correct, but boxing remained popular nonetheless.

After the Civil War social acceptance of boxing gained some adherents, in part due to the passage of the new Queensberry Rules in 1869. Fights called for three-minute rounds, ten-second counts after knock-downs, and mufflers or gloves. Into this new atmosphere came the first black world champion from our neighbor to the north. George Dixon was the first of three great Anglo-Africans to reign in their weight classes.

Dixon was born at Leston's Lane in Halifax, Nova Scotia, Canada, on July 29, 1870. His family had originally settled in Nova Scotia when large groups of blacks loyal to King George III during the Revolutionary War decided to leave the colonies. In the opinion of ring expert Nat Fleischer, "for all his ounces and inches, there never was a lad his equal."[4] Sam Austin, the editor of *The Police Gazette* (the major sports paper of the late 1800s), added that Dixon had no flaws.

He moved to Boston with his parents and became interested in boxing while working as an apprentice to a photographer who specialized in pugilists' photos. After training in a local gym the 5'3", 100-pound Dixon was spotted by Tom O'Rourke, who became his manager. He turned professional at age sixteen during a glorious time for the black athlete. Black jockeys were winning nearly all the important races like the Kentucky Derby; baseball players were still in the International League; and William H. Lewis was just six years away from becoming the first black All-America football player.

Dixon quickly learned the art of the body feint. Fans loved seeing him dart his head and upper body in and out to draw his opponents off guard. He fought three years before losing to another Canadian, George Wright. But soon he had financial backers and was able to post larger side-bets. (In these times, without a commissioner to regulate the sport, opposing boxers generally had to publicly state how much of their own money was put up for a fight. Though these sums usually came from patrons, it let the public know the gravity of a bout. The more important the bout, the higher the side-bet.)

On May 10, 1888, Dixon fought a nine-round draw against Tommy Kelly for the paperweight (105-pound limit) title but was denied it. So he sought the American bantamweight title against Cal McCarthy. This championship fight occurred on February 7, 1890, and ended in a no-contest decision after seventy rounds at the Union Athletic Club in Boston. In a second bout for this title on March 31, 1891, Dixon became the first black man to hold an American title in any sport by knocking out McCarthy in the twenty-second round. He had already become the first black boxer to win an international title when he KO'd the British featherweight champion, Nunc Wallace, on June 27, 1890.

But 1892 was an even more momentous year for Dixon and the sport. On June 27 he KO'd Fred Johnson in fourteen rounds at Coney Island, New York, to become the first black world titleholder—the new featherweight king—and $4,500 richer. And his bout on September 6 of that year was perhaps the most discussed of the decade and had social repercussions far beyond the boxing ring.

Dixon had never fought in the South. Of the three bouts he had fought in Washington, D.C., two were against other blacks. Now he was offered a bout in New Orleans at the private Olympia Club as part of a three-day boxing carnival. The main feature was the heavyweight title affair between the champion, John L. Sullivan, and "Gentleman" Jim Corbett on September 7. Dixon would fight white amateur Jack Skelly on September 6.

In 1892 New Orleans was very racially divided in the post-Reconstruction period. Racist Jim Crow laws prevailed, and no racially mixed public bouts were legal. But as the Olympia Club was private, no laws would be broken. In addition, a global flu epidemic was just receding and large gatherings were discouraged. Dixon secured a promise from the promoters to set aside seven hundred tickets for "people of color" to witness his performance. And what a performance it was!

His bout was billed as the world featherweight championship and is so listed in the record books. Dixon weighed 115 pounds to Skelly's 116.5. New electric indoor lights were used for the first time, and a winner-take-all purse of $17,500 awaited the winner, which could go only to Dixon if he won because Skelly was an amateur.

In the first round Skelly was peppered with shots from the more experienced champion as the white local fans winced in dismay. It was assumed that any experienced white boxer in peak condition could prevail over any black fighter. The promoters were almost sure Skelly was going to win, although Dixon was the reigning champion. But through the last four rounds it became "simply a question of how much punishment Skelly could absorb....Dixon broke Skelly's nose with a right-hand swing.

The blood came spurting from the injury....The sight was sickening....Finally in the eighth round, after a minute's work, Dixon crashed a right swing to the point of the jaw....Skelly...was counted out."[5] In some quarters of the city black citizens celebrated for two days.

But the morning papers on September 7 were swift and brutally frank in their assessment. From the *Chicago Tribune*: "white fans winced every time Dixon landed on Skelly. The sight was repugnant to some of the men from the South. A darky is alright in his place here, but the idea of sitting quietly by and seeing a colored boy pommel a white lad grates on Southerners."

From the *New Orleans Times-Democrat*: "What with bruises, lacerations and coagulated blood, Skelly's nose, mouth, and eye presented a horrible spectacle....some even turned away their heads in disgust...at that face already disfigured past recognition....It was a mistake to match a negro and a white man, a mistake to bring the races together on any terms of equality, even in the prize ring....It was not pleasant to see a white man applaud a negro for knocking another white man out."

Evidently nearly all the white spectators had come to the Olympia Club fully expecting a white amateur to handle a world champion, no matter what his color. The club itself, according to the September 11 *New Orleans Daily Picayune*, decided to "permit no more matches to be fought there, which ignore a respect for the color line." For his part, "Little Chocolate," as Dixon was called, said he would fight in New Orleans again if asked.

Dixon's win and the resulting racial animosity from whites was a prime factor in

limiting access for blacks to heavyweight
title bouts. It encouraged white boxers to
draw the color line, and it meant the absolute end of any more fights of its kind in the
segregated South.

On October 4, 1897, Dixon finally lost
his world featherweight title at Woodward's
Pavilion in San Francisco to Solly Smith,
whom he had previously beaten. He regained it over Dave Sullivan on November
11, 1898, on a disqualification in the tenth
round. Dixon thus became the first black
fighter to gain, lose, and regain a world
title. He lost it for good on January 9, 1900,
to Terry McGovern in New York on an
eighth-round knockout.

At the end Dixon was without friends
or his manager, O'Rourke. He had lost all
his ring earnings and admitted as much. He
was quoted as saying, "I hope that my
career will be a good lesson for others.... I
hope that they will remember my plight and
not follow the—Easy come, Easy go Methods—which has put me in the position
where I now find myself."[6]

He died January 6, 1909, in New York
City. His body lay in state at the Longacre
Athletic Club for two days until funds could
be amassed to send his remains to Boston.
George Dixon, the first black world boxing
champion, was buried in Mount Hope
Cemetery.

Dixon's stablemate under the man-
agership of O'Rourke was Joe Walcott,
sometimes known as "The Barbados De-
mon." Walcott was born March 13, 1873, in
Barbados, West Indies. Built like a fireplug,
he was only five feet, one and a half inches
tall and weighed 145 pounds at his best.

But what a fighter he was! Walcott simply
loved to mix it up in the ring. He won the
New England wrestling titles in the lightweight and middleweight classes—in the
same night!

Walcott was added to O'Rourke's roster of boxers from his position in Boston as
an elevator operator at the American House
Hotel. He hung around Jack Sheehan's
gymnasium and was soon beating everyone in his weight class. He turned professional at age seventeen in 1890 and won his
first bout, which netted him $2.50 at the
Music Hall. On August 22, 1893, he KO'd the
Australian lightweight champion, Jack
Hall.

But Walcott was a natural welterweight. In a match against George "Kid"
Lavigne, Walcott had to "train down" to the
lightweight limit. In fact, Lavigne's manager, Sam Fitzpatrick, forced O'Rourke to
agree that if Walcott did not stop Lavigne
inside of fifteen rounds, Walcott would lose
the bout. He did lose in fifteen rounds,
though he bloodied Lavigne unmercifully.
Special provisions like the foregoing were
common then.

After losing a bid for the world lightweight title against Lavigne on October 29,
1897, and a welterweight title bid to "Mysterious" Billy Smith in 1898, Walcott seemed
poised for his chance in 1900. But part of
his chance to fight for the welterweight title
again may have been an agreement to "take
a dive," or deliberately lose a few chosen
bouts. An eleventh-round loss to Tommy
West on August 27 certainly was fixed because he feared for his life. With no central
organization to control the sport, gamblers

bought and sold boxers at will. No black fighter between 1895 and 1906 could go undefeated, no matter how good he was.

Walcott's problem was that he did nothing to publicly disguise his blatantly inept performance. Nat Fleischer recalls that O'Rourke personally told him that "Walcott didn't dare to win that night. I got the tip...he must lose....If West had been stopped in that twelfth round...I'd probably have been laying nice, peaceful and natural on the next slab."[7]

New York had passed the Horton Law in 1896 rather than ban boxing outright. This law allowed private clubs to stage bouts, provided both the clubs and the boxers were registered by the state. It also lifted restrictions on the numbers of rounds and decisions by referees, and it forbade side-bets. But because of Walcott's showing, the Horton Law was replaced on August 30 by the Lewis Law, which mandated professional boxing on a club-membership basis only. That remained in effect until 1911. Despite these problems Walcott earned and defeated Jim "Rube" Ferns for the welterweight title on December 18, 1901. He won every round until it was stopped in the fifth after a KO. Walcott thus became the second black champion, but his laurel was not a world title.

After losing his welterweight crown to Aaron "Dixie Kid" Brown on April 30, 1904—the first time a title held by a black boxer was lost to another black boxer— Walcott fought a draw with Joe Gans for the world title on September 30 of that year. Brown had outgrown the welterweight class and abdicated his championship, so Wal-

cott claimed it, and his claim was generally recognized. He finally lost it to Billy "Honey" Mellody after recovering from a gun accident that left his friend dead and his right hand shattered.

Walcott fought on until 1911. He later became a fireman on a freighter, a porter at New York City's Majestic Theater, and a handyman at Madison Square Garden. He had spent all his earnings and died in an automobile accident in Massillon, Ohio, in 1935.

"The Dixie Kid" held the welterweight title only six months—from April 30, 1904, until October 4 of that year, when he abdicated. He fought on through 1914 as a middleweight.

The last of the black champions from the British Commonwealth was another Virgin Islander, Peter Jackson. Jackson came from Fredericksted, where he was born on July 3, 1861. At age six he was taken to Australia to live and began taking boxing lessons at age seventeen from Larry Foley. He won the Australian heavyweight title on September 25, 1886, from Tom Leeds in thirty seconds of the first round. He thus became the first black man to win a national boxing crown.

Jackson sailed for America in 1888 to fight the leading heavyweights, but racism immediately halted his plans. He had to settle for fighting George Godfrey, who was *The Police Gazette*'s "Colored Champion." *The Police Gazette* named colored champions in almost every weight class, in part to stimulate interest among its black readers and in part to appease the racist sentiments of its other ethnic readers. Baseball was squeezing the last blacks out of the major leagues, and the *Gazette* merely reflected the general feelings of antipathy toward black athletes.

Already twenty-eight in 1889, the 6' 1½", 192-pound boxer was running out of time if he hoped to annex the world title. As good as he was and with the Australian title to his credit, he could find few whites to fight. He decided to go to England, but not before expressing the hope that "here in your America, the opportunity which I have been seeking will come to me."[8] He was so wrong. Few periods in American history can match the racism toward blacks and Orientals of the late nineteenth century.

One white man who pointedly refused to meet Jackson was America's first national sports hero, John L. Sullivan, better known as "The Boston Strong Boy." Sullivan was the world heavyweight champion in 1889, but when approached about fights with blacks, he said, "I will not fight a negro. I never have, and I never shall."[9] But in truth Sullivan *had* fought a black man in Tombstone, Arizona.

In 1884, a year before he won the title, Sullivan was touring the Southwest and challenging all comers to stay in the ring with him for two rounds for five hundred dollars. A "near giant [black] named Jim, who rode for John H. Slaughter" took up the challenge. The *Tombstone Epitaph* recalls that Sullivan and Jim met in Schiefflin Hall, and when the fight began, Jim got in the first lick, "a looping round house swing that caught Sullivan high on the head and threw him off balance." But that was it. Sullivan finished him off handily, and Jim was "carried out feet first like a ton of coal."[10] This

encounter may not have been official, but it happened nonetheless.

Jackson captured the British title from Jim Smith on November 11, 1889, on a foul in the second round. (British boxers were evidently still using dirty tactics seventy-nine years after the Tom Cribb–Tom Molineaux bout.) On May 21, 1891, the thirty-year-old Jackson had his most famous bout, with a future champion, James Corbett. At the California Athletic Club in San Francisco, the two boxers fought a sixty-one round draw. Experts rate this as one of the sport's most acclaimed fights. A year later, Corbett won the world championship from Sullivan at the aforementioned boxing carnival in New Orleans.

Sadly, after winning the heavyweight title, Corbett also drew the color line, thus depriving younger black heavyweights of a chance for glory. In a possible attempt at atonement for this, Corbett wrote in his autobiography that Jackson was the best fighter he had ever seen. Jackson's most poignant plea came in a lengthy letter published in the July 3, 1893, *Rocky Mountain News* of Denver, Colorado.

It said, in part, "Before age has impaired my powers I hope to have the pleasure of again meeting James J. Corbett in the ring. Not that I have a feelng of animosity for him. On the contrary, I like him very much....Corbett defeated the best fighter that ever lived, John L. Sullivan....So it comes about that Corbett, being champion of America, and your humble servant practically holding the championship of England and Australia, the three fight-countries of the universe, either of us, should one defeat the other, would be the champion pugilist of the world....I was very sorry when he took on Charles Mitchell of England and passed me by....The champion's proposition that I put myself in condition and be prepared to take Mitchell's place...is foolish.

"I ask in all fairness, what earthly chance have I of meeting the champion next December?...I have never challenged Corbett and I never will....Age is now coming on me—I am thirty-two....I hope to get on a match with him....Boxing I think, is a manly sport....It is not for every man to be a fighter....If a man is fainthearted he should never step over the ropes....The man whose heart fails him suffers...like the poor wretch on the way to the galllows."

It is clear that Corbett promised Jackson a rematch but that someone persuaded him to renege. Even Corbett's conscience as a sportsman was not strong enough to meet the Australian and English champion, embodied in Jackson. Racial antagonism in America was that strong in the early 1890s. Equally as poignant, two years later in 1895, was another open letter, written this time by the white sports editor of the influential New York *Sun*, Charles A. Dana. His missive was the most provocative piece of racist sports journalism yet seen in America and caused a sensation that lasted for years afterward.

Dana wrote, "We are in the midst of a growing menace. The black man is rapidly forging to the front ranks in athletics, especially in the field of fisticuffs. We are in the midst of a black rise against white supremacy....Less than a year ago Peter Jackson could have whipped the world—Corbett, [Robert] Fitzsimmons,...but the white race is saved from having at the head of pugilism a Negro....There are two Negroes in the ring today who can thrash any white man breathing in their respective classes...George Dixon...and Joe Walcott....If the Negro is capable of developing such prowess in those divisions of boxing, what is going to stop him from making the same progress in the heavier ranks?

"What America needs now is another John L. Sullivan....How is it that these sable champions spring up all at once? Is it because they are far better than their white brethren or is the white race deteriorating?...Wake up, you pugilists of the white race! Are you going to permit yourself to be passed by the black race?...Some say that the 'colored brother' is not a man of the highest courage, but I doubt that....He has always been made to believe that he belongs to an inferior race....But...the Negro has evinced as much courage in combat as the white man."

Because the New York *Sun* was one of the sports world's most-read papers, Dana's commentary was a bombshell. He openly appealed to the worst in the white sporting public and reinforced the popular notion that black athletes in all sports lacked heart. Fifteen years after Dana's piece appeared, his racist theories caused the downfall of the most acclaimed white heavyweight champion since Sullivan.

With few opportunities, Peter Jackson's career was short and bittersweet. He had thirty-five wins, three losses, and one draw. He returned to Australia and died of tuberculosis on July 13, 1901, at forty-one.

He was buried with honor at Toowong Cemetery in Roma, Queensland, and his gravestone is engraved with words that wished for him eternal peace:

SLEEP, PETER, SLEEP, *brave champion.*
   All hushed,
will gather around where snow-white
   flowers, moist-eyed,
we fling within the grave.
The fight is done.
Sleep, Peter, Sleep.
The hero's rest is there
in mother earth's broad breast.

Joe Gans

The first African-American to win a world title was born in Baltimore, Maryland, on November 25, 1874. His name at birth was Joseph Gaines, but it was later shortened to Joe Gans. At full maturity he stood 5'6¼" and weighed 133 pounds. His nickname at the height of his powers was "The Old Master."

Gans was found along the docks of Baltimore, where he first toiled as an oyster shucker. Like other black boys his age, he went to the Monumental Theater to see whatever was on the program. One night the theater featured a battle royal in which several youngsters were all put in the ring at one time and told to fight it out until only one remained. Gans won this affair and attracted the attention of boxing enthusiast and restaurant owner Al Hereford.

The gentle Gans was genuinely surprised that someone like Hereford showed interest in him. Hereford supposedly replied, "That's my funeral, not yours. I'm satisfied to take a chance."[11] Turning professional in 1891, Gans was one of the busiest fighters on record. In his first nine years he lost only twice. One of these losses was to another famous black boxer, Bobby Dobbs, who, although a natural welterweight, fought anybody and everybody. Dobbs had been born a slave in Knoxville, Tennessee in 1858.

After the loss to Dobbs in 1897, Gans was thought to be champion material with a string of victories laced with knockouts. He landed a shot at the world lightweight title against Frank Erne on March 23, 1900, but was KO'd in the twelfth round. His fighting skills were nevertheless obvious. He piled up more knockouts until he fought a bout on December 13 of that year against Terry McGovern in Chicago. Gans "took a dive" and lost in the second round to blows that observers declared would not harm an infant. It was obviously a fixed bout, and the resulting stink caused the Chicago City Council to ban the sport. He deserved the shame he felt, although he may have feared for his life just as Joe Walcott had before him. Some even felt he had taken a dive against Erne as well.

A year and a half after his disgraceful display against McGovern, Gans got his second chance at the world lightweight crown. Fighting in Fort Erie, Ontario, Canada, he KO'd Erne in the first round to become the first native-born African-American to win a world crown. A right to the chin caught Erne off balance, followed by a left to the jaw and another right to the jaw, and down went Erne for good. Erne was still on the canvas when referee Johnny White counted him out.

Gans then began gaining weight. He fought as a welterweight although he would lose the weight to defend his lightweight title. This up and down in weight took its toll. He was forced to defend the title against Jimmy Britt, who was not above using foul tactics to his advantage. In the second round Gans went down and was delivered a low blow, which drew a warning from referee Ed Graney. Britt ignored the warning. In the fifth round Gans again went down, and Britt clouted Gans on the side of the head while he was on his knees. Instead of going to a neutral corner as Graney instructed, Britt hovered atop Gans and struck when he could.

Finally, Graney would take no more and disqualified Britt for repeated fouls. Then all hell broke loose. Britt took swings at Graney, and they both hit the deck until police arrived to separate them. So Gans retained his title on a foul. But to remove any doubt about his superiority, Gans defeated Britt in 1907 in six rounds. The tactics used by Britt would have been unthinkable for a black boxer to use against a white opponent in a championship fight.

Gans was then challenged by Oscar M. "Battling Nelson" Nielson of Denmark, who was the new world lightweight champion. After the Britt win in 1904, Gans relinquished his world lightweight title and actually won the vacant world welterweight title from Mike Sullivan on January 19, 1906. Gans could hardly refuse—the money was so tempting. Nelson and Gans then agreed to a "fight to a finish" at Goldfield, Nevada, on September 3. The promoter was Tex Rickard, who would figure very prominently in a later bout between Jack Johnson and Jim Jeffries.

The $34,000 purse was divided into $11,000 for Gans and $23,000 for Nelson. Billy Nolan, Nelson's manager, insisted on this split because he knew Gans was short of money. In addition, Gans had to reduce to the 133-pound limit at age thirty-two. Furthermore, Nolan insisted that Gans had to make the weight on the day of the fight in his boxing clothes. Gans had to agree because he needed the money. No matter; the fight was a classic.

Under a brutal Nevada sun, Gans reportedly vomited four times and broke his right hand in the thirty-third round. Ever the model of sportsmanship, he twice bent over to pick up Nelson after knocking him down. Nelson was not so kind. In the forty-second round, by then half blind from punches, Nelson lashed out with a vicious blow to the groin. Without hesitation, referee George Siler ordered Nelson to his corner and awarded Gans the fight on a foul. Gans thus regained his old world lightweight title.

However, his victory caused the first serious outbreaks of racial violence against blacks as a result of a boxing match. Police reported incidents across the country attributed to the bout. William Conway, a black bar patron in Flushing, New York, had his skull fractured by three white customers. Anthony Roberts, a black doorman at the St. Urban Apartments on New York City's Central Park West, told police he fought off two white attackers with a razor and a small pistol.

Gans regained his title, but he was losing another battle. He had tuberculosis and knew he was going to die. He retained his world lightweight crown with four successful defenses and ordered his manager to book another match with Nelson. With a wife and two children, he wanted to provide for their future. Gans and Nelson met on Independence Day in 1908, and although Gans was "The Old Master" for five rounds, he could not hang on. He went down three times in the seventeenth and final round as Nelson regained his lost title. They met one last time in Colma, California, on September 9, and Nelson again prevailed with a knockout in the twenty-first round.

In the spring of 1909 Gans went to Prescott, Arizona, to try to arrest his deadly affliction. But realizing intuitively that he was near death, he asked his friend Kid North to take him home before he expired. He just made it, dying in his mother's arms as his wife and children stood nearby. Joseph (Gaines) Gans was buried in the Mount Auburn Cemetery in Baltimore on August 13, 1910. He left his family financially secure and his reputation restored.

Gans was not alone among black boxers in the lower weight classes. The aforementioned Aaron "Dixie Kid" Brown was widely respected, although he had a pitiful end. Brown committed suicide by jumping from a hotel window. Frank "The Harlem Coffee Cooler" Craig hailed from New York City and fought as a middleweight around 1900. Sim Thompkins adopted the nickname "Young Peter Jackson" and was a Baltimore-based welterweight during the Joe Gans era. Charles Henry "Jack" Blackburn was known as "The Philadelphia Comet" and mixed it up with Sam Langford and Gans several times. Blackburn became best known as Joe Louis' trainer after spending some prison time for a shooting.

Sam Langford was one of the best of his time and could have been world middleweight champion. He was born in Nova Scotia, Canada, on March 4, 1886, and fought in more different weight classes than anyone else. Though only 5'6" his weight varied between 150 and 190 pounds. Be-

cause black fighters had such difficulty booking bouts against whites, he fought other blacks over and over: Joe Jeanette eighteen times, Sam McVey fifteen times, Jim Barry twelve times, Jack Johnson once. It was strongly rumored that Jack Johnson reneged on an oral promise to fight him when he became heavyweight champion. Langford and others like him before World War I had to endure discriminatory treatment not meted out to other ethnic groups.

Gans' death closed out the second era of the African-American boxer that had begun with the Tom Cribb–William Richmond fight in 1805. Authorities allowed blacks to contest for world titles in all weight classes but the heavyweight division before 1908. Gans and his contemporaries—George Dixon, Joe Walcott, Peter Jackson, Bobby Dobbs, and many others—proved to all that blacks could garner their share of honors if given the chance. It was well into the first decade of the century before the first black heavyweight challenger for the world crown could prove his worth. And the sport has not been the same since then.

John Arthur Johnson

Athletes from myriad sports acquired monikers or nicknames that enlivened their marquee value and described some obvious talent or celebrated their hometown. Not so with John Arthur Johnson, who was born in Galveston, Texas, on March 31, 1878. He was known simply as "L'il Arthur" as a boy and Jack Johnson as a man. History invested him with the opportunity to batter down the last serious barrier to blacks in sports.

Starting with John L. Sullivan and ending with Jim Jeffries on his retirement in 1905, white world heavyweight champions cooperated with boxing officials to maintain it as a bastion of white supremacy. Looking back on what motives could have driven them to take this approach, it seems contradictory to at once deny the black man the chance to prove himself while espousing the notion that he was innately a coward. Surely a coward would have been no competition against a world champion. The most plausible answer was the general feeling throughout the nation around 1900 that blacks were socially, physically, and mentally inferior to whites, even divinely ordained so.

Major league baseball had barred blacks since 1885. The jockeys had been denied their license renewals. Marshall Taylor was literally run off some of the velodromes. College football teams had quotas for blacks. Black tennis players were not acceptable on the grass courts of Newport, Rhode Island. In this supportive atmosphere, it was palpably easy for white heavyweight champions to draw the color line and not be accused of ducking a likely black contender. For white America truly believed then that no black man had a chance anyway, though some sports writers had their doubts.

Johnson came from a family of three boys and three girls and was a favored child. His mother, Tina, and sister Lucy were especially fond of him. His father was much more strict, insisting that he work alongside him at his janitorial duties. After finishing the fifth grade, Johnson quit school and embarked on a string of jobs that took him far beyond Galveston. He worked on a milk wagon for $1.25 per week; in Gregory's Livery Stables; as a baker's apprentice. At thirteen he tried to run away from Galveston as a stowaway aboard a moving freight train, only to find out later that the train had just shifted around in the yard itself.

He heard about Steve Brodie, the man who jumped off the Brooklyn Bridge and lived to tell about it, and yearned to meet him. Johnson finally did meet Brodie after smuggling himself onto a steamship. When caught, he had to work as a cook's helper to pay for his trip. But the ill treatment he received at the hands of whites in many occupations left a vein of resentment and repressed anger and frustration in him. Later, as one of his biographers, Finis Farr, noted, "He could make people angry by the expression on his face."[12]

From New York his wanderlust took him to Boston, where his leg was broken by a horse while he was working at the racetrack. He was still only fifteen. Homesick, he headed back to Galveston for a job on the docks as a stevedore. There he had to fight just to keep his place. After taking a few lickings, his sister Lucy shamed him into defending himself, and he eventually prevailed against the bully of the wharf.

At sixteen he headed for Dallas, where his boss in a carriage shop, Walter Lewis, happened to be an ex-boxer. Offered free lessons, Johnson took them and tested his new skills against Bob Thompson, who traveled as part of a troupe of boxers. Although he took a licking for the required four rounds, he collected twenty-five dollars for his time and decided fighting was more profitable than building buggies. From 1895 through 1897 he traveled and boxed for a living. He even suffered the indignity of battles royal and spent some time as Joe Walcott's sparring partner.

Back home in Galveston in 1897, he married Mary Austin, a black woman, and had his first serious bout against Joe Choynsky, a noted Polish-Jewish heavyweight, on February 25, 1901. He was KO'd in three rounds. Both fighters spent three weeks in jail since boxing was illegal in Texas. Johnson, however, used his time incarcerated wisely, taking more lessons from Choynsky. It would not be his last time in jail.

Johnson and Austin were divorced in 1902. He took up with Clara Kerr, another black woman. By then a determined fighter, he signed on with Frank Corella as his manager, who arranged vaudeville appearances as well. It was quite common for black boxers to augment their ring earnings with theatrical exhibitions when traveling across the country. Johnson's stint included a harmonica solo, a bass fiddle routine, a dance routine, and the wide smile of his that bared a bright golden tooth.

In the ring Johnson was acclaimed the best black boxer alive on February 3, 1903, when he defeated "Denver" Ed Martin for the Negro heavyweight crown. The average white fight fan, however, knew very little of these affairs. In 1903 and 1904, for instance, all his opponents were black. Few whites desiring a shot at the world title would bother boxing a noted black heavyweight, for they had everything to lose. If they won, the public would say, "So what." If they lost, the public would say, "You must not be very good to lose to a black fighter."

Black heavyweights of the period tended to be older than their white counter-

parts. First, it took longer for them to establish their reputations. Second, a good young fighter without early backing or promotion usually quit and learned a trade. Third, they had to have white managers to book their bouts, and these managers were willing to take on only proven properties. Fourth, some of them were part-timers. And fifth, many of them had committed themselves to boxing before Sullivan and company began drawing the color line.

In 1903 world champion Jim Jeffries echoed the old Sullivan line by declaring, "I will not fight a negro! If the public demands that I should fight Johnson I will surely have to decline. If Johnson wants to fight for the championship he will have to fight somebody besides me. If I am defeated, the championship will go to a white man, for I will not fight a colored man. Now mind, I am not shrinking from this match because I am afraid of Johnson, for I think I could lick him as I have the rest."[13] Jeffries was not maligned for thinking this way. It looked hopeless for any black heavyweight to dream of fighting for the world title at the end of 1903.

The following year Johnson started to publicly question Jeffries's abilities, which Johnson claimed were hidden behind "the color line." It was the image of the uppity black man challenging the strongest white man in the world to a fight. But Jeffries would not be budged. He retired in May 1905, citing a lack of competition—white competition, that is. Johnson then turned his attention to Marvin Hart, the new world titleholder, though he had lost to Hart four months before Hart became champion. He also lost on a second-round foul to Joe Jeanette, a black heavyweight.

Hart then lost to the Canadian Tommy Burns, so Johnson again readjusted his aim. But the retired Jeffries was still on his mind. Burns, like the other champions before him, drew the color line, although his reputation was not nearly as dynamic. He stood 5′ 7″ and weighed only 175 pounds. Johnson had to establish a record that was uncontestable. He was undefeated in 1906 and 1907.

One of his wins was over Bob Fitzsimmons, the former world champion. Johnson was thus the first black man to score a victory over a world heavyweight champion. Meanwhile, his new manager Sam Fitzpatrick sought every means possible to arrange a date with Burns. Burns kept refusing, so Fitzpatrick and Johnson decided to literally chase Burns wherever he went. Burns made plans to go to Australia, so Johnson got there ahead of time. When Burns found out that Johnson was already in Australia, he stayed in the United States.

Several newspapers—including the St. Louis *Post-Dispatch* and the New York *Sun*—now demanded Burns defend himself and his title against Johnson. Another former world champion, James Corbett, said, "Tommy Burns would lick Jack Johnson if they ever came together."[14] From England, Burns had to say something, so he boasted that "I'll take care of Johnson when I return to the United States."[15] Johnson, though, had no intention of letting Burns return to the United States before fighting him.

London's National Sporting Club wanted to stage the fight, and Johnson and Fitzpatrick went there to open discussions. But Johnson was made to wait out on the sidewalk while Fitzpatrick was ushered inside. Johnson was furious but Burns mooted the discussions when he departed for France. Johnson followed. Burns then departed for Australia; Johnson followed after hearing King Edward VII refer to Burns as a Yankee bluffer—which must have been doubly damning since Burns was a Canadian, not an American.

Finally Burns could run no more, and he agreed to meet his black challenger. Actually, if some wise and clairvoyant seer had been asked to name the most logical place for the first world heavyweight title bout between a white and a black boxer, Australia would have been it. Still largely unexplored and underpopulated and possessing a rugged frontier spirit, the Aussies were quite hospitable to black athletes. Peter Jackson had been popular there, and so was cyclist Marshall Taylor.

The fight date was set for December 26, 1908, with a purse of $40,000, split $35,000 for Burns and $5,000 for Johnson. Hugh "Huge Deal" McIntosh was the promoter of this bout at Rushcutter's Bay in Sydney. Before the fight Burns said to a New York *World* reporter, "I will bet a few plunks that the colored man will not make good! I'll fight him and whip him, as sure as my name is Tommy Burns."[16] Burns still believed that black fighters were basically cowards.

Johnson was more measured in his response. "Burns has embedded in his brain the belief that I have a yellow streak, that I am not game....I am here to assure the sporting patrons of Australia that nothing like that will happen. I have not lost heart."[17] Johnson even opened his training to the public and delighted some startled reporters when he bet a friend that he could outrun a kangaroo and did so. By his own admission he did "lots of road work but comparatively little boxing, giving my attention to ball and bag punching."[18] Still, just before round one Burns was a 3-to-2 favorite.

Twenty-six thousand fans, reporters, sportswriters, and local notables and two women attended the fight. Johnson, thirty, and Burns, twenty-seven, weighed 195 and 180 pounds, respectively, although Johnson was almost six inches taller at 6' 1¾". The opening bell sounded at 11:15 A.M., and Johnson immediately began berating his opponent, "Who told you I was yellow? You're white Tommy—white as the flag of surrender!"[19] And down went Burns from a right uppercut.

After the first round, bettors started hedging their wagers. Following round two the odds were even. By the eighth round Burns' eyes were almost closed, and he was bleeding from the mouth. No mouthpieces were worn in those days. Johnson talked constantly, inviting Burns to approach and take his best shot. After the thirteenth round, McIntosh consulted with police about stopping the fight. But Burns' aides said he would fight on. In the fourteenth round Burns was staggered twice by rights to the head and combinations. The police finally called a halt, and John Arthur Johnson, a descendant of the Koromantee tribe of West Africa, was the new world heavyweight champion.

While the *Washington Post*'s J. Ed Grillo reported Johnson's victory as a popular one, Johnson himself was frank and forthright: "I never doubted the issue from the beginning. I knew I was too good for Burns. I have forgotten more about fighting than Burns ever knew."[20]

Tommy Burns was also honest. He said, "Race prejudice was rampant in my mind. The idea of a black man challenging me was beyond enduring. Hatred made me tense."[21] Johnson had startled Burns and Fitzpatrick before the fight by asking Burns if he and McIntosh were good friends. When Burns replied that "there are none better,"[22] Johnson insisted McIntosh referee the match. Fitzpatrick gulped, but Johnson held his ground. Johnson wanted to make sure there would be no problems afterward on this matter.

Two other ringside commentators made noteworthy pronouncements. One was former heavyweight champion John L. Sullivan, a guest columnist for the *New York Times*. He cynically said that "the negro can't assume that title [heavyweight champion]....I can't see where Johnson will be given a high position in the general public."[23]

The other commentator wrote one of the most famous passages ever penned in sports. He was author Jack London, of *Call Of The Wild* fame. London must have felt sorely piqued at Johnson's victory because his tone was emotional yet conciliatory. He wrote, "The fight!—There was no fight!...It had all the seeming of a playful Ethiopian at loggerheads with a small white man—of a grown man cuffing a naughty child....But one thing now remains. Jim Jeffries must emerge from his alfalfa farm and remove the golden smile from Jack Johnson's face. Jeff, it's up to you!"[24]

So Jim Jeffries became the "Great White Hope" to save his race. But he was four and a half years retired and overweight. Johnson had his own troubles. Following his breakup with Clara Kerr, he had forsworn black women, thinking they could not be trusted. In her place came Belle Schrieber, a white woman. In Australia, however, he was accompanied by Hattie McClay, whom the Aussie press referred to as "that New York Irish girl." Back home in Galveston, the local black community had planned a welcome reception, but they asked Johnson not to bring McClay. Johnson told them to go to hell.

In New York City, blacks had no such southern qualms and welcomed him with a brass band at Grand Central Station. The black press wanted Johnson to defend his title against a black challenger. But he refused, as Jeffries began softening his opposition to a bout. Johnson then fired Fitzpatrick and took on George Little and Sig Hart as his new managers. Sam Berger, Jeffries' manager, thought a Johnson-Jeffries fight was as good as a license to print money.

Jeffries was finally persuaded to come out of retirement, and the two parties met on December 1, 1909, at the Albany Hotel in New York City to work out the largest and richest proposition in sports history. Johnson had to agree to fight in the United States, to limit the bout to from twenty to one hundred rounds, to allow clubs to bid for the site rights, to post—along with Jeffries—a five-thousand-dollar good faith bond, and to allow Jeffries to split the proceeds either sixty-forty or seventy-five-twenty-five as he saw fit.

Six of the world's best-known promoters offered sealed bids with a five-thousand-dollar nonrefundable bid fee. They were Ed Graney, Jack Gleason, Jimmy Coffroth and Tom McCary, Hugh "Huge Deal" McIntosh, and George Lewis "Tex" Rickard. It came down to McCary and Rickard. McCary offered the fighters the entire purse plus $110,000, but they had to sign in twenty-four hours. Rickard then explained his bid of $101,000, including $20,000 immediately, $20,000 sixty days thence, and another $50,000 forty-eight hours before the bout. Jeffries and Johnson asked for twenty-four hours to think about it.

The next day Rickard showed up with $20,000 in solid gold to show he meant business, and he won the bid. But just before they were about to sign, the police intervened and threatened to jail anyone who signed anything because of the Lewis Law, which allowed only club bouts. The group simply got up, took a ferry across the Hudson River to the Naegeli Hotel in Hoboken, New Jersey, and signed the papers. After considering Salt Lake City, San Francisco was chosen as the site for July 4, 1910. This proposal constituted the largest legitimate business deal ever consummated by an African-American to that time.

The thirty-four-year old Jeffries began his weight-reducing regimen in Carlsbad, California, and then at the Rowardennan Hotel near San Francisco. Johnson and Duryea went to spend Christmas in London to fulfill vaudeville engagements, and he managed to get into all sorts of trouble.

After being arrested in London twice for "breaking furniture" and "using foul language," Johnson made his way to San Francisco. The psyching began at once. Jim Corbett, a part of Jeffries' camp, said "Take it from me, the black boy has a yellow streak, and Jeff will bring it out when he gets him into the ring."[25] The February 5, 1910, *Chicago Defender*, a black paper, said,

"The Future Welfare of His People Forms a Part of the Stake."

Problems then came in bunches. On March 24 Johnson was jailed in New York City's Tombs prison for roughing up another black man, Norman Pinder. He then fired George Little, one of his managers. On June 15 the Governor of California, James C. Gillette, bowed to pressure from religious groups and canceled California as the venue. Fortunately Rickard had a friend in Nevada Governor Denver Dickerson, who agreed to Reno as a site. Once the materials were in place the arena was built in three days.

Jeffries began getting nervous. He changed the money split to sixty-forty, although he had a confirmed offer of $608,000 for a "Grand Tour of Champions" beginning July 8—if he won. Johnson was offered no such tour. Upon arriving in Reno, Jeffries made the following statement: "When the gloves are knotted on my hands, and I stand ready to defend what is really my title, it will be at the request of the public, which forced me out of retirement. I realize full well what depends on me, and I am not going to disappoint the public. That portion of the white race that has been looking to me to defend its athletic superiority may feel assured that I am fit to do my very best. If Johnson defeats me, I will shake his hand and declare him the greatest fighter the world has ever known."[26] It was an extraordinarily racist statement from a man who hadn't fought in five years.

Johnson's entourage included Billy Delaney, his trainer and former trainer for both Jeffries and Corbett; Tom Flannigan; "Professor" Burns; Sig Hart; Barney "Doc" Furey; George "Kid" Cotton; Dave Mills;

Stanley Ketchel, the former world middleweight champion; and Frank Sutton. In his prefight comments he said, "Every fighter on the eve of his fight declares that he hopes the best man wins....if Mr. Jeffries knocks me out or gains a decision over me, I will go into his corner and congratulate him as soon as I am able....I mean it...I will proclaim Mr. Jeffries king of them all."[27] The world's press was sending out over a million words a day from Reno just before the bout. Thirty thousand people showed up for a place in an arena that held only eighteen thousand.

Official ticket prices ranged from ten to fifty dollars, and there were few scalpers. Curiously, two black boxers, Bob Armstrong and Sam Langford, joined the Jeffries camp. Langford was surely jealous and wanted a bit of revenge from Johnson for reneging on an agreement to fight him after becoming champion.

John L. Sullivan was once again a *New York Times* guest columnist but was afraid to say publicly beforehand that he thought Johnson would win. Joe Choynsky and Tommy Burns opted for Jeffries. Battling Nelson picked Johnson. On Saturday, July 2, Rickard duly paid the $101,000 to former New York Congressman Tim Sullivan for safekeeping. The fighters were ready and the war of words was over.

Writer Norman Mailer once penned a book about a bout between Muhammad Ali and Joe Frazier called *The Fight*. But that fight did not even closely approximate the Johnson-Jeffries bout in overall athletic, social, and racial importance. The morning of July 4 was a clear, powder blue. For breakfast Johnson had four lamb cutlets, three scrambled eggs, and several slices of steak. Jeffries had fruit, toast, and tea. They agreed to dispense with the traditional prefight handshake—an obvious insult to Johnson, which he calmly ignored.

Johnson entered the ring wearing a floor-length robe with velvet lining; Jeffries wore street clothes minus a shirt. Johnson bowed to all four sides of the ring. When asked to call a flip of a coin to see who would get the shady corner looking away from the sun, Johnson interrupted and told Jeffries he could take any corner he desired. Jeffries chose the shady side. When they doffed their outer garments, Jeffries was wearing purple trunks; Johnson wore navy blue trunks with an American flag draped through the belt loops. Jeffries was attempting the near impossible. He had not fought in nearly six years but was unbeaten in twenty-one fights. Still, he was a solid 5-to-3 favorite.

The fight began one hour late, at three o'clock. A serious Johnson easily won the first two rounds as Jeffries clinched at every opportunity. In round four Jack suffered a cut lip from an uppercut as both fighters talked incessantly. Rickard reminded them that this "was a fight not a talkfest."[28] At the end of the fifth round most experts believed Jeffries had little chance. His punches had no crispness and were off target and generally ineffective, and he was tiring.

Johnson taunted not only Jeffries but his backers at ringside as well. To Sullivan he said while clinching, "John, I thought this fellow could hit."[29] To Corbett at the end of the seventh round, he bellowed over Jeffries' shoulder, "Too late now to do anything, Jim; your man's all in."[30] The ninth and tenth rounds were all Johnson as he did his heaviest damage with uppercuts. (In those days fighters did not wear mouthpieces.) In the eleventh Jeffries was spitting blood and hugged at every opportunity.

Jeffries knew that if he fell at the feet of a black man it would symbolize the failure of the white race. The myth of the natural superiority of the white man over the black man had brought Jeffries out of retirement in the first place, and now he was paying the price. In round thirteen Jeffries was a pitiful sight as Johnson allowed Jeffries to hit him at will while laughing at the feeble attempts.

The end came at two minutes twenty-five seconds into the fifteenth round. A left uppercut sent Jeffries down on both knees near the west side of the ring. The referee counted. Jeffries rested one foot on the canvas and was up at the count of nine. Johnson hit him with a left at point-blank range "full on the face," which sent him through the ropes. Again Jeffries came back to be met with a right to the ear. Corbett cried out, "Oh don't Jack; don't hit him!"[31] Johnson ignored him and sent another left home. Jeffries sank to the floor sideways.

Rickard counted again. Eight seconds later Jeffries' seconds rushed into the ring—in clear violation of the rules—to help him. Delaney broke through and demanded that Rickard give the fight to Johnson. Delaney did not realize that Jeffries' camp was throwing in the towel. John Arthur Johnson was now the undisputed world heavyweight champion.

Johnson was uncompromising in his postfight comments. "I won from Mr. Jeffries because I outclassed him in every department....I was certain I would be the victor. I never changed my mind at any time.... I believe we both fought fairly.... He joked me and I joked him. I told him I knew he was a bear but I was a gorilla and would defeat him."[32]

From Jeffries: "I lost my fight... because I did not have the snap of youth.... I believed in my own heart that all the old-time dash was there. ... It simply was not there and that's all there is to it.... I guess it's my own fault.... They started calling for me and mentioning me as 'the white man's hope.' I guess my pride got the better of my judgement."[33] Later Jeffries admitted that "I never could have whipped Johnson at my best. I couldn't have hit him."[34]

The fighters cleaned up financially. Johnson got $110,600—$50,000 for the movie rights and $60,600 as his share of the proceeds. Jeffries got $90,400—$50,000 for the movie rights and $40,400 as his share. There was no federal or state income tax at all. Forty years later, Jeffries still regretted his comeback attempt. He died a wealthy man at seventy-seven.

While the crowds dispersed peacefully in Reno, there was pandemonium and bloodshed elsewhere over Johnson's unpopular victory. Page four of the July 5 *New York Times* read like a police precinct bulletin board: "THREE KILLED IN VIDALIA [Georgia] ... OMAHA NEGRO KILLED ... TWO NEGROES SLAIN ... BLACKS SHOOT UP TOWN ... HOUSTON MAN KILLS NEGRO ... NEGRO SHOOTS WHITE MAN ... NEGRO HURT IN PHILADELPHIA ... OUTBREAKS IN NEW ORLEANS ... POLICE CLUB RIOTING NEGROES ... MOB BEATS NEGROES IN MACON [Georgia] ... 70 ARRESTED IN BALTIMORE ... ALMOST LYNCH NEGRO." In all, thirteen blacks were killed and hundreds were wounded as angry whites retaliated over the loss of their Great White Hope.

White town councils in Washington, D.C., Atlanta, Baltimore, St. Louis, Cincinnati, and other cities banned films of the fight. Congress passed a quickie law banning the distribution of the films across state lines for commercial purposes. One can only wonder what the reaction would have been had Jeffries won. As Talladega College Professor Wil Pickens wrote in the July 29, 1910, *Chicago Defender,* "[I]f Jeffries had won the fight, it would have aroused no resentment in the Negro race against the white race. The Negroes would have forgotten it in about fifteen minutes."

Travels and Travails

Johnson did not enjoy a period of idolatry or social acceptance. Whites considered him too uppity, mainly because he had a white wife. So he headed for Europe and some vaudeville engagements managed by his nephew Gus Rhodes. He did not fight at all in 1911. He married Etta Duryea and opened his own saloon called Café de Champion at 42 West Thirty-first Street in Chicago, which featured famous black chanteuse Bricktop. He just refused to change his lifestyle. He had one fight in 1912, a ninth-round KO over Jim Flynn.

On September 11, 1912, Etta committed suicide by shooting herself. A month later Johnson himself was shot in the foot by one of his musicians over another white woman, Lucille Cameron, who later became his secretary. Cameron's mother threatened to charge Johnson with abduction. Cameron was held in late October for questioning under the Mann Act, which made it a crime to transport anyone across state lines for immoral purposes. On November 1, 1912, his café's liquor license was revoked. On November 7, Johnson was formally indicted by a grand jury of violating the Mann Act. (The presiding judge, of all people, was Kennesaw Mountain Landis, who would be singularly responsible for keeping blacks out of major league baseball when he became the commissioner.) But the person in question was not Cameron; it was Belle Schrieber, who had agreed to serve as a government witness. White America meant to punish Johnson one way or another.

Said Charles Erberstein, Schrieber's lawyer, "Jack Johnson has insulted every white woman in the United States."[35] Booker T. Washington was even asked to give a statement. He replied through his secretary, Emmett J. Scott, "Jack Johnson's case will be settled in due time in the courts....this is another illustration of the most irreparable injury that a wrong action on the part of a single individual may do to a whole race. It shows the folly of those who think that they alone will be held responsible for the evil that they do....No one can do so much injury to the Negro race as the Negro himself....I do not believe it is necessary for me to say that the honest, sober elements of the Negro people of the United States is severe in condemnation of the kind of immorality which Jack Johnson is at present charged....I do not mean to, as I said at the beginning, say how far Jack Johnson is or is not guilty of the charges."[36]

Johnson was handcuffed, jailed, and released on bail of $32,000 in collateral property. His indictment listed eleven counts: three counts of prostitution; two counts of debauchery; three counts of unlawful sexual intercourse; two counts of crimes against nature; and one count of inducement to prostitution. Schrieber must have been quite graphic in her evidence. Johnson married the eighteen-year-old Cameron eight days after her release on November 25. But at his trial on May 13, 1913, the jury returned a guilty verdict after deliberating only one hour and forty-five minutes. On June 4 he was sentenced to a year and a day and was fined a thousand dollars by Judge George Carpenter.

To evade jail for these ridiculous charges, Johnson hatched an escape worthy of a John Le Carré novel. He sent his wife to Toronto and arranged a swap with Andrew "Rube" Foster, the black owner of the Chicago American Giants baseball team. (Both Foster and Johnson were big, dark-complexioned, and bald-headed.) Disguised as a member of Foster's squad, Johnson slipped by American authorities in Hamilton, Ontario, on a train that left from Chicago's Englewood Station. Johnson got Foster to agree to switch the train's route to Buffalo through Canada, although Foster never knew about Johnson's escape plans.

When the train got to Hamilton, Johnson and his nephew off-loaded. They were met by his former manager, Tom Flanagan, who drove them to Toronto to meet his wife. Johnson, his wife, and his nephew left Canada on June 29, 1913, aboard the steamer *Corinthian*. Although he did not know it at the time, he would remain outside the United States just three weeks short of seven years—all because of the racism in his native country.

Johnson Loses His Title

His European theatrical engagements were canceled. In Paris he wound up fighting Jim Johnson, a black boxer, in his only serious bout of 1913. This was the first world heavyweight title fight between two black fighters. Johnson broke his arm in this ten-round draw. He was not paid for fighting Frank Moran the following year because World War I broke out the next day, June 28, 1914. On to Russia where, after meeting Rasputin, he was asked to leave. Back to Paris, where he was unwelcome. So he headed for England. They asked him to leave. He was, for a time, a man without a country.

Back home, the black press kept up with him. In the August issue of *Crisis*, the official organ of the National Association for the Advancement of Colored People (NAACP), the esteemed W.E.B. DuBois offered this assessment: "Some pretend to object to Mr. Johnson's character. But we have yet to hear, in the case of white America, that marital troubles have disqualified prizefighters or ball players or even statesmen. It comes down then, after all, to this unforgiveable blackness. Wherefore we conclude that at present prizefighting is very, very immoral, and that we must rely on football and war for pastimes until Mr. Johnson retires or permits himself to be 'knocked out.'" Immoral or not, the average black man in the street was still very much a Johnson fan.

To help Johnson—supposedly—Jack Curley proposed to Johnson in late 1914 that he fight Jess Willard, a 6'6", 250-pound giant. Curley intimated that if Johnson accepted his thirty-thousand-dollar offer, he might be able to return home to see his mother without a jail sentence. Unfortunately, Curley's partner, Tom Jones, was Willard's manager. Johnson agreed, and after being turned down by Pancho Villa in Mexico, he persuaded the president of Cuba, General Mario Menocal, to agree to stage the fight at the Oriental Racetrack in Havana.

Johnson and Willard met on April 5, 1915, in front of thirty-two thousand fans, for which the fighters were paid thirty thousand and ten thousand dollars, respectively. Willard, from Pottawatomie County, Kansas, brought an 18-to-3-to-1 record into the ring. He had never so much as donned a pair of gloves until he was twenty-four. Johnson was then thirty-seven years old.

Johnson won the first four rounds, laughing at his clumsy opponent's efforts. The crowd, which contained the largest group of blacks ever to watch a title fight, was for Johnson. Round eight was Willard's best, but nothing of consequence happened for another seventeen rounds. The twenty-sixth round, though, was one of the most analyzed in all of boxing history.

Johnson was way ahead on points. Willard shot a left jab to Johnson's face and then a right to the stomach. After a clinch, referee Jack Welch ordered a "break," and then Willard rushed and scored with a left to the body. Another jab at Johnson's head, and he was no longer the heavyweight champion. He was counted out with his knees bent in the air and his hands shading his eyes from the sun. After the count of ten, he was up immediately and left the ring.

It appeared that Johnson "threw" the fight in the twenty-sixth round. During that last clinch Johnson supposedly looked over Willard's shoulder and signaled to his wife to leave with Curley. The thirty thousand dollars due him was not paid in full before the bout, and as the story goes, the rest was paid during the last round. In his autobiography he wrote of an "additional percentage which Willard's manager (Curley's partner) owed me if I lived up to my agreement to lie down."[37] Most boxing historians believe Johnson did indeed tank the bout—a disgraceful performance from a world champion in any sport. Historians are also in agreement that Johnson won every round except possibly the twenty-fifth.

Johnson probably lied to reporters afterward, saying, "Willard was too much for me. I just didn't have it."[38] Nat Fleischer said he had Johnson's affidavit in a safe in his office, in which he "declares he faked the knockout according to arrangement with Curley."[39] Finis Farr thought that "Jack's tale of being advised to throw the fight to Willard was fantasy."[40] In any event he lost, and a riot followed at the racetrack. To worsen matters, Willard announced two days later that he, too, would thereafter draw the color line.

Prison and the End

Curley was not able to secure a jailproof return to the United States for Johnson. Johnson returned to England, where he was fined 1,075 pounds for punching a theater owner in the eye over the rental of the fight films. He was expelled in January 1916 and went to Spain for three years, where he fought bulls and played in a movie, *False Nobility.* His mother died in 1917, and he pined over her loss.

He then headed for Mexico again and tried to make a go of it as a wrestler, bullfighter, and boxer. He was even accused at one point by American authorities of spreading social equality propaganda among blacks down there. Finally, Johnson convinced himself that he could run no more. A Chicago politician, Tom Cary, persuaded him to give himself up.

So on July 20, 1920—six years, eleven months, and ten days after leaving—Johnson surrendered to U.S. authorities in San Diego, California. At Leavenworth Prison, he served only eight months of his original sentence because of good behavior. (The warden there was his old friend Denver Dickerson, the ex-Governor of Nevada.) He was even made the prison's physical director. He was released on July 9, 1921, after delivering an inspirational address to the inmates.

Back in Chicago he was accorded a warm welcome, and he made speeches for a living on various subjects. In 1924 he even spoke at a Ku Klux Klan rally in Danville, Illinois. In 1925 he was divorced from Lucille Cameron and married Irene Marie Pineau, his fourth wife and third white wife.

He was the most dominant force in all of boxing for the first twenty years of this century. Nearly every nonpartisan expert agrees that had he not been forced into exile, he would have had as fine a record as Joe Louis. That he was hounded for his choice in women was, on the one hand, unfortunate for him but, on the other hand, more a testament to the miscarriages of America's ideals of equality, fair play, and justice.

John Arthur Johnson died in a car accident on June 10, 1946, near Raleigh, North Carolina. He was, in this author's opinion, the most significant black athlete in history.

Notes

1. Chalk Monograph, p. 23.
2. Frederick Douglass, op. cit., p. 145.
3. Ibid., p. 148.
4. Nat Fleischer, *Black Dynamite.* vol. 3., p. 6.
5. Ibid., p. 45.
6. Ibid., p. 121.
7. Ibid., p. 235.
8. Ibid., vol. 1., p. 139.
9. Chalk, *Pioneers in Black Sport,* p. 142.
10. Durham and Jones, op. cit., p. 111–12.
11. Fleischer, op. cit., vol. 3, p.131.
12. Finis Farr, p. 39.
13. Chalk, op. cit., p. 240.
14. Quoted in Farr, op. cit., p. 49.
15. Ibid.
16. Quoted in ibid., p. 56.
17. Quoted in ibid., p. 58.
18. Jack Johnson, *In the Ring and Out.* (Chicago: National Sports Publishing, 1927), p. 160.
19. *The New York Times,* December 27, 1908.
20. Ibid.
21. Farr, op. cit., p. 61.
22. Johnson, op. cit., p. 164.
23. *The New York Times,* op. cit.
24. Quoted in Farr, op. cit., p. 61.
25. Quoted in Farr, op. cit., p. 82.
26. Quoted in ibid., p. 107.
27. Quoted in ibid., p. 107.
28. *The New York Times,* July 5, 1910.
29. Quoted in ibid.
30. Quoted in ibid.
31. Quoted in ibid.
32. Quoted in ibid.
33. Quoted in ibid.
34. Quoted in Farr, op. cit., p. 119.
35. Quoted in Chalk, op. cit., p. 154.
36. Telegram from the Tuskegee Institute, October 23, 1912.
37. Jack Johnson, *Johnson Is a Dandy,* p. 199.
38. Quoted in Farr, op. cit., p. 204.
39. Fleischer, op. cit., vol. 4, p. 116.
40. Farr, op. cit., p. 199.

Chapter 2

Horse Racing

Early History:
The Arabians

One of the most thrilling of sensations is felt atop a thoroughbred at full cry. One can move faster astride a horse than by any other nonmechanical means. Classical mythology even sought to combine ancient dreams of soaring like eagles with the very real power of domesticated horses. The result was Pegasus, the imaginary winged horse.

Although horses have been around for millennia, the thoroughbred evolved on the Arabian peninsula in the seventeenth century. Experts say the religion of Islam was spread throughout the Middle East not only because of the fanaticism of its followers but also because of the horses they rode. For the Muslim male during the time of the Prophet Muhammad, the ability to handle an Arabian steed in battle was a supreme test of manhood. Specifically, these marvelous animals were bred for speed, endurance, and strength.

Historian Charles Parmer recalls the story of how the Prophet Muhammad himself first chose the very best for breeding. "Having more worlds to conquer and needing mounts with stamina and speed, he pent up his war horses on desert ground for two blistering days within sight of running water. On the third day the bars were lowered. The fevered animals dashed for the stream. Muhammad raised a finger, his trumpeters sounded the charge....most beasts ignored the call, stopped and drank; a stalwart few flung ears forward, lept the stream and swept ahead in battle formation. These Spartan ones were given life tenure of the Muslim paddocks, their only duty to propagate. Their weaker-hearted brethren met ignominious death."[1]

Roughly a thousand years later, three of these Arabian horses were imported into England within a span of thirty-five years: the Byerly Turk in 1689, the Darley Arabian in 1704, and the Godolphin Barb in 1724. To this day, every horse known as a thoroughbred can trace its pedigree back to one of these three Arabians. All thoroughbreds are entered into *The General Stud Book*, begun during the reign of Queen Anne of England. The export of these magnificent animals to America began in the 1730s.

American Thoroughbreds Before the Civil War

In 1665 in what is now Garden City, Long Island, New York, the first American horse race was held on a track laid out by the

English governor, Richard Nicholls. It was
the most important sports event held in
America to date. No thoroughbreds were
entered, but by the early 1700s every sizable
town had its own course, usually built by
slaves. Boston had such a problem with
racing along its town roads that it banned
the activity in 1677.

But the combination of five events
superseded any moves to stop the sport.
One, Virginia passed a law in 1705 permitting slaves to be listed as property. Two, the
Stud Book made the sport exclusive. Three,
wealthy Americans imported thoroughbreds and began breeding their own. Four,
the patronage of racing in England passed
from royalty to the nobility. And, five, the
Racing Calendar began publishing news
and results of horses, owners, trainers, and
jockeys. This all happened within thirty
years.

The 1705 Virginia law was important
because the care of horses was extremely
labor intensive and there was no assurance
of a return on investment, so only the well-
to-do could afford it. Slaves listed as
property meant that costs could be kept
low. The patronage of the English nobility
meant that more people would become
involved, thereby expanding breeding ex-
ponentially. The underlying driving force
was, of course, the same on both sides of
the Atlantic Ocean: gambling. Thomas
Jefferson himself noted as much when he
said, "[A] young [American] gentleman
goes to England, he learns drinking, horse
racing, and boxing...the peculiarities of
English education."[2]

Racing was not strictly confined to the
wealthy. On Race Day at the typical county
court house, the common folk—some free

blacks included—raced their "brag nags,"
and bets were taken in tobacco, rice, cotton, sugar, corn, and, yes, slaves. But when
the plantation owners got together "on the
day of the running, laborers, farmers, and
slaves gathered on the track while ladies of
the aristocracy watched from their car-
riages, and their gentlemen hovered near
on horseback."[3] Most of these horses were
trained and cared for by blacks.

After the Revolutionary War more scientific methods were used, and horse
owners and trainers realized that the rider,
or jockey, was frequently more important
than the horse itself. By 1800 in the South,
the vast majority of jockeys were diminutive
slaves who had grown up around horses all
their lives. In the North, owners continued
importing English jockeys or they used
local whites. Thus, black trainers and jockeys were the first African-Americans involved completely in sport.

The first such jockey was known as
"Monkey" Simon, whom many believed was
the best jockey of his day. He commanded
upward of a hundred dollars per ride for
himself or his master and was not averse to
a little "back talk" to his superiors. Some-
time in May 1806, so the story goes, General
Andrew Jackson was wounded in a duel
and spent much of his recovery time at the
Clover Bottom Race Course near Nashville,
Tennessee. Jackson had an "exchange"
with the 4' 6" tall Simon:

> "Monkey!" Jackson bellowed to Simon
> at some distance as a crowd gathered
> around sensing something dramatic.
>
> Slowly, Monkey Simon turned around.
> Flecking his boots with his whip, he
> looked up insolently: "You speakin' to me,
> white man?"

"Yes, to you! Now listen: None of your monkeyshines today. When my horse starts to pass you, don't you dare spit tobacco juice in his eyes—or in the eyes of my jockey. Understand?"

Simon glared. Turning his head, he spat against a post. Then said: "General, I've rid ag'in many of yo nags, but none ever got close enough to catch my spit."[4]

Even if this story is only half true, it is doubtful that Jackson took too much offense at Simon's remarks.

These colorfully clad daredevils were also very superstitious. Accounts relate that jockeys believed that winning a race depended upon more than just a good ride. In 1814, General Jackson reportedly imported a crack black jockey named Dick to ride his horse against a local favorite. Jackson's horse won because his imported jockey told his weaker-hearted opposing rider that he (Jackson's jockey) would cast a spell on him if he did not let him lead for the first mile and a quarter.

Despite their superstitions, black jockeys continued to inspire confidence in their owners and bettors. Nowhere was this more graphically illustrated than in the heralded Match Races of 1823, 1836, 1876, 1878, and 1883. These were, in their times, the most popular sports events in the country, and black jockeys played a key part. Whenever horses' reputations from different sections of the country assumed mythic proportions, someone suggested a special race just between them. They were "matched" for one big race, and the outcome was decided by a series of "heats"— much longer than today's races.

In 1823, American Eclipse, representing the North, and Henry, representing the South, squared off before sixty thousand people. It was the largest crowd ever assembled in one place in the Western Hemisphere. The third Match Race was held in 1876 between Aristedes—the First Kentucky Derby winner—and Ten Broeck. Frank Harper, Ten Broeck's owner, picked William "Billy" Walker to ride him. H. Price McGrath, Aristedes' owner, was so sure his horse was going to win that he accepted all bets and did not bother to record them. He told his bettors his little red horse would keep the books. And it did, winning by forty lengths.

In the Match Race held in Louisville in May 1878, Ten Broeck again lined up but this time next to Molly McCarthy in a race to be decided by the best-of-three four-mile heats. A quarter of a million dollars was wagered locally, and there was a five-thousand-dollar side-bet. William Walker was in the saddle again atop Ten Broeck. As luck would have it, Molly McCarthy broke down during the first heat and could not continue.

Local blacks were so taken by the race that one of them made up the following ditty:

I bet my money on Ten Broeck, cause I
    knowed he'd win de race
He made Miss Molly bite the dust, an' she
    ain't showed her face.

But just before the Civil War the image of the black jockey took a turn for the worse. There were charges of dishonesty, of "pulling mounts" (holding a horse back), taking bribes, cheating owners, and associating with gamblers. Unfortunately, this view prevailed for the next sixty years and was used by some to get them off the tracks for good.

Abe Hawkins, an ex-slave who had a fine reputation as a rider, later fell into disrepute. In May 1851, the *Spirit of the Times* reported that Hawkins was expelled from the Metarie (Louisiana) Jockey Club for "throwing" a race he was about to win by slowing his horse.

The Civil War put a stop to nearly all racing in the South as men rode their own horses into battle. When it was over, there was a country to put back together, horses to replace, and 4.5 million new black citizens. It also gave rise to the greatest black athletic performances of the nineteenth century.

A Glorious Half-Century: 1861–1911

The astounding accomplishments of black jockeys occurred within fifty years, beginning with the onset of the Civil War. The loss of horses of all breeds had been enormous during this conflict, but enough basic stock was left to begin anew. Tracks were rebuilt, and an unprecedented succession of events ensued.

Stakes races made their first appearance, including the Travers (1864), Belmont (1867), Champagne (1867), Flash (1869), and Kenner (1870). Handicap races began with the Saratoga Cup (1865), Jerome (1866), Ladies (1868), and Dixie (1870). Abe Hawkins was prominent in this decade in winning the Travers in 1866 and the inaugural Jerome Handicap that same year. His fame was such that the April 12, 1866, *New Orleans Times* said of him, "He is probably the best rider on the continent, is a dwarf in size but well formed, and 'knows the ropes like a book!'" He was just one of dozens of his kind in the post-Civil War era.

Concurrent with the inauguration of new races came a new way of betting. It was called pari-mutuel, a French expression meaning "among ourselves," and it enabled an almost unlimited number of fans to bet. Instead of bargaining directly with a "tout," or bookie, a bettor simply placed bets in a pool with others; the odds were determined by the amount of money bet on certain horses. Although it angered the bookies, it pleased track owners and made the entire sport richer. The pari-mutuel system enabled investors to build the famous tracks at Monmouth, New Jersey; Pimlico, Maryland; and Churchill Downs, Kentucky.

The most important race at Churchill Downs was the Kentucky Derby, which is the premier event in the sport today. The first "run for the roses," as this race is referred to, was on May 17, 1875, in Louisville before ten thousand spectators. In 1875 it did not have the fame it has today, but because of its social importance, it soon had no rival. By 1890, M. Lewis Clark, the race director, had made it *the* greatest social event in the South, save possibly the Mardi Gras in New Orleans.

On that Monday fifteen horses lined up in two rows at the starting line. Fourteen of the fifteen jockeys were black. The odds-on favorite to win was one of two entries by H. Price McGrath—Aristedes and Chesapeake. Oliver Lewis was atop Aristedes. McGrath's plan was for Lewis to take Aristedes out front early to set a killing pace and let Chesapeake come through to win in the end. But it did not happen that way. Chesapeake faltered, and Aristedes, the smallest horse in the field, came home the winner. The success of events like the Kentucky Derby also changed the standard length of races, from the old "heats" concept to the shorter 1 ¼ to 1 ½-mile lengths.

Isaac Murphy

The inaugural year of the Kentucky Derby was also the major race debut of the greatest black athlete of the nineteenth century, Isaac Murphy. Murphy was born Isaac Burns on New Year's Day 1861 on the Fayette County, Kentucky, farm of David Tanner. His father, James, was a bricklayer who fought in the Union Army and died in a Confederate prison camp. His family then moved to the home of his maternal grandfather, Green Murphy, (hence the name change), an auctioneer and bellringer. When he was twelve his "Uncle Eli" added two years to his real age to secure a jockey apprentice license. He then was contracted to ride for his mother's employer, Richard Owings, and his partner, James T. Williams.

Apprentices like Murphy usually lived at the tracks, sleeping near the stalls and beginning as exercise riders. All tried to become a hand rider rather than a whip rider. Hand riders were so in tune with the horse that the whip was needed infrequently. To be known as a hand rider was a high compliment. Murphy was the most phenomenal hand jockey the world had yet seen.

Murphy's first major victory was at Louisville in 1875 astride Lady Greenfield; then at Lexington, Kentucky, on September 15, 1876, at the Crab Orchard Course aboard Glentina. In 1877 he rode Vera Cruz to victory in the St. Leger. Two years later, he finished second in the Kentucky Derby, and he won the Travers, Kenner, and Clark Handicaps—all aboard Falsetto. By 1882, he was riding for the Fleetwood Stables at a salary of ten thousand dollars per year, plus twenty-five dollars for every winning ride and fifteen dollars for every loss. He got married, and he and his wife, Lucy, lived at 143 North Eastern Avenue in Lexington, Kentucky.

Married life must have suited him since he won the Tobacco Woodburn and Hindoo (later called Latonia) Stakes atop Leonatus. Leonatus was trained by Raleigh Colston, a retired black jockey. But 1884 was stellar. Murphy won six races, including the Kentucky Derby, on four different horses. Murphy's first Kentucky Derby win is described in *The Kentucky Derby Diamond Jubilee:* "Bob Miles beat the flag and jumped into a two-length lead, followed by Powhatan III, Audrain, the favorite and Admiral. Buchanan, fractious at the post, was away poorly, but Isaac Murphy, his Negro jockey, saved ground for three-quarters of a mile, and then Murphy called upon him for his best effort. Buchanan moved to first quickly with gigantic strides, eased up to the final eighth, and won by two lengths."[5]

He continued winning and changed his contract to E.J. "Lucky" Baldwin in 1886 for ten thousand dollars per year and became an owner himself, with Playfellow. In 1890 he became the first jockey to win two Kentucky Derbies, these times aboard Riley. He repeated the following year for an unprecedented third win plus five other major events. He was at the very top of his profession, which commanded the largest spectator attendance of any sport in America. But his wins came at a price that all jockeys had to pay.

The bane of them all was excess weight. On August 26, 1890, he was grounded for finishing in a dizzy state aboard Firenze in the Monmouth Handicap.

Most people believed he had slightly succumbed to champagne and dieting. *The New York Times* of August 27 noted that "Murphy's trouble is probably due to the fact that on Sunday he fell into the clutches of a gang of politicians who called themselves the Salvatore Club...because they won a lot of money backing Salvatore in his races....there was drinking." Whether true or not, he was slowing down, and he won only six races in 1891.

Murphy's reputation, however, remained solid despite the widespread view that black jockeys were unsavory. Reported the *Louisville Times* on May 15, 1981, "Isaac Murphy...is a quiet, polite young man, who never made a bet in his life, never swore, and never was caught telling a lie. His integrity and honor are the pride of the Turf, and many of the best horsemen pronounce him the greatest jockey that ever mounted a horse."

In 1892 he won only two races, but his three Kentucky Derby wins stood until 1930, when Earle Sande won his third Derby. Eddie Arcaro finally broke the record in 1948 when he won his fourth aboard Citation. Of Murphy's ability, one expert commented, "A horse could jump straight up and down, yet Murphy never raised off his back." "He seemed part of the horse. He would just lay down on his mount's neck and bring him home."[6]

Speaking of himself, Murphy tried to impart some advice to up-and-coming jockeys when he said, "You just ride to win. They get you to pull a horse in a selling race and when it comes to a stake race, they get Isaac to ride. A jockey that will sell out to one man will sell out to another. Just be honest. And you'll have no trouble and

plenty of money."[7] He died on February 12, 1896, at age thirty-five of pneumonia. Dieting and possibly too much champagne had left him vulnerable to disease. He left his wife thirty thousand dollars, but it was not enough to cover all his debts. Lucy Murphy was herself later buried in a pauper's grave.

Murphy's funeral was attended by blacks and whites alike. Although buried in Old Number 2 Cemetery in Lexington, through neglect his gravesite was lost for generations. But Frank Barries, Jr., finally found the site, and Murphy was reburied in a Lexington park near the grave of the great thoroughbred Man o' War. He rode in 1,412 races and won 628, for a winning percentage of 44 percent.

Immediately after Murphy's death, L. P. Tarlton, the famed trainer, penned these words in *The Thoroughbred Record:* "I have seen all the great jockeys of England and this country for years back, but, all in all Isaac Murphy is the greatest of them all."[8] But Isaac Murphy himself had the last word on his ability: "I am proud of my calling just as I am of my record, and I believe my life will be recorded a success, though the reputation I enjoy was earned both in the stables and in the saddle. It is a great honor to be classed one of America's greatest jockeys."[9]

The Supporting Cast

Isaac Murphy was not alone in his success. From roughly 1800 until the eve of World War I, black jockeys had few peers in their profession. In the South before the Civil War, slave jockeys were given names associated with the classics, like Cato, Pompei, Scipio, and Caesar. A jockey named Cato won aboard Wagner in victories over Gey Eagle in 1839 at Louisville. In those days the jockeys hardly received much acclaim. The owners were accorded the plaudits.

Once major races were reinstituted after the Civil War, the black jockey received his due. From 1880 through 1905 they captured thirteen Kentucky Derbies, seven Alabama Stakes, twelve Clark Handicaps, nine Clipsetta Stakes, eight First Specials, eight Great Western Handicaps, seven Kenner Stakes, ten Kentucky Oaks, twelve Latonia Derbies, seven Latonia Oaks, seven Second Specials, seven St. Louis Derbies, five Tennessee Derbies, and six Tidal Stakes. The overwhelming majority of these victories were on southern tracks.

In the latter part of the 1870s, William "Billy" Walker was the leading jockey. In 1877 he won the Kentucky Derby aboard Baden-Baden and the Dixie Handicap. Oliver Lewis won the first Kentucky Derby in 1875. Others in the 1870s and 1880s included Shelby "Pike" Barnes; John Stoval, who rode home four winners in one day on October 1, 1881; Alonzo Clayton; George Lewis (Oliver's brother); Spider Anderson; Erskine Henderson; George Withers; Ed West; Robert "Tiny" Williams; Babe Hurd; and James "Soup" Perkins.

Those who bridged the 1880s and 1890s were Monk Overton, who won six races at Washington Park in Homewood, Illinois, in one day on July 10, 1891; Tom Britton; Anthony Hamilton; Harry Ray; Jess Conley; Pete Clay; Andrew Hamilton; and Abe Clayton. But two in particular—Willie Simms and "Soup" Perkins—were superior jockeys.

On June 23, 1893, Simms won five of six races at Sheepshead Bay, New York, and he did it again on August 24, 1894. He won the Kentucky Derby twice (1896 at 1898), the Latonia Derby, the Belmont Stakes twice, and the Second Special four times. He rode constantly, most of the time contracted to Michael F. Dwyer and Richard Croker. His patrons took him to England, where he was successful in winning aboard Euteegallalee and Banquet for owner Harry Reed. In the end he earned more money than Murphy—$300,000, as compared to around $250,000 for Murphy. After 1890, jockeys and owners stood to earn considerably more money because railroad track gauges were standardized throughout much of the nation, making travel easier. (Before 1890 there had been constant on-loading and off-loading of horses when rail gauges changed on different tracks.)

Perkins was born in 1880 and rode five of six winners at age thirteen at Lexington in 1893. Noted the *Morning Transcript* of October 21, 1893, "IT WAS A PERKINS DAY—THE BOY JOCKEY BREAKS ALL PREVIOUS RECORDS—HE RIDES FIVE OF THE WINNERS." Eight months later at Saratoga he did it again. He won the 1895 Kentucky Derby atop Halma, which was the first Derby winner to sire another Derby winner—Alan-a-Dale.

In the twilight years of the black jockey's dominance, Jimmy Lee and Jimmy Winkfield were top draws. Both could look back on twelve Kentucky Derby wins for their brethren in the first twenty-two meetings of this vaunted race. But racism was slowly taking precedence over performance. The Reconstruction era in the South was long past by 1890, and racist Jim Crow laws were the order of the day—no matter how good the ability of a black jockey.

Charles Parmer took note of Lee's diffi-
culties: "He remained a quiet, courteous
fellow....But some of his compatriots of
color became a trifle cocky in the jockey
rooms; especially in the East. The white
boys retaliated by ganging up against the
black riders on the rails. A black boy would
be pocketed, thrust back in a race; or his
mount would be bumped out of contention
on a white boy's stirrup, and toss him out of
the saddle....those white fellows would
slash out and cut the nearest Negro
rider....they literally ran the black boys off
the track."[10]

Lee went out in style, anyway. From
1907 to 1909 he won ten major races,
including the Kentucky Oaks, the Travers,
and the California Derby. Four of these wins
were aboard Sir Martin.

Lee's friend and fellow rider was
Jimmy Winkfield, one of the true legends in
the sport. He, too, went to Europe, but not
before making his mark here, which included two Kentucky Derby wins in 1901
and 1902: aboard His Eminence and Alan-
a-Dale, respectively. In 1900 he was third at
the Derby and in 1903, second. He left
behind the best record there: two wins, one
second, and one third. He was the last
black jockey to win it.

Winkfield was born in Chilesburg,
Kentucky, on April 12, 1882, and began
working in the stables at Latonia at age
fifteen for eight dollars a month. But he
developed a sullied reputation. He was
once grounded for a year for causing an
accident and holding back Alan-a-Dale in a
time trial so he could ride him in the 1902
Kentucky Derby. A white rider was promised the faster of two horses owned by
Major McDowell for that race. Winkfield

simply tricked both McDowell and the
white jockey and won the race himself.
Alan-a-Dale, however, did not race again
that year because of bad legs, of which
Winkfield knew all along.

In 1904, Winkfield went to Russia to
race for Michael Lazzareff. He lived a sump-
tuous life in Moscow's National Hotel until
the Bolshevik Revolution. He managed to
escape and made his way to France, where
he won the Prix du President de la Républi-
que in 1923 atop Bahadur. He retired at age
forty-eight and became a trainer in France
until World War II. Back at work in the
United States, he one day gave a mount to a
promising young jockey—William Hartack—in Charleston, West Virginia. Hartack
later won five Kentucky Derbies. Winkfield
died in 1974 at age ninety-three and was
named to the Jockey Hall of Fame at
Pimlico.

Black jockeys enjoyed an unprecedented streak of good fortune until racism
forced them off the tracks. No civil rights
groups came to their aid then, and most
had unfortunate endings. The Jockey Club
was formed in 1894 to license riders, and
they systematically denied the relisting of
blacks. The ebony-skinned riders were just
too good and made too much money to suit
the whites in charge.

In the first decade of this century only
a handful were left: Willie and J. Hicks
(brothers), Jess Conley, C. Bonner, Dan
Austin, Leroy Williams, Atkin Williams, and
E. Crowhurst. None made much money,
and few found steady work. Near the end of
the decade R. Simpson, C. and M. Dishmon
(brothers), Johnny Hudgins, Clarence Reed,
and Charlie Gregg tried to hang on. Nothing
happened, and no one cared. Jess Conley

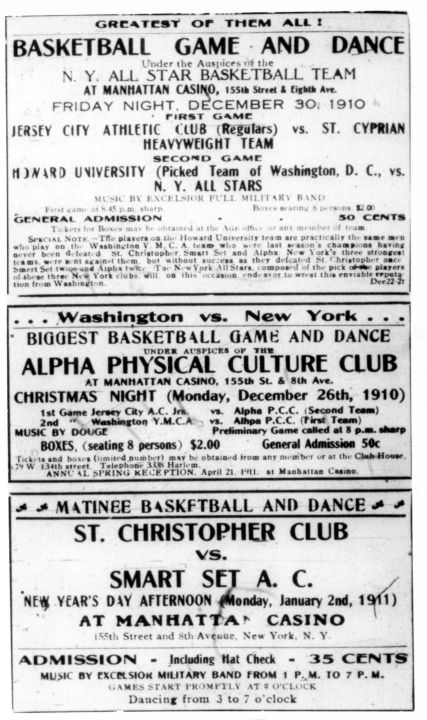

GREATEST OF THEM ALL!

BASKETBALL GAME AND DANCE

Under the Auspices of the
N. Y. ALL STAR BASKETBALL TEAM
AT MANHATTAN CASINO, 155th Street & Eighth Ave.

FRIDAY NIGHT, DECEMBER 30, 1910

FIRST GAME
JERSEY CITY ATHLETIC CLUB (Regulars) vs. ST. CYPRIAN HEAVYWEIGHT TEAM

SECOND GAME
H)WARD UNIVERSITY (Picked Team of Washington, D. C., vs. N. Y. ALL STARS

MUSIC BY EXCELSIOR FULL MILITARY BAND

First game at 8.45 p.m. sharp.　　　　Boxes seating 8 persons. $2.00

GENERAL ADMISSION - **50 CENTS**

Tickets for Boxes may be obtained at the AGE office or any member of team.

SPECIAL NOTE.—The players on the Howard University team are practically the same men who play on the Washington Y. M. C. A. team who were last season's champions having never been defeated St. Christopher, Smart Set and Alpha, New York's three strongest teams, were sent against them, but without success as they defeated St. Christopher once Smart Set twice and Alpha twice. The New York All Stars, composed of the pick of the players of these three New York clubs, will, on this occasion, endeavor to wrest this enviable reputation from Washington.
Dec22-2t

. . . Washington vs. New York . . .

BIGGEST BASKETBALL GAME AND DANCE
UNDER AUSPICES OF THE
ALPHA PHYSICAL CULTURE CLUB
AT MANHATTAN CASINO, 155th St. & 8th Ave.

CHRISTMAS NIGHT (Monday, December 26th, 1910)

1st Game Jersey City A.C. Jrs.　vs.　Alpha P.C.C. (Second Team)
2nd　"　Washington Y.M.C.A　vs.　Alhpa P.C.C. (First Team)

MUSIC BY DOUGE　　Preliminary Game called at 8 p.m. sharp

BOXES, (seating 8 persons) $2.00　　General Admission 50c

Tickets and boxes (limited number) may be obtained from any member or at the Club House, 79 W. 134th street. Telephone 3338 Harlem.
ANNUAL SPRING RECEPTION, April 21, 1911, at Manhattan Casino.

✄ ✄ MATINEE BASKETBALL AND DANCE ✄ ✄

ST. CHRISTOPHER CLUB
VS.
SMART SET A. C.

NEW YEAR'S DAY AFTERNOON (Monday, January 2nd, 1911)

AT MANHATTAN CASINO
155th Street and 8th Avenue, New York, N. Y.

ADMISSION - Including Hat Check - 35 CENTS
MUSIC BY EXCELSIOR MILITARY BAND FROM 1 P. M. TO 7 P. M.
GAMES START PROMPTLY AT 2 O'CLOCK
Dancing from 3 to 7 o'clock

A notice of a basketball game and a dance, 1910. *(Source unknown)*

William Henry Beckett, as he appeared in the school year book of the Springfield Young Men's Christian Association Training School (now Springfield College), in 1907. *(Courtesy of Springfield College)*

Jesse Stahl (1883–1938). Only the second black elected to the National Cowboy Hall of Fame (as of 1985), he was a big powerful man, about 6 feet 2 inches and 220 pounds. Stahl was quick, coordinated, and also a proficient bulldogger. Shown here about 1918. *(Newman Photo:* Who's Who in Rodeo *by Willard Porter, Oklahoma City: Powder River Book Company, 1984, page 125)*

Jack Johnson and Joe Jeannette square off against each other. The two had fought nine times, and four contests were no decisions; Johnson lost one on a foul, won two, and two were called draws. This photo dates from around 1908. *(Courtesy of Jack Hay)*

BOB ARMSTRONG.   "DENVER" ED. MARTIN.

Bob Armstrong, born in 1873, 6 feet, 190 pounds, fought between 1895 and 1903. He had thirty-six fights (thirteen knockouts, twelve decisions, three draws, and eight losses). He is shown about 1902. He once served as sparring partner for Jim Jeffries, and also Jack Johnson.

Denver Ed Martin, born September 10, 1881, 6 feet 3 inches and 203 pounds, fought between 1899 and 1921. He had thirty-two fights (eighteen knockouts, eight losses, one draw, one no decision, and four won via decision). *(*The Mirror of Life, *London, England, July, 1902)*

The "Dixie Kid," Aaron L. Brown, was born in Fulton, Missouri, on December 23, 1883. He is shown in England at the age of twenty-eight in 1911. The Dixie Kid fought in England, France, Ireland, and Scotland from 1911 until World War I started.
(The Mirror of Life, *London, England, July 1911*)

Joe Walcott, of Barbados, the first black world welterweight titleholder, about 1892. (The Mirror of Life, *London, England, July 1892*)

BOBBY DOBBS

Robert "Bobby" Dobbs was born in Cartersville, Georgia, in 1869. A top lightweight and welterweight, he is shown here in 1897, at the age of twenty-eight. (The Mirror of Life, *London, England, June 1898*)

An etching of Tom Molineaux, left, and Joe Cribb, 1810. (*Source unknown*)

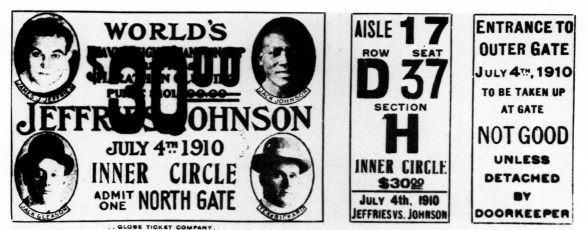

A $30 ticket to the Jack Johnson–Jim Jeffries bout on July 4, 1910. *(Courtesy of the Nevada Historical Society)*

Jack Johnson and his handlers at the Jim Jeffries bout on July 4, 1910, in Reno, Nevada. *(Courtesy of the Nevada Historical Society)*

Jack Johnson's training camp at Rick's Resort in Reno, June 1910. *(Courtesy of the Nevada Historical Society)*

Joe Gans, first native-born black American world lightweight titleholder, in 1906. *(Source unknown)*

Jack Johnson, about 1911. *(Courtesy of the Nevada Historical Society)*

Edward Dudley Brown, better known as "Brown Dick," a Hall of Famer in the trainer category. In his early racing career, Brown Dick was also a jockey. He is shown here about 1895. *(Courtesy of Jim Bolus, racing writer for the* Courier-Journal *of Louisville, Kentucky)*

Jimmy Winkfield, in his colors, about 1901. *(Courtesy of Jim Bolus)*

Isaac Burns Murphy in his colors, about 1890.
(From Champions of American Sport, *New York: Harry N. Abrams–Abbeville Press, Inc., 1984, page 111)*

Oliver Lewis, winner of the first Kentucky Derby in 1875—shown about 1888. *(Courtesy of Jim Bolus)*

A nattily attired Isaac Murphy and friends in the 1890s. *(Courtesy of Jim Bolus)*

Edward Frankin Geers (1851–1924), shown here about 1920. One of the all-time great harness horse racers, Geers began driving in his native Tennessee and popularized the pacing horse.
(Courtesy of Jim Bolus)

American artist Frederick Remington was noted for his pictures of spirited horses and western subjects. In this picture, he is capturing the "false start" at a horse race. Isaac Murphy, the jockey, is shown at left.

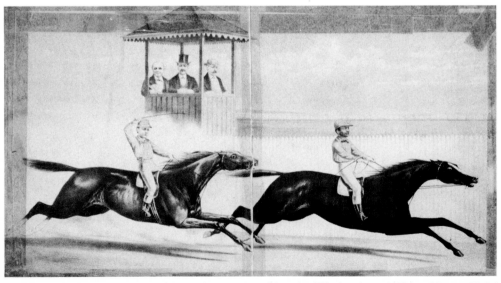

A Currier & Ives print: "Harry Bassett and Longfellow in their great races." Just after 1870, these horses held the public eye with their stirring contests at Long Branch and Saratoga. Harry Bassett won the Belmont Stakes in 1871, as racing interest spread in the land.

A beaming Sol Butler receiving his medal for winning the broad jump (now called the long jump) at the 1919 Inter-Allied Games in Paris, France. (Story of the Inter-Allied Games, 1919, *United States Army, 1920*)

George Poage winning his second bronze medal in the 200-meter hurdles, finishing third at the 1904 Olympics at St. Louis, Missouri. Harry Hillman won the gold medal and Frank Castleman, the silver medal. *(Courtesy of the United States Olympic Committee)*

George Poage, sitting on grass at left, on the 1903 University of Wisconsin track team. He competed in the 1904 Olympics. *(Courtesy of the University of Wisconsin)*

Theodore "Ted" Cable, second row, second from right, and Alexander Louis Jackson, second row, third from right, on Harvard University track team, in 1912. *(Courtesy of Harvard University)*

Napoleon Bonaparte Marshall, second row from top, at right, on 1895 Harvard University track team. *(Courtesy of Harvard Unive*

Ed Gourdin, seated third from right, on 1919 Harvard University track team. *(Courtesy of Harvard University)*

Howard Porter Drew, of the University of Southern California track team, wins 100-yard dash in 1914.
(Courtesy of the University of Southern California)

was the last black to ride in the Kentucky Derby, finishing third atop Colston—named for Black trainer Raleigh Colston—in 1911. Except for the steeplechase events, it was all over after a century of excellence.

John Stoval died in 1900, when a horse fell on him. Tom Britton committed suicide in 1901 with carbolic acid. Joe Harris was killed in 1909. Few jockeys managed to invest any of their winnings. In retrospect, the sport of horse racing is the only instance where the participation of blacks stopped almost completely while the sport itself continued—a sad commentary on American life.

The Trainers

Blacks have been training horses since they were introduced into the colonies in the seventeenth century. After the Revolutionary War the northern states clung to their imported or local trainers, but down South, as Parmer wrote, "Before 1861...horse trainers...usually were black slaves with canny horse sense."[11] They were, in fact, the first African-Americans to work exclusively in a sporting endeavor. That tradition continued until roughly 1900 with tremendous success.

Out in the untamed West, before Native Americans were forced to reservations, the black trainer's reputation was widespread: "whenever the Indians were subdued and the settlements secured, some proposed a horse race. When the race was run, frequently Negroes were participants. Whether they were owners, riders, or trainers, they were at the starting post or the finish line."[12] Then there was "Silver" Walker, a black barber who bred

and trained his own stable in Idaho in the 1870s.

John "Jack" Fisher was famed in California in the late 1800s. He was born a slave in St. Louis, Missouri, and early on became a stableboy and houseboy. But E.J. "Lucky" Baldwin brought him to Rancho Santa Anita in Southern California to care for his horses. Most trainers, however, were retired jockeys who managed to persuade owners of their horse knowledge.

Edward "Brown Dick" Brown trained Baden-Baden who won the 1877 Kentucky Derby. William "Bill" Bird trained Buchanan, Isaac Murphy's first Derby winner. Alex Perry guided Joe Cotton, the 1885 Derby victor. Others mentioned in the records included William Perkins (Soup's brother), Billy Walker, Raleigh Colston, Albert Cooper, Dudley Allen, James Williams, George Holt, Frank Taylor, and Jimmy Winkfield (in Europe and Russia). Ed Brown is rumored to have earned nearly $250,000 in his career as a rider, trainer, and owner. But they, too, were forced out in the early 1900s. The only avenue left was steeplechase racing.

The Steeplechasers

After being forced out of "flat" racing, as events like the Kentucky Derby are called, some black riders turned to the steeplechase. Instead of racing around a flat track, horse and rider wind their way around a longer course beset with obstacles of various kinds—water jumps, hedge rows, railings, and the like. Uncanny judgment of pace, timing, and the competition is necessary for success.

What Isaac Murphy was to flat racing,

Charlie Smoot was to steeplechasing after World War I. He was a three-time winner of the prestigious Beverwyck Steeplechase— in 1916, 1926, and 1933. In 1927 he rode home ten winners in fifty-three mounts—an astounding record.

Others gave it a try and made names for themselves. Sam Bush of Baltimore won the Prix Nagne aboard Despote in 1923 and later the Prix Richard Henry atop Boy Prince. Paul McGinnis captured twenty-eight races in 1936. Nott Brooks, Wilbert Breland, Jimmy Dupree, Frederick Brooks, Angus Scott, Johnny Mason, Lester Franklin, Leon J. Goines, and A. Simms all worked before World War II. Goines raced principally in Canada and Mexico and once won seventeen events in twenty-one starts. He retired to train the stable of Deborah Everett of the DuPont family.

This event was not without its black trainers: Matthew Smart, George Miller, Marshall Lilly, Pete Green, and Tom Bass. Bass trained steeplechase and show horses at his stable in Mexico, Missouri. He displayed some of his handiwork at the 1890 St. Louis Exposition.

Though not with the same luster as their flat-turf cousins, the black steeplechasers represented themselves creditably. It remains another example of excellence where opportunity beckoned.

Here and There

In selected spots in the racing world after the depression, blacks continued to find niches where they could work. Some are still at it today: Fred Treadwell comes immediately to mind.

Treadwell was born in 1885 on Long Island, New York, and worked for the William Post family, who were avid polo enthusiasts. His parents were servants for the Posts, and he in time became a trainer of polo ponies and an accomplished polo player himself in the 1930s. But he never rode in official games because of his color. His name never appeared in the United States Polo Players Registry.

But he did appear in games opposite some famous players like Tommy Hitchcock, General George Patton, and Will Rogers, Sr. Hitchcock noted Treadwell's plight in saying, "The only thing against him is his color."[13] Will Rogers added, "Polo is a gentlemen's game, but the only gentlemen I know in the game is Fred Treadwell."[14] A little condescending perhaps, but kind words just the same.

Concurrent with Treadwell was an assorted lot of blacks who made their living as clockers, hotwalkers, trainers, exercise boys, grooms, and stable hands. They are not forgotten. The trainers included Henry Loudon, Elzy Brown, Arthur Perrossier, William Buckner, Carl Sitgraves, Willie Mitchell, Clifford Scott (Chicago), Odell Livingston, and Frank Tyler. In 1937, George Miller trained Gray Gold, which finished eighth in that year's Kentucky Derby. Raymond White trained American Eagle, a 1944 Kentucky Derby entrant, and King Bay, which won the Francis Peabody Memorial in 1947.

In 1947 seventeen-year-old Ronald James became the first black entry at the National Horse Show at New York's Madison Square Garden. He rode his own mount, Candida, in the MacClay Trophy Class, the Children's Hunter Class, and the Children's Hack Hunter Class. He also qualified at the Bethlehem (Connecticut) Horse Show.

Another trainer of show horses was Sullivan Davis, born in Owen, Virginia, in 1910. He was steering horses at age fifteen and then moved to his own quarters in Montvale, New Jersey. He won four Saddle Seat Medals, three National Horse Show Good Hands titles, and the 1972 Walter Devereaux Sportsmanship Trophy.

After World War II the "sport of kings" was not as firmly tied to blue-blooded, "old money" society. New tracks were built and old ones refurbished. Traditions changed. In 1952 a young sixteen-year-old from Columbia, South Carolina, Hosea Lee Richardson, made history by becoming the first black rider at Miami's Tropical Park. He had ridden his first winner at Chicago's Washington Park in 1951. In 1964 Robert McCurdy of Atlantic City, New Jersey, also rode at Tropical Park. Al Brown rode for Georgeanna Foster, a black female trainer from Long Island, New York. Foster was joined as trainers in the 1960s by Sylvia Bishop of Charleston, West Virginia, Chester Ross, and Marshall Lilly.

Louis Durousseau was a special case. He overcame racial prejudice to ride at Santa Anita on December 26, 1968. A Cajun from Louisiana, he made over $100,000 per year, according to *Ebony* magazine. He was forbidden to ride there in the early 1960s, but the intervention of Earl Warren, Jr., saved the day. There have been no outstanding black jockeys since Durousseau.

Summary

From the earliest presence of horse racing as a sport here in America, blacks have been involved. Proscribed by race, servitude, and class from initial participation, black jockeys later became the very model

for the profession. They performed so well that their white peers felt threatened and arranged for their eviction from the profession. But the records established leave no doubt of superior accomplishment. The saddest commentary, though, is that this "sport of kings" was the only athletic endeavor in which the primary black participant was completely eradicated, not to return. In other sports like baseball and football, blacks were denied full participation for a time but returned in force. Not so in horse racing. Isaac Murphy, so highly admired during his time for his skills and character, would have been ashamed of his sport.

Notes

1. Charles Parmer, *For Gold and Glory.* (New York: Carrick and Evans, 1939).
2. Quoted in Rader, op. cit., p. 34.
3. Parmer, op. cit., p. 45.
4. Parmer, op. cit., p. 61.
5. George B. Leach, *The Kentucky Derby Diamond Jubilee.* (New York: Gibbs, Inman, 1949), p. 35.
6. Peter T. Chew, "Ike and Wink," *The Kentucky Derby: The First 100 Years.* (Boston: Houghton Mifflin), p. 1202.
7. Quoted in ibid.
8. Quoted in ibid.
9. Quoted in Joseph Flory, "Famous Blacks in Thoroughbred Racing," *Backstretch* (April 1980):37.
10. Parmer, op. cit., p. 150.
11. Parmer, op. cit., p. 114.
12. Durham and Johnson, op. cit., p. 170.
13. Kansas City *Call,* May 31, 1933.
14. Quoted in Franklin O. Smith, "Historically Speaking." *Black Sports* 4 (August 1974):53.

Chapter 3

Cycling

It is difficult to believe now that cycling was once the third or fourth most popular spectator sport in America. Back in the 1890s, when cars were extremely rare, bicycles—or velocipedes, as they were called then—propelled people faster than any other mechanical means except trains. The citizenry was fascinated by the sight of a rider approaching at fifty miles per hour astride a two-wheeled contraption.

The first velocipedes were made in the 1860s and had large front wheels and smaller rear ones—both made of iron. What a bumpy ride that must have been! Nevertheless, by 1868 the first race was staged in Paris. America saw its first bikes around 1878, but their cost was the equivalent of a half a year's salary for most people. Finally, in 1888 John Boyd Dunlop invented the pneumatic tire filled with air and the cycling craze began. Assembly-line production techniques brought the price down, and in 1893 there were over a million bikes on the nation's roads and paths.

Marshall "Major" Taylor

Cylcing has the distinction of being the first sport in which a national title was won by a native-born African-American. Marshall Taylor was born in Indianapolis, Indiana,

on November 21, 1878, in a family of eight children. His father, Gilbert, served in the Union Army during the Civil War. Young Marshall began as a trick rider for a local cycling shop and raced in a few amateur events when possible. The prize he won after his first victory was a watch and a dinner set.

When Taylor started, there were two categories of cycling events that proved popular with the public: the strenuous six-day "go as you please" affairs and the sprints of distances from a quarter of a mile to two miles. America had entered a decidedly macho period in its history, and stamina and strength were highly valued. These qualities matched the mood of the country. Horse races were typically four-mile heats until the late 1880s, and distance races at track meets were more important that the 100-yard dash, which was over in ten seconds or so. Fans wanted to see a struggle, so lengthier events were more appealing. Although Taylor participated in both cycling events, he eventually specialized in sprints.

He found the time to ride because Louis "Birdie" Munger, a white ex-cyclist and bicycle manufacturer, graciously assisted him from the beginning. Taylor worked in Munger's plant and was given all the benefit of Munger's experience. Munger publicly proclaimed to friends that Taylor would one day be the champion cyclist.

Taylor's early success did not come without a high price. Like other riders in sprint events, he was sometimes pocketed, jostled, bumped, and elbowed in making his way through half a dozen competitors on a narrow track. Racism was also a heavy burden. He sought to make his local YMCA his training base as a member of the See-Saw Circle Club, a black club, but was forced to go elsewhere. The best black cyclist at the time was Henry "The St. Louis Flyer" Stewart. Taylor finally settled in Worcester, Massachusetts, in 1895 with the YMCA and the Albion Cycle Club, another black group. After winning most of his amateur races, he decided to become a professional in 1896 at the young age of eighteen.

As a professional, he found a circuit organized by the League of American Wheelmen (LAW), which had been formed in 1880. There were even a few blacks in LAW meets. Taylor surprised himself by winning his first professional start—a half-mile handicap—at Madison Square Garden. As he and his fellow black riders continued to make creditable showings, white riders began reacting the way white jockeys were reacting at the time to black jockeys—they demanded that blacks be ejected from the LAW. Taylor's first major victory had been a ten-mile road race in Lexington, Kentucky, in 1891. But after winning an amateur one-mile event there in 1893, he never raced seriously in the South again.

Southern white LAW riders had constantly complained about blacks as far back as 1892. W. C. Grivat, the president of the Louisiana LAW, formally petitioned the national body for "forcing obnoxious [black] company upon southern wheelmen."[1] H.E. Raymond, the LAW National President, was in a dilemma, as black riders were welcomed on northern tracks. Raymond sent the following note to Grivat:

> While I am a thorough northerner I can still appreciate the feelings of the southern wheelman on the negro questions, and...with the class distinction so arbitrary in your section, it would be most unwise for the league to accept applications of negroes for members in any of the Southern states. It is at the same time more or less unfair to ask us to cut out the negro up here, where he is not so obnoxious and does not rub up against us as frequently as he does in the South."[2]

Southern affiliates then framed the problem as "the blacks versus us whites," to which Raymond replied, "There is no question of our accepting the negro in preference to the wheelman of the South. If it should be narrowed down to a question such as that, we should undoubtedly decide that we want our Southern brothers in the league in preference to the negroes of the country."[3]

Then the Southern LAW lobby asked for a ruling on membership for "whites only." Once again Raymond replied cautiously: "We, all of us, both north and south, have a feeling of antipathy toward the colored brother, but he is not so prominent or so likely to apply for membership in the LAW in the north as he is in the south."[4] Grivat managed to persuade the national body to consider the possibility that the LAW might lose its southern affiliates. In the winter of 1892–93, white southern LAW members began resigning, and the national body began expelling black members at its annual convention. But a motion to completely revise the membership requirements fell short of the two-thirds needed for ratification.

A year later the bylaws were changed to reserve membership for whites only, and southern dissidents returned to the LAW. Part of the vehement and emotional hatred by black riders must have come from the George Dixon–Jack Skelly prize fight in New Orleans in September 1892. Dixon, a Black boxer making his first appearance in the deep South, pulverized the white amateur Skelly in front of a mostly white audience. The local white press thereafter editorialized to ban mixed sports between blacks and whites.

By 1896, Taylor was allowed to race in selected LAW professional events although he was not a member. (The LAW was still an amateur group but placed a two-dollar tax on professionals and made them register.) He took full advantage and was a genuine threat at any distance up to a mile and was feared at two-mile lengths. In 1897 he won two key first-place victories in LAW one-mile open events in Boston and Providence, Rhode Island, and placed second in the half-mile at Providence. In truth, Taylor might have won the American championship on total points that year, but southern race directors refused to accept his entry. After winning the Boston event, W. E. Becker, a fellow white rider, proceeded to grab Taylor by the throat and choke him until police intervened.

To protect himself, Taylor joined the American Cycle Racing Association to race as a team member with Fred Titus and Edward Taylor—both white. In going after the Championship of America, he had to end with the highest scoring average in the Grand Circuit races. But meet promoters in Baltimore and St. Louis and at the Woodside track in Philadelphia rejected his applications. He was in the strange position of having the LAW refusing him membership but allowing him to race, while some northern meets rejected his application outright.

Near the end of the 1898 season, authorities were not sure who should be declared the national champion. Some of the professionals had seceded from the LAW jurisdiction and upset the tabulations of point totals. Finally, it was left to Charles M. Mears, the Ohio State Handicap official, to sort it out. Mears declared Taylor the winner, who "in all classes or races throughout the season scored the greatest number of victories."[5]

Taylor's point total of 121 made him the nation's first black national champion in any sport. He compiled twenty-one first-place victories, thirteen second-place berths, and eleven third-place showings, to 113 points for second-place Arthur Gardner.

However, to mar his victory the LAW declared Tom Butler its champion based on points totaled under their auspices. Fortunately, the LAW ceased to matter anymore in professional racing after 1898 because the National Cycling Association (NCA) was formed, which more specifically represented the aims of those who cycled for a living. As fate would have it, Taylor was the last professional to quit the LAW, even though they had denied him membership. He hung on with the LAW because the NCA had arranged inferior accommodations for him at a meet in Cape Girardeau, Missouri, and it wanted to force him to race on Sundays. A very religious man, Taylor refused, although it cost him untold trouble. (Sixty-nine years later, Muhammad Ali, the reigning heavyweight boxing champion, made a similar decision, which cost him time and money.)

When another outlaw group, the American Racing Cyclists' Union, formed, it too barred all blacks from membership. But the most important magazine of the sport, the *Cycling Gazette,* uttered the most racist statement of all. It editorialized that "Boycotting against Major Taylor too long delayed...white bicycle racers have drawn the color line...in the interest of the LAW and to the end that there might be no invidious criticism on the action of the white riders, we could have wished that they had boycotted Major Taylor before he had defeated them all. It looks now as if the ease with which this ebony wonder cut down records and carried away first money in all the big contests in which he entered had as much to do with the action of the white flyers as their active self-love."[6]

In 1899 Taylor was determined to win the American title with no encumbrances. Luckily, he competed in and won the World One-Mile Sprint Championship in Montreal and then set a world record at that distance in Chicago. He was now an American and world champion and the most acclaimed black athlete in the world aside from boxer, Joe Gans and jockey Jimmy Winkfield. He won the American title in 1899 and again in 1900. Yet few realize the emotional toll of the racism of his fellow competitors.

At his best Taylor was earning twenty thousand dollars per year. He continued to race and in 1901 traveled to Europe to test himself against foreign competition. For the next few years he spent part of his season in Europe and part in America. However, in 1903 he went to Australia and was so enamored of the warm hospitality he received that he named his daughter Sydney after that nation's capital city. After taking three years off from 1905 to 1907, he returned and promptly set new world records in the quarter-mile sprint—in 25.4 seconds from a standing start (1908)—and in the half-mile sprint—in 42.2 seconds from a standstill.

He left behind a professional record second only to Isaac Murphy's in the previous century and as accomplished a career performance as an athlete could ask. He was lauded by presidents, including Theodore Roosevelt, who told him, "I am always glad to shake the hand of any man who has accomplished something worthwhile in life.... [W]henever I run across an individual who stands out as a peer over all the others in any profession or vocation, it is indeed a wonderful distinction."[7]

Major Taylor was one of the most gifted and persevering athletes this nation has ever produced.

Notes

1. Quoted in Somers, op. cit., p. 222.
2. Quoted in ibid., p. 223.
3. Quoted in ibid.
4. Quoted in ibid.
5. Marshall Taylor, *The Fastest Bicycle Rider in the World.* (Worcester, Mass.: Wormley, 1928), p. 27.
6. Quoted in ibid., p. 34.
7. Quoted in ibid., p. 421.

Chapter 4

Track and Field

Early History

Running for some people today seems genetically programmed. They must run, jog, amble, or mope along, or else they will suffer psychological damage. Ancient man *had* to run, or he would not have eaten. Survival depended on the swiftness of some of those prehistoric tribesmen. Consequently, nearly every society has prized its fleetest runners, and even monarchs have been known to try it as sport. King Amenophis II of Egypt (c. 1438 B.C.) was a skilled archer, strong rower, and swift runner. Perhaps the most famous example is Phidippides, the messenger who ran twenty-six miles from the plains of Marathon to tell his countrymen of victory in battle.

At the Olympic Games in pre-Christian Greece, the ideal athlete was the winner of the five-event pentathlon, of which two were field activities—javelin and discus— and the other a 200-meter dash. The very first event in that first Olympics in 776 B.C. was a foot race of approximately 200 meters.

African runners were familiar to these Greeks. The historian Herodotus referred to the athletic skills of "Aethiopians" (the Greek word for all Africans at one time) in saying they were "exceedingly fleet of foot—more so than any people of whom we have information."[1] Herodotus probably had in mind the Africans of the savannah grasslands, who indeed had to run great distances to hunt game. Hunting parties were honored in their villages, and training runs were held to determine who could withstand their rigors. In all but the most densely vegetated parts of Africa, the swiftest and strongest runners were not only honored but necessary for group survival.

As late as the 1930s, French anthropologist Charles Beart mentioned what he thought was a wondrous phenomenon. He lived in Ougadougou (now in Burkina Faso) and thought it faster to send a package to Niamey by an African porter than by mail.

African slaves brought this love of running, and jumping and their natural swiftness to America and engaged in many races among themselves. (Here they encountered Native Americans, who shared their love of running. Some Native American tribes made fleetness a standard part of their rites of passage for young males.) Girls ran, too, as had their African ancestors. The passage of time and assimilation into European customs did not dim this craving: "most slave children thought of themselves as skillful 'athletes'; their white counterparts were generally felt to be less competent physically, unable to dance, run, jump, or throw."[2]

William Johnson, the free black barber who kept a diary from 1835 until 1852, wrote of frolicking with his sons. "I made a jump or 2 with the boys this Evening and beat Bill Nix about six inches in a one-half hamon Jump." (A hamon jump was a jump with no running start.) Ex-slave and civil rights leader Frederick Douglass wrote in his autobiography that "the majority [of slaves] spent the holidays in sports, ball-playing, wrestling, boxing, foot racing.[3] Even the intellectual William E. B. DuBois mentioned in his book *The Souls Of Black Folk* the elation a black boy felt at defeating a white boy in a foot race when he had no other way to assert himself.

But not all racing activities before the Emancipation Proclamation banned blacks. The Highland Games, organized by some Scottish-American groups, welcomed blacks, and the YMCAs organized events at their Colored branches as early as 1853. There were also professional walking races—"pedestrianism," as it was called—in the period from the 1830s to the 1880s. The horse-drawn trolleys in New York City made pedestrianism one of the first mass-attendance sports in the country along with boat racing. Francis Smith in the 1830s and Frank Hart in the 1870s were noted black walkers.

These early walking and running events usually pitted one ethnic group against another for prizes approaching a thousand dollars. Promoters made sure to invite runners who claimed Irish, English,

Native American, and Scottish ancestry. The English assumed they were superior in mind and body, and they were frequently at pains to prove it. Of an 1844 race featuring an assortment of nationalities and racial strains, Benjamin G. Rader noted that "It was the trial of the Indian against the white man, on the point in which the red man boasts his superiority. It was the trial of the peculiar American physique against the long-held supremacy of the English muscular endurance."[4] But after the Civil War, running became a true sport with specialized training and exacting demands. Within half a century the black man literally ran away with the records in running and jumping.

Athletics Becomes Organized

Just as boxing became distinct from barroom brawls and football evolved from wild, undisciplined team sport, so track—or "athletics," as it is called in the rest of the world—emerged from casual racing. Oxford and Cambridge Universities in England held their first dual meet in 1864, an event so well received that the British Empire Games were held two years later. Britain's dominions were worldwide in the mid-1800s, and they wanted athletic events to show off the finest British subjects. What better way to do that than by staging some games to see who could go the fastest, and farthest, with most endurance.

Here in America the New York Athletic Club (NYAC) was organized in 1866. It promoted its first meet in 1871. No blacks or other "disdained" ethnics belonged to the NYAC or other groups with "elite" membership, although everyone seemed interested in the posted results of contests. After all, runners required only a pair of shoes, and anyone with a watch could time the distances. The assumption was made by some that unless a runner belonged to one of these clubs, neither his efforts nor his times were to be taken seriously: "a superior athlete, unless he be black, a recent immigrant, or too crude in social demeanor, could expect little difficulty in finding a club that would grant him membership."[5]

Pedestrianism was dead by 1880. The inaugural intercollegiate meet was held in 1873, and the first National Amateur Track event was sponsored by the NYAC in 1876. The races in this first "national" affair included the 100-yard dash, the 120-yard high hurdles, the one-mile run, the three-mile run, and the seven-mile walk. These runs became the standard, pivotal events of all meets thereafter for a quarter-century. Notice that of the five races, three are distance runs. Endurance was then thought to be more important than short-distance speed.

The Amateur Athletic Union (AAU) was formed in 1888. It, too, reserved membership for young men of high social standing who fit the phrase "gentleman player." There was an opening of sorts on April 21, 1895, when the Penn Relay Carnival in Philadelphia began. It allowed anyone who was qualified to run in the team-oriented relays.

Denied admittance to national meets before 1895, blacks had to content themselves with their own arrangements, sponsored by groups like the Odd Fellows and colleges. Black institutions in the South held "Special Days" when intramural activities were contested. To be sure, equipment was crude and facilities were substandard, but the attempt was made nevertheless. Academics were more pressing than athletics.

Early Black College and Public School Programs

Most black colleges stressed physical training early in their history. But Tuskegee Institute (now Tuskegee University) went a step further in 1890 when it hired James B. Washington, the school's bookkeeper, as its first sports director. Washington had learned the basics of baseball and running while at Hampton Institute (now Hampton University). Three years later in 1893, Tuskegee staged the first major black college track meet, using members of its military cadet battalions.

The events included—other than close-order drill—running, jumping, relays, weight throwing, broad jumping, wall scaling, standing broad jumping, tug-of-war, and a centipede race. There was no aping the format of the NYAC or AAU meets. The relays were deemed especially important in fostering teamwork, dedicated coordination of athletes, and persistence. Blacks were doubly damned at the time because northerners believed *all* southerners—black and white—were lazy, and said so. Caspar Whitney, Walter Camp's collaborator in the All-America football selections, said in *Harper's Weekly* magazine that "The Southerner is prone to 'drifting', and by the pleasantest route....The athletic wave that has swept over the South has put new spirit into the young men, and lessened the receipts of saloons to an appreciable degree."[6]

Most sports administrators used manuals prepared by the YMCA and the A.G. Spaulding Company that laid out the requirements for facilities and training techniques. The most important contribution, however, came from black athletes who had returned from varsity participation in white schools up North. Most of these students received their admittance slips precisely because they showed promise in some sport. Some black institutions thus served as part of a "farm system" for certain white colleges.

Around the turn of the century, a black student from the South had to be a graduate of a black college before entering a white school as a freshman. It is not surprising, therefore, that a handful of white colleges had a long history of black participation while others had none at all. The idea that athletic talent could earn a place in a prestigious northern school was well grounded by the 1890s.

Matthew Bullock was a good example of this phenomenon. He was a star at Dartmouth and then organized the first intercollegiate track meet in 1907 for black colleges in the Southeast. From his base at Atlanta Baptist College (now Morehouse) he combined the best features of the Olympics and the Ivy League meets and the peculiarities of the triple-departmentalized black schools to field a successful event.

A year before Bullock's efforts in Atlanta, Harvard-trained Edwin B. Henderson sponsored the first intercity meet for black schoolboys in Washington, D.C., on May 30, 1906. Under the auspices of the Interscholastic Athletic Association (ISAA), nearly a hundred men and boys competed from the following schools: Howard University; the Washington, D.C., Colored YMCA; the "M" Street High School (now Dunbar); Armstrong Technical High School; Baltimore High School; and Wilmington (Delaware) High. It was a resounding success.

Blacks seemed to have found a formula that was enunciated by Colston R. Stewart a half a century later in the December 1951 *Negro History Bulletin*: "first, organized sport sifted down from the colleges and schools to the public; second, Negroes migrating North and entering public schools...; third, weaving their way onto track teams and community play associations...; fourth, there were more schools in the South for Negroes with athletic facilities...; and fifth, the Penn Relays Carnival began."

Strangely, some disinterest set in just before World War I. Poor facilities, uneven coaching, and competition from baseball in the spring made college track programs unappealing for a time. In the 1913 *ISAA Handbook*, Virginia Union University reported that "Track work has received little or no attention." However, the Colored (now Central) Intercollegiate Athletic Association (CIAA) was formed in 1912; it began to provide the organizational framework to advance the sport's cause after World War I.

Public school track programs had an interesting beginning. The precedent was set at Eton, the English secondary school for its upper class, in the early 1800s. The typical black public school in the South before 1900 was a one-room, dilapidated

frame building. The best situation was a
school connected with a black college that
typically had a preparatory section included. Northern blacks had it a bit better,
but unless the school system was integrated, the facilities were vastly inferior.
One solution was the Public Schools Athletic League (PSAL).

The PSAL began in New York City to
help occupy the city's youth in useful activities. Blacks took part immediately, and
the ISAA encouraged its members to participate. The Smart Set Club, an organization formed in Brooklyn, New York, was so
encouraged by the PSAL movement that it
staged the first large indoor meet ever
organized by blacks. Held on March 31,
1910, in Brooklyn's 14th Regiment Armory,
the meet attracted over twenty-five hundred
participants. Smart Set's reputation was further enhanced since it was the only black
club allowed to enter relay teams in national AAU meets, though the club itself
was not an AAU-affiliated organization.

The PSAL divided boys in track, swimming, and skating into four weight classes:
midget, or less than 80 pounds; lightweight, or less than 95 pounds; middleweight, or less than 115 pounds; and
unlimited. Girls had their own set of events:
short-distance dashes, baseball throws,
and short-distance swimming.

Black clubs in New York City in 1910
banded together to form the Vulcan Athletic
League (VAL) to stage events in basketball,
football, baseball, and track. Thus, on the
eve of World War I black schoolboys—and
some girls—had the ISAA, PSAL, the VAL,
the Colored YMCAs, and the Sears,
Roebuck–sponsored meets in Chicago to
assist them in track activities. Later still, the

Police Athletic Leagues (PALs) started programs. The clubs had been encouraged by
the successes of other blacks at white
colleges, and in the Olympics and even
those in other sports, like world champion
cyclist Marshall Taylor.

Fortunately, Edwin B. Henderson recorded the best times and distances of
blacks. He included them in the 1913 *ISAA
Handbook*. Not including blacks who
starred on varsity squads at white colleges,
he listed the following results—which may
look very surprising in the 1980s:[7]

100-yard dash--------------------10.2 seconds
440-yard run----------------------54.2 seconds
1-mile run -----------------------5.25 minutes
220-yard hurdles ---------------27 seconds
12-pound hammer-------------121 feet
220-yard dash--------------------23.6 seconds
880-yard run----------------------2 min. 15.6 sec.
120-yard hurdles ---------------18.6 seconds
12-pound shot------------------40' 3½"
High Jump -----------------------5' 8"
Broad Jump --------------------21' 7"
Discus Throw-------------------81' 3"
Pole Vault-------------------------9' 6"
2-mile run -------------------------11 min. 47 sec.

Stars at White Colleges

America's white colleges began track competition as an adjunct to rowing races in
1873. In 1852 James Gordon Bennett, a
wealthy sportsman, had invited crew teams
from Harvard and Yale to come to Lake
Winnepesaukee in New York to race for his
hotel guests. He added a two-mile run. The
race proved so popular that other intercollegiate meets were soon arranged with
the help of elite clubs in the Northeast.

Black America's first track star, William Tecumseh Sherman Jackson, emerged from this marriage of club and college. He attended Amherst College in Massachusetts from 1890 to 1892. There he played football with the first black All-America selectee, William Henry Lewis. Jackson received his early running experience at Virginia Normal and Industrial Institute (now Virginia State University), where he excelled at the half-mile run.

While at Amherst he set a school record of 2 minutes 5.4 seconds for the 880-yard run, and drew raves from critics. Said the *Worcester* (Massachusetts) *Telegram* on May 29, 1980, of one of his dual meets, "In it were an even dozen flyers....But it remained for a new man to carry off the honors...W.T.S. Jackson, Amherst....The last is a Negro and an athlete of speed and stamina....Jackson forged ahead, winning in the remarkable time of 2:08.2. Considering the track and the wind it was one of the biggest efforts of the day."

At the time blacks were not perceived as being naturally fast or enduring on the tracks, since most neither had the benefit of training nor were allowed to participate in meets sponsored by the elite clubs. Jackson's performance, however, set some to thinking about the supposed "natural" advantages of his race.

The next star performer was Napoleon Bonaparte Marshall of Harvard, who ran from 1895 to 1897. His specialty was the quarter-mile. Marshall was born of well-to-do parents in Washington, D.C., on July 30, 1873, and had attended the well-heeled Phillips Andover Preparatory School before enrolling at Harvard. His best time for the 440-yard dash was 51.2, which he set as a

sophomore. The record at the time was 49.6, set by Thomas E. Burke of Boston University.

Two other pre-1900 names were Spencer Dickerson, a quarter-miler at the University of Chicago in 1896–97, and G.C.H. Burleigh at the University of Illinois, who scored a 16.6-second time for the 120-yard high hurdles. Most observers today would assume that blacks excelled at shorter dashes in the beginning since that is their forte at present. But nearly every noted performer on the cinder paths until 1910 was a distance specialist. In the 1890s endurance was more highly prized than sheer speed over a hundred yards—for people as well as horses.

The first black champion on the track was Philadelphia-born John Baxter "Doc" Taylor, who attended the University of Pennsylvania in 1904 and 1907–1980. (He mysteriously left for the years 1905–06.) He went to racially mixed Central High School and Brown Preparatory before college. In 1904, wasting no time, he broke the Intercollegiate Amateur Athletic Association of America (ICAAAA) 440-yard-dash mark with a new time of 49.2 seconds. He repeated as ICAAAA victor in 1907 and 1908. He was coached part-time by the then dean of track coaches, Michael C. Murphy, who was an Olympic instructor in 1912.

On May 30, 1907, Taylor set a new mark of 48.8 in the ICAAAA Championships and was joined on the Penn squad by two other blacks—Howard Smith and Dewey Rogers, both half-milers. At the 1908 Olympic Games in London, Taylor was involved in a contretemps during a 400-meter race. There were severe disagreements between the American and British teams, and officials ordered the 400-meter finals rerun when they claimed that Taylor's teammate, J. C. Carpenter, deliberately ran wide and in front of Lieutenant Wyndham Halswelle, the British favorite, near the finish line.

The British, who had stationed officials around the track at twenty-yard intervals, cried "Foul!" and removed the tape at the finish line before the race was finished. Taylor was physically pulled off the track just before a half-hour argument between the Americans and the British. Carpenter was disqualified, and the race was ordered rerun with strings to divide the lanes. Taylor and his other teammate, W. C. Robbins, refused to cooperate. Halswelle ran the race alone and won the Gold Medal. Taylor did run the third leg on a first-place effort in the 4-by-400-meter medley relay in a combined time of 3:29.4 minutes. It was the first gold medal performance by a black American in Olympic history. The other black participant at London, W. C. Holmes, did not place in the standing broad jump.

Taylor returned to Philadelphia a hero and made plans to open a veterinary medical practice; but he suddenly died of typhoid pneumonia on December 2, 1908. He was only twenty-six.

Taylor's immediate predecessor in the Olympics was George Poage, who competed in 1904 at St. Louis, representing the Milwaukee Athletic Club. Poage won a bronze medal in the 400-meter hurdles, which featured four Americans from first to fourth place. (The winner, Harry Hillman, was a bank teller who never attended college and who advised swallowing whole raw eggs to enhance one's stomach and wind.) In the 400-meter run, Poage placed sixth. He ran the 100-yard dash, the 200-

yard dash, the 220-yard hurdles, and the 440-yard dash at the University of Wisconsin. John B. Taylor broke Poage's collegiate record of forty nine seconds in the 440-yard dash in 1907.

One year after Taylor's performance in London, black America's first star in field events entered Harvard. He was Theodore "Ted" Cable, a five-foot-nine-inch, 185-pounder from Indianapolis, Indiana. Born in 1891, he graduated from Shortridge High School in his hometown and enrolled at Phillips Andover Academy. At Harvard he had not planned to do any sports activities, but he answered coach Pat Quinn's call for freshmen in the weight events. He wound up a team member in the 220-yard dash, the hammer throw, and the broad jump.

In the 1912 Harvard-Yale meet, Cable won the hammer throw with a heave of 154' 11¼", the first black to do so in a field event. He topped that off with a victory in the broad jump of 22' 10¼". At the Intercollegiate finals on May 18 at Cambridge, Massachusetts, he won the hammer throw, thus becoming its first black winner, too. He missed out on an Olympic berth that year, finishing third in the hammer throw trials and fourth in the hop, skip, and jump event. He repeated as Intercollegiate hammer-throw champion in 1913 at 162' 4½" and placed second at the AAU in the thirty-nine-pound weight throw. Alexander Louis Jackson joined Cable at Harvard in 1913 as a hurdler. From Englewood, New Jersey, Jackson first ran in meets sponsored by the Vulcan Athletic League. Those early pioneering efforts had begun paying dividends.

No one, though, was ready for Howard Porter Drew of Lexington, Virginia. He was the first in a continuing line of blacks known as "the world's fastest humans." Drew was born on June 28, 1890, and entered high school in Springfield, Massachusetts, at age twenty-one after working at a railroad depot. In 1910 this speedster won the National Junior 100-yard and 220-yard dash titles in 10 and 21.8 seconds, respectively. He repeated these victories in 1911. But 1912 was his banner year.

The 5' 9" Drew defeated the favored Ralph Craig of the University of Michigan in the Olympic Trials on June 8 in a time of 10.8 seconds for 100 meters. That equaled the existing Olympic record. But when he got to Stockholm for the Games, he pulled up lame after qualifying in his heat, and he could not run in the final. Nevertheless he recovered, and on November 11 of that year he lowered the 100-meter record to 10.2 seconds at an indoor meet at the 23rd Regiment Armory in Brooklyn.

On September 12 he captured the AAU 100-yard dash, finishing a full yard ahead of A. T. Myer. Then he equaled the American record in the 70-yard dash at 7.5 seconds and later broke it on December 7 with a clocking of 7.2 seconds. Reporters who were used to blacks doing well in distance races were perplexed by Drew's showing, since he seldom trained. Some say he injured himself in Stockholm precisely because he was forced to train as an American team member. The *New York Tribune* writer said, "It seems incredible that a man without fear of life and not the slightest desire to catch a train can impel himself to such prodigious speed."[8]

From the American coach, Mike Murphy, came the comment that "Never in my life have I seen any sprinter with such wonderful leg action...why, his legs fly back and forth just like pistons....Trainers and experts say that he has the quickest start of any man ever seen upon the track."[9]

In 1913 Drew again won the AAU titles in the 100-yard and 220-yard dashes, holding the world record in the latter at 22.8 seconds. But that most coveted of speed marks—the 100-yard dash—was equaled by him on September 1 at Charter Oak Park in Hartford, Connecticut. He sped the distance in 9.6 seconds, to write his name alongside Arthur Duffey's from 1902. He decided to enter the University of Southern California, and in 1914 he was a co-holder of the 220-yard dash record at 21.2 seconds.

Unfortunately, there were no Olympics in 1916 because of World War I, so after switching to and graduating from Drake University, he entered the Army and prepared for the Inter-Allied Games in Paris in 1919. He failed to qualify for the 1920 Olympics but was named to an All-America list of track stars in 1918, which represented the best of all time. Alan J. Gould, the Associated Press sports editor, said it for everyone: "Drew was the greatest of them all."[10] Drew and Andy Ward, the AAU winner in the 100-meter and 200-meter, could have done well in an Olympics in 1916.

A contemporary of Howard P. Drew was another world record holder, Henry Binga Dismond of Richmond, Virginia. After surpassing the quarter-mile competition at home, he went to Howard University and then to the University of Chicago, where he was tutored by Amos Alonzo Stagg. In 1913 he ran a 47.8-second time for 440 yards and was hailed as the second coming of John B. Taylor. Two years later he managed to equal the world record held by

Ted Meredith at 47.4. Between seasons he competed for the Smart Set Club and the Loughlin Lyceum.

Other quarter-milers included Cecil Lewis at the University of Chicago; James E. Meredith at Penn; and Irving T. Howe of Boston's English High School and later of Dartmouth and Colby College. W. Randolph Granger, of Barringer High School in Newark, New Jersey, ran the half-mile at Dartmouth; J. Ferguson was a two-miler at Ohio State via West Virginia Institute (now West Virginia State); Howard Martin ran at the University of Cincinnati; Jim Ravenelle was a quarter-miler at NYU; Ben Johnson competed in dashes at Springfield (Massachusetts); Fred "Duke" Slater tossed the shot put at Iowa; and football giant Paul Robeson threw the weights at Rutgers.

Edward Solomon Butler was an exception. He was the first African-American to star abroad in more than one event. John B. Taylor had earned glory in the London Olympics for his specialty, but Butler could do everything. He hailed from Wichita, Kansas, where he was born in 1895. His family had been part of the large migration of blacks to Kansas in 1879. Beginning at Hutchinson High School, he followed his coach to Rock Island (Illinois) High School and flourished.

At a scholastic meet there, Butler won all five events he entered: the 100-yard, the 220-yard, the 440-yard, the high jump, and the broad jump titles. Illinois officials thereafter passed a rule then limiting entrants to two events. He also played football and basketball. Entering Dubuque (Iowa) University in 1915, he immediately set records that stood until the depression. Noted the *Des Moines Register* of December 13, 1915,

"Butler is the fastest man who ever set foot on Hawkeye soil."

After graduation he found himself in the Inter-Allied Games in 1919, where he made the third-longest long jump in history—24′ 9½″, only 2¼″ behind the world record. He returned to America with five medals and two diplomas after the King of Montenegro presented his awards to him.

Black runners had come quite a distance since W.T.S. Jackson began at Amherst. They began at the middle-distance events and ended World War I with a reputation for all-around swiftness.

Military Successes

Black soldiers gained much acclaim in the Army. Before 1900 only a handful had had any formal training, but they had made good showings at military meets. In 1908 black military units won the track team titles in all three Philippine Department contests. The 9th Cavalry won the Luzon meet over the white 3rd Cavalry, 10th Cavalry (Black), 5th Field Artillery, and 26th, 29th, and 30th Infantries. The 24th Infantry won the Visayas meet, and the 25th Infantry captured the Mindanao events.

The following year, Private George Washington of the 25th Infantry won the 100-yard, 220-yard, and 880-yard events in the Philippines Championships. On February 26, 1916, a Private Gilbert (no first name could be found) equaled the world mark in the 100-yard dash at 9.6 seconds in Honolulu. Sergeant Schley C. Williamson was easily the Army's fastest soldier from 1917 through 1920, clocking 9.8 seconds for 100 yards. As in football and basketball, black soldiers took tremendous pride in their athletic accomplishments. With superior facilities and a high level of general fitness, they were always ready to race.

By 1920 the black runner was an enigma to most experts. The white man still theorized that *he* was physically and mentally superior. Jack Johnson, the black former heavyweight champion, had lost his title, and no black heavyweights were given a chance for another seventeen years. What began as ideas about black musculature to explain why they were distance runners soon had to be altered to account for Howard P. Drew and Private Gilbert. In fact, white theorists had to invert their racist notions completely for a time. Beginning with Drew and Butler, black athletes dominated the dash and jumping events. Before World War II closed another chapter in the saga of track and field, several more blacks made the timers check their watches in disbelief, especially one named James Cleveland "Jesse" Owens.

Notes

1. *Horizon History of Africa,* vol. 1, p. 184.
2. David K. Wiggins, "The Play of Slave Children in the Plantation Communities of the Old South, 1820–1860." *Journal of Sports History* 7(Summer 1980): 32.
3. Frederick Douglass, op. cit., p. 145.
4. Rader, op. cit., p. 40.
5. Rader, op. cit., p. 60.
6. Somers, op. cit., p. 246.
7. *ISAA Handbook* (1913), p. 123.
8. Quoted in Henderson, *The Negro in Sport.* (1949), p. 50.
9. Quoted in ibid., p. 51.
10. Alan J. Gould, The Associated Press, April 5, 1928.

Baseball

Early History:
English Roots

Like many ball games played in America, baseball had its roots in the English countryside. The English called their version "chunny," but the Irish, the Scottish, and later the German immigrants here called it "base ball." There is even a record of American soldiers playing a game called "base" on April 7, 1778, at Valley Forge. In 1886, Princeton students played "baste ball." But the most common term for the game just before the Civil War was "towne ball."

Historian John Hope Franklin noted that slaves certainly played their share of towne ball, using balls made of cloth bound around boiled chicken feathers. Local rules prevailed. In his massive and authoritative history of slave life, John Blassingame wrote of the testimony of Henry Baker, born in 1854 in Alabama, "At dat time we played what we called 'Town Ball.'...we had bases en we run frum one base tuh de udder 'cause ef de runner wuz hit wid de ball he wuz out. We allus made de ball out a cotton en rags. We played wid de niggers on de plantation."[1] They must have had some rough games indeed.

First Organizations

The first established team was formed in New York City by a well-financed, blue-blooded group that called themselves the Knickerbockers. Organized by Alexander Cartwright, a bookshop owner, they sought to enforce a high standard of membership, rule enforcement, and amateurism. "[C]ommon laborers, poor immigrants, or black Americans need not have applied for membership," noted sports historian William J. Baker.[2]

There were two competing styles of play: the Massachusetts and the New York. The Massachusetts style had the bases set in a diamond or oblong shape. Players ran up and back and were put "out" by being "plugged" or "soaked"—hit by the ball. In the New York game the bases were set in a square pattern, and the runners had to touch the bases before a fielder touched that base or him. The New York style won out, and Cartwright eventually put the bases ninety feet apart, as they are today; he replaced "soaking" with tagging, determined that three outs forced a change of sides, allowed fielders to make outs by catching a ball in the air or on one bounce or touching a base, seated an umpire at a table along the third-base line, made the pitcher toss the ball underhanded from forty-five feet away, disallowed gloves, and decided that games ended when a team scored twenty-one runs. Not too different from today.

But the Knickerbockers lost their first game 23 to 1, so they found out quickly that social pedigree did not necessarily win games. Besides, clubs sprang up all over the map, and competition was keen. Urban ethnics took tremendous pride in their club squads. The Irish and German clubs began to treat the sport like an ethnic heirloom. Free blacks also formed sides and played against one another.

In 1858 the National Association of Baseball Players (NABBP) was formed and initially included blacks who played on some member clubs. There was opposition, but they still played. In 1859 the first college game was contested between Amherst and Williams. Then the Civil War spread the New York game even more far afield. On Christmas Day 1862, there was a game at Hilton Head Island witnessed by thousands.

After the war urban blacks formed clubs at a quick rate. Some were made up of social club members, and some were made up of men who worked at prestigious white clubs. In New Orleans, for instance, black employees of the Boston and Pickwick clubs played against other black teams with names like the Unions, Aetnas, Fischers, Orleans, and the Dumonts. They even organized a citywide Negro Championship. These games were frequently attended by the black elite to the accompaniment of brass bands. But more and more white players were playing as professionals, paving the way for a national effort.

The National Sport

At the end of the Civil War baseball was the divided nation's most popular sport. There were clubs everywhere, and officials began making rule changes to enhance spectator appeal. While the elite clubs in Boston, New York, and Philadelphia abhorred professionalism, the ethnics could care less about such niceties. They wanted to win and make money. The Cincinnati Red Stockings in 1869 became the first all-professional team whose players derived their sole income from baseball.

Two years before the Red Stockings' debut, the NABBP decided to ban all blacks from participation. The Nominating Committee's statement left no doubt where its sentiments stood: "It is not presumed by your committee that any club who have applied are composed of persons of color, or any portion of them; and the recommendations of your committee in this report are based upon this view, and they unanimously report against the admission of any club which may be composed of one or more colored persons."[3] Strong stuff, though every club owner was a northerner. The pressure came from the Irish and German clubs to keep blacks out.

There was one positive bit of change in 1867: The "boxscore" was invented by Henry Chadwick as a means of cataloging the many statistics during games. He even started his own newspaper, *The Chronicle,* which carried the latest batting averages. These innovations came at a propitious time since more and more fathers were working at "wage" jobs rather than at a traditional family trade. Baseball was becoming a prime instrument of socialization for some of the nation's youth. But illegal gambling on games became rampant, and in some quarters the sport developed a seedy image. The *New York Times* called professional baseball players dissipated gladiators.

Blacks, meanwhile, played among themselves and sometimes advertised for competition. In Houston, Texas, the *Daily Houston Telegraph* of July 14, 1868, printed the following challenge from a side: "Black Ballers—There is a Baseball club in this city, composed of colored boys bearing the aggressive title of 'Six Shooter Jims'. They wish us to state that they will play a match game with any other colored club in the state."

Black teams positively flourished in the Northeast, and intercity games were quite common. In October 1867 the Brooklyn *Daily Union* published this account of a pending game between the Philadelphia Excelsiors and the Brooklyn Uniques and the Monitors: "These organizations are composed of very respectable colored people, well-to-do in the world...and includes many first class players. The visitors will receive all due attention from their colored brethren of Brooklyn; and we trust, for the good of the fraternity, that none of the 'white trash' who disgrace white clubs, by following and brawling for them, will be allowed to mar the pleasure of these social colored gatherings."[4]

These team members were probably from the black upper class, inasmuch as they had the resources to travel to play games—no easy task right after the Civil War. (The game, incidentally, was won by the Excelsiors over the Uniques, 42 to 37.)

Some of these players were so extraordinarily good that they tried to fit in somewhere to play professionally full-time. The first to be found was Bud Fowler (née John W. Jackson), who played for a local white team in New Castle, Pennsylvania. He had begun for an all-black squad called the Washington Mutuals. Perhaps it is no accident that Fowler succeeded—he was born at Cooperstown, New York, the birthplace of modern baseball, in 1850. Fowler's presence on the team attested to the exceptions made for some black players.

A year before Fowler began at New Castle, white professionals formed the National Association of Professional Baseball Players (NAPBBP), which replaced the NABBP. It strove to raise salaries and conditions for its members as rivalries heated up. But its members seldom lived up to contracts and switched teams willy-nilly. In its place in 1876 arose the National League of Professional Baseball Clubs (NLPBBC). But the NLPBBC invested its power in the *owners,* not in the players. It also banned Sunday games, betting, and blacks. The following season they instituted the dreaded "reserve clause," which saved five players from each roster who were not to be considered for trades.

Recalcitrants led by the Cincinnati Red Stockings formed the rival American Association of Baseball Clubs in 1880. A team in Toledo entered the American Association in 1884. On its squad was a young black player named Moses Fleetwood Walker— the first black player in what is called organized baseball.

Moses F. Walker grew up a privileged boy. He was born free on October 7, 1857. His father was a doctor practicing in

Steubenville, Ohio. At twenty-one he entered the preparatory department at Oberlin College. He became a catcher on the school team and was elected captain in 1880. The following year he was involved in a racial incident in a game with a team from Louisville, Kentucky. No matter—he was graduated in 1882 and entered the University of Michigan Law School. The summer of 1882 he followed the basepaths of Bud Fowler and played for New Castle.

Moses' brother Weldy also entered Oberlin's preparatory department in 1881 and played varsity ball. The next year found him on the varsity squad of the University of Michigan, where its school paper wrote of him in October 1882, "We are glad to welcome Weldy, and are willing to harbor any more [Walkers] if they are as good a baseballist as Weldy's brother."

Moses Walker left law school in 1884 to catch full-time for the Toledo Mudhens in the Northwestern League. He had signed with them the year before and had a nasty racial contretemps with Adrian "Cap" Anson, the star of the Red Stockings. Weldy joined Walker on July 11, 1884, and played five games. But their troubles were just starting.

The National League and the American Association signed a "peace agreement" in 1882 that maintained reserve players and protected territory. Moses Walker was not on Toledo's reserve list, although he played forty-two games as their starting catcher. Perhaps Toledo manager Charles Norton was worried about protecting a Negro when everyone else was trying to get them out.

The American Association had two distinctly southern cities, and Louisville was one of them. Walker was jeered there the same year the great black jockey Isaac Murphy won his first Kentucky Derby. The Toledo *Blade* noted that "Walker . . . is one of the most reliable men in the club, but his poor playing in a city where the color line is closely drawn as it is in Louisville."[5]

Then came a "letter" to Norton warning of trouble if Walker played at Richmond. It read:

Richmond, Virginia
September 5, 1884

Manager, Toledo Baseball Club
Dear Sir:

We the undersigned, do hereby warn you not to put up Walker, the Negro catcher, the days you play in Richmond, as we could mention the names of seventy-five determined men who have sworn to mob Walker, if he comes on the grounds in a suit. We hope you will listen to our words of warning, so there will be no trouble, and if you do not, there certainly will be. We only write this to prevent much bloodshed, as you alone can prevent.

Bill Frick	James Kendrick
Dynx Dunn	Bob Roseman.

It was later discovered that the letter was a hoax. But Norton left Walker at home anyway. The Toledo *Blade* said Walker was ill, which of course was not true. In any event, in 1884 he batted .251 in forty-six games, with four doubles, two triples, and a .888 fielding average—ranking him twenty-sixth among American Association catchers. For the record, Walker played against the following American Association teams: New York Metropolitans, Columbus Buckeyes, Louisville Eclipses, St. Louis Browns, Cin-

cinnati Reds, Baltimore Orioles, Philadelphia Athletics, Brooklyn Atlantics,
Pittsburgh Alleghenys, Indianapolis Hoosiers, and the Washington Nationals. He
did not play against the Richmond
Virginians.

The success of the Walkers and Fowler
led other black players and teams to believe
they could succeed as well. It was less clear
whether the two Organized Ball leagues
would eventually take them in. But enough
evidence existed and enough support from
black communities was forthcoming to
give it a try. They had little to lose, for the
national sport was now established—and it
was racist.

First Black Professional Teams

That black professional teams would arise
was in no doubt. That the first one did so by
accident is surprising. In 1883 the United
States Supreme Court declared the Civil
Rights Law of 1875 to be unconstitutional,
so black athletes were under no illusions
about legal assistance to play Organized
Ball. The first squad surfaced in Babylon,
Long Island, and, aware of the racial diffi-
culties ahead, planned accordingly.

In Babylon in the summer of 1885 the
Argyle Hotel's headwaiter, Frank
Thompson, organized his fellow black waiters into a team. There is still some doubt as
to who named the team the Cuban Giants,
but the rationale is clear. Most baseball
teams of the era were called Giants, but the
first name usually designated some city or
neighborhood. The name Cuban was specifically used because the team wanted the
public to think they were not American, but
Cuban or foreign. To further convince spec-

tators, they spoke a gibberish on the field
that many took to be pidgin Spanish. Such
was the weight of racism in their minds.

But they were good as well. Reported
the October 10, 1885, *South Side Signal* of
Babylon, "The colored baseball team who,
during the summer played many excellent
games on the Argyle grounds, have, since
leaving Babylon, tried conclusion with several of the leading clubs. One of their losses
was to the New York Metropolitans, 11-3.
The 'Mets' finished in seventh place in the
American Association that year." The original members of that team were: Ben
Holmes, captain, at third base; A. Randolph
at third base; Ben Boyd at second base;
William Eggleston at shortstop; Guy Day
catching; George Parego, Frank Harris, and
R. Motin pitching; Milton Dabney in left
field; and Charles Nichols in right field.

In time, as Solomon White pointed out
in his historic tome *Official Baseball
Guide,* the Cuban Giants "were heralded
everywhere as marvels of the baseball
world."[6] In nine games in Babylon that first
season, the Cuban Giants had a 6-2-1
record.

There had been some black semiprofessional nines (baseball teams are
sometimes referred to as nines) before the
Cuban Giants. In 1884 the all-black New
York Gorhams played an exhibition against
the Cape May (New Jersey) Collegians in
front of President Chester A. Arthur. In
Charleston, Memphis, Atlanta, and New
Orleans local teams continued to attract
large crowds. Even in the late 1880s, when
Reconstruction had ended, there were a few
games played between all-white and all-
black nines. The May 18, 1887, *New Orleans
Pelican* wrote of a victory of the all-black

Pickwicks over a white team: "The playing of the colored club was far above the average ballplaying and elicited hearty and generous applause from the large crowd in attendance, which was about evenly divided between white and black."

Meanwhile the Cuban Giants consolidated their lineup in the fall of 1885 when their new white owner, John L. Lang, signed three players from the all-black Philadelphia Orions—second baseman George Williams, shortstop Abe Harrison, and pitcher Shep Trusty. This move, noted White, "on the part of Lang was one of the most important and valuable acts in the history of colored baseball. It made the boys from Babylon the strongest independent team in the East, and the novelty of a team of colored players with that distinction made them a valuable asset."[7] It is assumed by many that Frank Thompson gave up the team because he did not want to leave his job as headwaiter at the Argyle Hotel.

White owners showed interest when it became obvious there was money to be made when black teams were booked properly. Few black men could do that because they lacked the connections and the trust to make deals; and professional baseball already had a dubious image. Lang then gave way in 1886 to Walter Cook, another white businessman from Trenton, New Jersey, who hired S. K. Govern, a black man, to manage the squad. Solomon White said the players were thrilled by the sale.

This 1886 Cuban Giants team was the best in the nineteenth century. The lineup included: Clarence Williams catching, George Stovey and Shep Trusty pitching, Jack Frye at first base, George Williams at second base, Ben Holmes at third base, Abe Harrison at shortstop, Billy White in left field, Ben Boyd in center field, and Arthur Thomas in right field. Frye and Stovey must have pulled double duty that season because records show them also at Lewiston and Jersey City, respectively.

Salaries were paid according to position. Pitchers and catchers got eighteen dollars per week plus expenses; infielders got fifteen dollars per week plus expenses; and outfielders got twelve dollars per week plus expenses. By contrast, white major leaguers were making around $1,750 a season, which was three times the average working man's wage. No wonder white players did not want blacks playing with them.

The best black players, however, were always torn between playing for an all-black squad or trying to play for a mixed team for higher pay. The owners of minor league teams were sometimes willing to let blacks play if they were good—and why not? Everyone knew they could not play in the major leagues, so many owners had little to lose if their white players did not object.

League Formation Attempts and Championships

As local black teams stabilized, attempts were made to form leagues. In 1886 the Southern League of Colored Base Ballists was organized, but it collapsed after a few games. Rivalries and intercity games continued nonetheless. Dale Somers noted that "Teams of black athletes from St. Louis and Memphis came to the city [New Orleans] in the late 1880's, and local Negroes travelled to Mobile and Natchez for contests.... [I]n

1889 a Memphis Nine played the P.B.S. Pinchbacks for the 'Championship of the South.'" But *integrated* ball came to an abrupt end in New Orleans in 1890.

There was another attempt in 1887. The League of Colored Baseball Clubs (LCBC) was formed of the Boston Resolutes, New York Gorhams, Philadelphia Pythians, Washington Capitol Citys, Pittsburgh Keystones, Norfolk (Virginia) Red Stockings, Cincinnati Crowns, Lord Baltimores, and Louisville Fall Citys. The president was Walter Brown, the black manager of the Pittsburgh squad. It, too, soon folded because the distances between cities was too great. Another reason was that the years between 1885 and 1890 were known as the "money period." Players had a chance of playing with all-black sides or trying out for a higher-paying mixed-race team. The LCBC was even recognized in the national agreement between the National League and the American Association as an official minor league.

Black teams in this six-year span were sorely hurt by the jumping of key performers from team to team. George Stovey, for example, played for the Cuban Giants in 1886 and the International League Newark team in 1887. He was the first premier black pitcher, and his services were in demand. A left-hander, he won thirty-four games for Newark and lost fifteen. But they released him on September 30 because, as *The Sporting Life* of July 14 noted, "Several [white] representatives declared that many of the best players in the [International] league were anxious to leave on account of the colored element." A third reason for the difficulty was that the Cuban Giants never joined the black league. Its white owners kept them out because more money was to be made otherwise.

In the end it was not the reneging on agreements that was the undoing of black players. It was racism. In 1887 several white players threatened to quit if blacks played, and Adrian "Cap" Anson refused to allow his team to play against Newark unless Moses F. Walker and George Stovey were benched. John M. Ward, a player/lawyer who helped found the Brotherhood of Professional Baseball Players in 1885, wanted to sign blacks, but Anson was adamant in saying "No negroes."

The most public protest came in 1887, when Chris Von der Ahe, president of the St. Louis Browns, received a letter from his players just before a game was to be played against the Cuban Giants. This game was scheduled for Sunday, September 11, at West Farms, New York. Fifteen thousand fans were expected. Von der Ahe was given the letter in Philadelphia's Continental Hotel dining room the night before by one of his players, James O'Neill. It read:[8]

Philadelphia, Penn.
September 10

To Chris Von der Ahe, Esq.
Dear Sir:
We, the undersigned members of the St. Louis baseball club, do not agree to play against negroes tomorrow. We will cheerfully play against white people at anytime, and think by refusing to play we are only doing what is right, taking everything into consideration.

W. A. Lathram	John Boyle
J. E. O'Neill	R. L. Caruthers
W. E. Gleasoin	W. H. Robinson
Charles King	Curt Welch

The game was canceled. The major league champion Detroit Tigers *did* play them and won 6 to 4 in a game not decided until the ninth inning.

Weldy Walker adamantly refused to take his dismissal from Akron (Tri-State League) at the end of 1887 lying down. He penned the following letter to the League president:[9]

> Steubenville, Ohio
> March 5
>
> Mr. McDermit,
> President Tri-State League
> I take the liberty of addressing you be-cause...the law permitting colored men to sign was repealed...February 23....I am ascertaining the reason of such an action. I have grievances, it is a question with me whether individual loss serves the public good....This is the only question...in all cases that convince beyond doubt that you...have not been impartial and unpre-judiced in your consideration of...the 'Na-tional Game.'...The law is a disgrace to the present age...and casts derision at the laws of Ohio....There is now the same accom-modation made for the colored patron of the game as the white....There should be some broader cause—such as lack of abil-ity, behavior and intelligence—for barring a player, rather than his color....
> Yours truly,
> Weldy W. Walker

Walker's elegant but biting riposte received many supporters. The Syracuse *Standard* said, "The...directors should...take steps toward rescinding...the rule forbid-ding...colored players."[10] The Newark *Call* noted that "If anywhere in the world the social barriers are broken down it is on the ball field...the objection to colored men is ridiculous."[11] A few weeks later the rule was indeed rescinded—only to be replaced by an even more insidious "gentlemen's agree-ment" that lasted until 1945.

But despite the imminent demise of blacks in Organized Ball, they made quite a showing in 1887. There were more of them on white minor league teams that year than at any other time. The player with the longest tenure was Frank Grant, a five-foot-seven-inch, 155-pound pitcher who re-mained on the Buffalo roster for three years. The light-skinned Grant was born in Pitts-field, Massachusetts, in 1867 and played for his hometown Graylocks team and a Platts-burgh, New York, nine before entering organized baseball in Meriden (Connecti-cut). In 1886 Grant batted .340 in forty-five games for Buffalo. He used shin guards to protect himself from white players who tried to spike him while sliding.

Black teams decided they had to play their own series of playoffs among them-selves, so a tournament was held in 1888 in New York City among the four best clubs. It was immediately deemed the first Colored Championships of America. Using a round-robin format, the Cuban Giants won first place, the Pittsburgh Keystones were sec-ond, the New York Gorhams were third, and the Norfolk Red Stockings were fourth. J. M. Bright, part owner of the Giants, donated a silver ball as the prize.

After watching the games the *Sporting News* reporter commented that "There are players among these colored men that are equal to any white men on the ball field. If you don't think so, go and see the Cuban Giants play. This club...would play a favorable game against such clubs as the New Yorks or Chicagos."[12] In early 1889 the Gorhams and the Giants joined with six other white teams to form the Middle States or Pennsylvania League—the first all-black *teams* to appear in an organized league. The squad from Harrisburg, Pennsylvania, won the pennant.

This Middle States League changed its name to the Eastern Interstate League in late 1889, but the Gorhams refused to follow. The Giants came back but changed their base of operations to York, Pennsylvania, and then changed their name to the York Monarchs after playing sixty-five games as the Giants. The best guess is that they had to adjust or lose their special place with white teams. Another complication was that while the York Monarchs were playing, J. M. Bright assembled a new team and called it the Cuban Giants—confusing but true.

By the end of 1889 the black presence in Organized Ball had disappeared. Buffalo released Frank Grant in 1888; Syracuse released pitcher Robert Higgins, who went back to his Memphis barbershop; and finally Moses F. Walker was released by Syracuse at the end of 1889. The *Sporting News* soberly assessed the situation: "race prejudice exists in professional baseball to a marked degree, and the unfortunate son of Africa who makes his living as a member of a team of white professionals has a rocky road to travel."[13]

Black teams subsequently began to squabble among themselves, for there were dozens of good players and they had nowhere else to play. In the Colored Championships of 1889 the Gorhams won a two-game series against the Cuban Giants.

When the Cuban Giants returned in 1890 to play in the Eastern Interstate League (the Middle State League's new name), *Sporting Life*'s Official Baseball Guide produced the first authentic batting averages. Some sample numbers included: George Williams, .371; Solomon White, .358; William Selden, .326; Arthur Thomas, .317; Jack Frye, .303; and Billy White, .291.

Just in time out West in Lincoln, Nebraska, the Lincoln Giants were formed in 1890—the first black professional team west of the Mississippi River. Unfortunately, they dissolved in less than one season. But the black player had proven he belonged from Maine to Mexico, and it was just a matter of time before he would be vindicated.

The Not-So-Gay Nineties

With segregation complete, black efforts turned to getting their own game in order. During the last decade of the nineteenth century Negro baseball became a truly integral part of black culture. In 1891, A. Davis, who ran the Gorhams, signed some players from the Monarchs and formed the Big Gorhams. Solomon White said that this aggregation was "without doubt one of the strongest teams ever gotten together, white or black."[14] Their record was an amazing one hundred wins and four losses, including thirty-nine wins in a row at one stretch. But, as had happened before, they disbanded after one season.

The only full-time professional team from 1892 to 1894 was the Cuban Giants. Black teams from 1891–94 merely survived, although some in cities with sizable black populations drew reasonably well. Others even resorted to clowning to amuse spectators. In 1895 the Page Fence Giants were formed by Bud Fowler and Grant "Home Run" Johnson. They traveled by train and staged parades just before games. Fowler explained that gimmicks were needed to counter the racism that drove him and his contemporaries out of white and mixed teams. He had done nothing else in life since 1872. Baseball was his life.

The Colored Championships resumed in 1895 when the Cuban X-Giants lost ten games to five in a series against the Page Fence Giants. The Cuban X-Giants, formed by E. B. Lamar, Jr., of New York, was another team that tried to capitalize on the fame of the original Cuban Giants. Black talent was so concentrated that pick-up teams could be quite good if one or two top performers were present. Such a team was the Chicago Unions, a local hit beginning in 1886.

The Chicago Unions played their games at their own field at Sixty-seventh Street and Langley. They toured the Midwest during the week and played to packed stands on Sunday afternoons. They became a professional nine in 1896. In their first twelve years of play, the Unions won 612 games, lost 118, and tied 12—for a .814 winning average. As a result of the strength of black teams by 1895, the Colored Championships had to be split into a West and an East series. For instance, in 1897 the Cuban X-Giants won the East title over the Genuine Cuban Giants two games to one at the Weehawken Grounds in New Jersey.

Lest this be confusing, "the Genuine Cuban Giants" was the new name for the original Cuban Giants team, which had changed owners and home bases so often.

Since the team started in 1885, their home city had changed from New York to Trenton to Hoboken to Johnstown and Glowersville (New York) to Pennsylvania to Ansonia (Connecticut). But they were still the most well-known black professional sports team in America.

The last team to make a splash was the Acme Colored Giants, organized by Harry Curtis, a well-meaning and colorful white showman. They played in the Iron and Oil League in Celeron, New York. This team was not very good and the press lambasted them unmercifully. Their record was eight wins and forty-one losses in a half-season in 1898. Their significance is that they were the last black group to be a part of an organized white league. The Iron and Oil League was not a part of Organized Ball; it was strictly local. Black teams and players were now completely missing from established leagues—organized and otherwise.

College Ball

Baseball was much more favored on the nation's campuses in the latter part of the last century than it is today. Football was just coming into its own with rules codification, but baseball was played by nearly every American boy on his local diamond.

The aforementioned Moses Fleetwood Walker led off the parade of black players on white college varsity squads, playing as catcher for Oberlin College in Ohio in 1878 and later at the University of Michigan Law School. His brother also played at Oberlin in 1881. In 1902 Merton P. Robinson followed Moses F. Walker as the school's second varsity catcher. In 1895 James Francis

Gregory was an infielder/outfielder at Amherst after having played at Howard University. *The Boston Globe* of May 12, 1896, said "Gregory makes brilliant plays for visitors" when Amherst played Harvard.

It was not unusual for black athletes to attend a black college before attending a white institution. Games between black and white schools were not unusual, either. In April 1894, Howard played Trinity College of Hartford, Connecticut, losing 34 to 17 in a game that *The Washington Post* noted was replete with hits and errors. In 1898 Howard lost to the Yale Law School team, 11 to 7. Howard just did not seem to do well against these schools.

Eugene Gregory played on Harvard's nine in 1897, and Frank Armstrong was seen on Cornell's (Iowa) team for three years, from 1898 to 1900. (Esteemed black leader Booker T. Washington visited Cornell one day in 1900 for a speech and later persuaded Armstrong to become his assistant.)

Following Armstrong was William Clarence Matthews, an infielder/outfielder at Harvard. Sports historian Ocania Chalk believes Matthews was the best black collegian of his time. In his first game, on April 5, 1902, he had two hits, scored two runs, and stole one base. Unfortunately, racism reared its ugly head when he was benched in games against the University of Virginia and the U.S. Naval Academy. Neither of those schools would play against blacks. He did play against the U.S. Military Academy. One of his opponents, a young cadet, got a hit: his name was Douglas MacArthur.

In 1905 Harvard took Georgetown University off its schedule because that school's captain, Sam Apperious of Selma,

Alabama, refused to play against Matthews. His batting average in 1904 was .300, and in 1905 it was .315. Matthews later entered Harvard's Law School before teaching at a black college. Though Matthews in all likelihood could have played in the major leagues on ability, his alma mater would not have encouraged such a move. All the Ivy League schools were bastions of amateurism. Noted the Harvard correspondent for *Sporting Life,* "Harvard will learn with much regret that William Clarence Matthews, the famous colored short stop, is to turn to the professional ranks."[15] White America seemed to try to control any opportunity for black men. He did play semiprofessional ball in Vermont for a summer.

Charles Lee Thomas was a special and storied case. In 1903 Thomas took over the catching duties of the Ohio Wesleyan team from Branch Rickey, the white former catcher and then team manager. During a trip, Thomas was denied accommodations at a motel his team was to use. The emotional duress this snubbing caused Thomas was enough to make Rickey promise himself that he might one day seek redress. As luck would have it, Rickey did make amends in 1945 when he signed Jackie Robinson, a black player, to a Brooklyn Dodger contract. Robinson was the first in Organized Ball since 1889. Thomas did graduate and became a dentist in 1908. Harold Parrot, Rickey's traveling secretary for the Dodgers, said, "Mr. Rickey certainly did remember the incident. It left an indelible impression on him all his life but he still had to be practical all the same."[16]

In 1905–06 George Walter Williams was a shortstop at the University of Vermont. He was joined by Fenwick Henri

Watkins in 1906. The following year the University of Alabama paid a forfeit of three hundred dollars rather than play against blacks at Vermont. In Wisconsin, Samuel Ransome won his letter in three sports, including baseball, at Beloit College. Booker T. Washington, Jr., the son of the famed black leader, was a catcher at Drummer Academy. Oscar Brown played at Syracuse in 1908, and Howard Robinson was a catcher at Oberlin. It seems that most black performers were catchers or outfielders but seldom pitched.

Cumberland Posey's story shows the lengths to which some athletes had to go to play. Posey was a light-skinned scion of a prominent black family from western Pennsylvania. Records list him on the varsity at the University of Pittsburgh in 1911. Records also list a Charles W. Cumbert as the second baseman at Duquesne University in Pennsylvania in 1916. Cumberland Posey and Charles W. Cumbert are the same person. He was driven off the team at Pittsburgh and, as his daughter, Ethel Posey Maddox, explained in 1973, "Cum Posey did attend Duquesne University. Since the Posey family was known to be black in race if not in color, I believe he was enrolled under the name of Cumbert."[17] It is the only such incident of a black athlete using a different name to play varsity sports at a white school.

Black College Baseball

Baseball at black colleges in the late 1800s was not a serious affair. When the American College Baseball Association formed in 1887, no black schools joined or were asked to join. Most games played were between classes on an intramural basis. The first recorded game was played when Atlanta Baptist (now Morehouse) and Atlanta University squared off in 1890. Some members of the Atlanta Baptist team included D. D. Crawford, Alfred D. Jones, James Bryant, W. E. Rainwater, and J. R. Epps. Perhaps a few of them were hoping that proficiency on the diamond would help them gain admission to prestigious white schools later on. It was not a coincidence that many blacks who matriculated at the Ivy League schools were talented athletes who had graduated from black colleges.

The nation's best-known black school, Howard University, began its athletic programs early. Regulation No. 70, published in 1872, stated that "From time to time, certain portions of the University grounds will be designated for purposes of recreation for each sex, and all outdoor recreation will be confined to these limits." Baseball was probably the first sport played there.

Students at Tuskegee actually petitioned for more playing time. In 1911 they asked President Booker T. Washington, stating that "We cannot finish a game of ball between the hours of three and four. We therefore petition that we be given Saturday afternoon, say from three o'clock till tea for baseball and other games."[18] The implication is that students had only one hour daily of free time and that Saturday was not exactly a day off, either.

Down in Atlanta in 1896 the black colleges formed a league with Atlanta University: Morris Brown, Clark, and Atlanta Baptist participated. Typical seasons consisted of five or six games. James M. Nabrit starred at Atlanta Baptist. His son, James,

Jr., later became president of Howard University.

In 1909 schools in the Nashville, Tennessee, area formed the Silk League, which included Fisk University, Roger Williams, Walden University, and Pearl High School. Pearl won the pennant the first year. It was not surprising to see high schools mixed in with colleges for athletics in those days. Secondary schools were played for the same reason that professional teams were played: There were not enough black colleges around to fill a schedule.

By the early 1900s every black school had a varsity nine. Administrators began governing the games, which had before been run by students. But try as they might, school officials could not stop games with teams that included professionals. Professional teams were always willing to play, they were constantly looking for new talent, and they were better players.

The presence of professionals finally elicited an official comment in the 1910 *Handbook* of the black-run Interscholastic Athletic Association (ISAA): "Honest professional sport does exist, but as a rule, when men put all their wits and strength into a contest to earn a livelihood, the ethics of the game usually is lowered; fair play generally is the lookout of the officials and not of the players; mean and unfair tactics are resorted to; spectators are hoodwinked; laying down, double-crossing and faking take the place of clean playing, and fairness of player to player and players to public become a secondary consideration."[19] It appeared that few professionals in any sport were held in high esteem by the

black elite, who were worried about their schools' academic reputations.

By 1910 baseball was the number-two sport on campuses, behind football. The best teams were Tuskegee, Biddle, Shaw, Howard, and Livingstone. In 1911 both Shaw and Biddle were 10 to 1 and Tuskegee was 17 to 1. It should be noted that the students made their own uniforms and bats, and the diamonds were maintained by students as well.

Finally, in 1912 the Colored (now Central) Intercollegiate Athletic Association (CIAA) was formed. This gave a tremendous boost to baseball and other sports. It differed from other attempted leagues and conferences in several respects. One, five prestigious schools agreed to join: Howard, Shaw, Lincoln (Pennsylvania), Virginia Union, and Hampton—no high schools. Two, in this mid-Atlantic area the high schools for blacks were among the best to be found, relatively speaking, and they fed their graduates to CIAA institutions. Three, within a six-hour train ride were enough black colleges to fill out any schedule. Four, the ISAA had done much of the organizational groundwork for the CIAA. And five, there was a broader commitment to make it work than ever before.

There was still one problem that frequently affected games: the tourist season. Black students were usually given the choicest jobs available, and school officials would not turn them down. Some black schools were even forced to arrange their classes around the vacations of rich, white northerners. Basketball and baseball suffered as a result. Charles Williams,

Hampton's athletic director, remarked in 1913 that baseball had not taken place that season the way other sports had because of the early closing of school, as well as the heavy academic load.

Even with all the problems, Easter Monday baseball became a spring tradition between 1900 and 1920. But baseball never recovered from the hiatus imposed by World War I. It was replaced by track as a spring sport, which enjoyed an international reputation.

The Independent Era of Professional Baseball

The independent era of black professional play spans the years 1899 to 1920. Nearly all the teams played only among themselves, except on special occasions when white nines played exhibitions against them. This twenty-one-year era was characterized by failed league formation attempts, by play in foreign countries for the first time, and by truly superior teams and players. Their appeal was also enhanced by the unprecedented migration of blacks from the South to northern factory jobs. Every one of these southern transplants knew of the game of baseball. Consequently, team owners and managers had a built-in constituency if they could market the sport properly.

Play was so uniformly good in the large cities that the 1899 unofficial Colored Championships were split between East and West races. That same year, the aforementioned Page Fence Giants changed their name to the Columbia Giants of Chicago and played their home games at

Thirty-ninth and Wentworth Streets. Chicago was becoming the black sports capital of America. It featured three teams with large followings. The Giants team members were: George Wilson, Miller (no first name), and Harry Buckner as pitchers; Burns (no first name) and George "Chappie" Johnson as catchers; Junior Johnson at first base; Charles Grant at second base; William Binga at third base; Grant "Home Run" Johnson at shortstop; John "Pat" Patterson, captain and left-fielder; Sherman Barton in center field; and Reynolds (no first name) in right field. Solomon White believed they were the finest black team ever assembled.

This squad made the Sunday afternoon game in Chicago a "must" on many social calendars. They even had separate uniforms for home and away games. Their chief rival was the Chicago Unions. This same scenario was acted out all across the country, although crowds were necessarily greater in the urban areas. Ticket prices averaged twenty-five cents for a bleacher seat and fifty cents for grandstand spots.

Not all ball parks were self contained then. The diamonds were dirt in the infield and in good repair for Sunday games only. Lockers and showers were nonexistent. Players changed before and after games at hotels or private homes. They were also responsible for their own equipment. As strange as it may seem, gloves did not become completely standard until the 1890s. It was initially considered unmanly to use gloves. Solomon White added that "bunts," too, were considered feminine. Player uniforms had no numbers—but there was no public address system to call them out anyway. Therefore, fans paid close attention to the action and argued among themselves as to whether their favorite player had got a hit or was charged with an error.

Batters enjoyed some relief in 1893 when the pitcher's mound was moved back to a distance of 60' 6" from home plate. It had been forty-five feet before. When a batter hit a home run, it was invariably an inside-the-park one since few parks had back fences. When balls were hit into the stands, they were retrieved, as they were expensive. Good ones were kept for Sunday games.

Then there was clowning. To enhance the entertainment value of games, some teams resorted to acting out funny routines. In particular, Abe Harrison and Bill Joyner were known as the game's premier funny men. Noted Solomon White, "If a player somersaults on a wet field, or another doffs his cap with a sly, unwonted grimace after making a great catch, it provokes heaven-splitting laughter."[20] That was the way it was when the independent era began around 1900 and the black player had no place else to play.

Managers had problems with star players. The big names were frequently laws unto themselves, and they sometimes behaved whimsically until the mid-1940s. Most players did not even know all the rules—and did not care to. They just wanted to play and get paid. Some asked for special accommodations when housing was the most grievous inconvenience. Yet they all realized that their collective success and four hundred dollars per season depended on unity.

The year 1900 brings to mind the weird saga of Charlie Grant, another light-skinned player who starred at second base for the Chicago Columbia Giants. During the winter of 1900–01, Grant worked as a bellhop at the Eastland Hotel Resort in Hot Springs, Arkansas, where the major league's Baltimore Orioles began spring training. John J. McGraw, the Orioles' manager, was looking for players. He noticed Grant playing with his fellow bellhops and waiters and was impressed. McGraw was determined to find a way to sign Grant in spite of the "gentlemen's agreement" not to hire blacks.

Looking at a map in the hotel lobby, McGraw noticed a small creek with the name Tokahama and decided to name the fair-skinned Grant after it: Charlie Grant would become Charlie Tokahama, a full-blooded Cherokee Indian. Grant went along with this ridiculous scheme and told people that his father was white and his mother was Cherokee. *Sporting Life* even described Tokahama as a "phenomenal fielder ...and...a good batter."[21] But rumors floated as to Tokahama's true identity.

Finally, Charles Comiskey, the Chicago White Sox president, found out and told his friends that "If Muggsy [McGraw] really keeps this Indian, I will get a Chinaman of my acquaintance and put him on third."[22] On April 20, 1901, *Sporting Life* let the world know that the experiment had failed. Grant, the son of a horse trainer, finished his career in baseball. He died in 1932 when a car blew a tire, jumped a curb in front of a building where he was janitor, and killed him.

That same spring the Chicago Union

Giants were organized by Frank C. Leland. They and the Philadelphia Giants were the two best teams from 1900 to 1910. The Philadelphia squad was formed in 1902 by Solomon White and Harry Smith and was owned by Walter Schlicter, a white businessman. The Philadelphia Giants' main rivals were the Cuban X-Giants. The Chicago Union Giants fought it out with the Algona Brownies, a team composed of players from the Chicago Unions and the Columbia Giants. Team formation and reformation was quite common then as players looked for the best deals they could find.

The 1903 season is memorable for the appearance of two premier pitchers, Andrew "Rube" Foster and Dan McClelland. Foster won four games in the East Colored Championships as his Cuban X-Giants defeated the Philadelphia Giants. McClelland pitched the first perfect game by a black twirler against the Pennsylvania Park Athletic Club. No opposing player got a hit, scored a run, or reached first base. Both Foster and McClelland looked on with curiosity later that fall as the major leagues began what they called a "World Series" between the champions of the National League and those of the American Association. Blacks were a bit wondrous that the term "World Series" was used when no blacks or teams from Central and South America were invited.

In 1905 a third attempt was made to form a league to include all the best black teams. The National Association of Colored Baseball Clubs of America and Cuba (NACBCAC) lasted just one season. (American blacks had been playing in Cuba since 1900.) In 1906 there was another stab at league formation: the International League of Independent Professional Baseball Clubs (ILIPBC), with J. Frelhoffer as president and John O'Rourke as secretary. But the ILIPBC was in reality a front for Nat Strong, a white booking agent who had ties to major league stadiums. Strong booked all games and took his fees off the top. The ILIPBC teams were the Philadelphia Giants, the Cuban X-Giants, the Quaker Giants, the Wilmington Giants, the Cuban Stars and Havana Stars from Cuba, and two white teams—the Philadelphia Professionals and the Riverton-Palmyrna Athletics. The Philadelphia Giants won the pennant, and the deciding game was played before the largest crowd ever to watch two black teams—ten thousand—at the American League Grounds on Labor Day, September 3.

More teams now had regional reputations. In the South one could hear of the Norfolk (Virginia) Red Stockings, the Louisville Fall Citys, the Meridian (Mississippi) Southern Giants, the Hot Springs (Arkansas) Majestic White Sox, the Memphis Tigers, the Pensacola Giants, and the Atlanta Deppens. Others included the Indianapolis ABC's, the Danville (Illinois) Unions, the Kansas City Giants, the West Balden Sprugels, the French Lick (Indiana) Plutos, the Topeka Giants, the Kansas City Royal Giants, and the St. Louis Giants. No wonder league formation attempts continued.

On February 16–17, 1908, a fifth try at a league was made in Chicago. Called the National Colored Professional Baseball League, it folded before the season started. But out of this confusion came pitcher

Andrew "Rube" Foster. Born in Calvert, Texas, on September 17, 1879, he began playing for the local Ft. Waco (Texas) Yellow Jackets and then for the Chicago Union Giants, the Cuban X-Giants, the Philadelphia Giants, and then Frank Leland's Chicago Leland Giants. Foster then persuaded Leland that if he (Foster) could negotiate with ballpark owners, he could get some of his Philadelphia Giants teammates to switch to Leland's squad. Leland bought the idea, and black baseball was never the same.

The 6' 4" Foster began running the Leland Giants, even though Frank Leland still owned them. In 1908 the Leland Giants joined the Chicago league and finished with a 108 to 18 record. A year later Foster took them out of the Chicago league and put them in the Park Owners Association (POA), in which all clubs had to own their stadiums. His team played at Sixty-ninth and Halsted Streets, which had three thousand grandstand seats, four hundred box seats, and a thousand bleacher seats. It was without a doubt the finest ballpark any black team had ever owned. The Leland Giants even played the major league Chicago Cubs in 1909.

In 1911, Foster formed his own team, the Chicago American Giants, after leading the Leland Giants to a 123-6 record in 1910. He was on his way and eventually became known as "the father of black baseball."

In the second decade of the independent era, black owners were more sure of themselves, although they argued constantly and jealousies arose. There still was neither enough trust nor the right connections with the major stadiums to effect a league. Local leagues like the semiprofessional New England Colored League (1909) did well.

The game itself was helped in 1911 when the Spaulding Company made a livelier ball. Balls before 1911 had had a leather covering over woolen yarn wrapped around a solid rubber core. The new balls had a cork center and were more tightly wound, which made them go faster and farther.

Black sports stars in general were more esteemed in 1910 than in 1890. In the previous decade such names as Marshall "Major" Taylor (cycling), John B. Taylor (track), Howard Porter Drew (track), and, of course, Jack Johnson had become the most recognized names in black America. Taking his place in this pantheon of athletes was a batter named John Henry Lloyd.

John Henry Lloyd was, next to "Rube" Foster, the best-known player of his time and many say the best black player ever. He was born on April 25, 1884, in Palatka, Florida. After he finished high school and stayed briefly with the Jacksonville (Florida) Young Receivers, he joined the Macon (Georgia) Acmes in 1905 as a catcher. The Cuban X-Giants signed him in 1906, and he won his first game with a double in the ninth inning. Then he went to the Philadelphia Giants because, as he said himself, "wherever the money was, that's where I was."[23]

He was so good that he received the nickname "the black Honus Wagner" after the famed major leaguer. In a bow to Lloyd's reputation, Wagner himself said, "I am honored to have John Lloyd called the Black Wagner. It is a privilege to have been compared to him."[24] In a series of six games in

Cuba in 1910 against the major league's Detroit Tigers, Lloyd played on the Havana Stars team, along with Grant "Home Run" Johnson, Preston Hill, and Bruce Petway. The Tigers' star was the incomparable Ty Cobb, the most feared batter in the game—.385 in 1910—and an avowed racist. Cobb's nickname was "The Georgia Peach."

In 1907 Cobb had a run-in with a black groundskeeper in Augusta, Georgia. In 1908 he was brought into court for knocking down Fred Collins, a black laborer who yelled at him for stepping into some freshly laid cement. Judge Edward Jeffries fined Cobb seventy-five dollars and then suspended the fine because he liked Cobb so much. In another 1910 incident Cobb climbed into the stands after a black spectator who had been heckling him. Noted one of Cobb's biographers, "Cobb...believed blacks to be fundamentally different and inferior to whites....he had no patience whatever with blacks who were insolent, fractious, unsubmissive."[25] There were many more just like Cobb in the major leagues.

In that Cuban series, Lloyd batted .500 against major league pitching in twenty-two at-bats. Cobb batted .370 in nineteen at-bats. The Havana Stars tied the Tigers in games at 3 to 3. American League President Byron Bancroft Johnson was so embarrassed that he made Nat Strong insert a clause in the contracts of major league teams playing in Cuba that said that no American blacks could play on any Cuban team when playing against American League clubs.

The black press was quick with its comments. The most incisive appeared in the December 4, 1910, Indianapolis *Freeman:* "The defeat of America's foremost teams stung like everything. The American scribes refused to write on the matter, it cut so deep, and was kept quiet....The clause was presented by Ban Johnson...as the defeat of Philadelphia and Detroit...was still fresh in his mind....John McGraw had the box-score....he could readily see that all the games were won by the Cubans by the work of the American colored players." This was further proof that the black player —and Lloyd in particular—were just as good as the major leaguers.

Two months after Lloyd & Company tied the Tigers, the Cincinnati Red Stockings signed two Cubans—Rafael Almeida and Armando Marsans—both of whom were dark-skinned. This move made some blacks think the majors might soon sign American blacks. No such luck.

There was another ill-fated attempt in December 1910 to form a league. What did excite some passions was the first All-Star Team as selected by the Indianapolis *Freeman* in 1911. That first historic list is as follows:

Harry Moore	first base	Leland Giants
Nate Harris	second base	Leland Giants
John Henry Lloyd	shortstop	Philadelphia Giants
Felix Wallace	third base	St. Paul Gophers
Frank Duncan	left field	Philadelphia Giants
Pete Hill	center field	Leland Giants
Andrew Payne	right field	Leland Giants
Bruce Petway	catcher	Philadelphia Giants
Pete Booker	catcher	Leland Giants
Rube Foster	pitcher	Leland Giants
Dan McClelland	pitcher	Leland Giants
Charles Dougherty	pitcher	Leland Giants

From 1911 to 16 the powerhouse teams were the New York Lincoln Giants, the Chicago American Giants, and the Indianapolis ABC's. Lloyd switched to the New York Lincoln Giants in 1911; its white team owner, Jess McMahon, had a powerful squad indeed. Lloyd promptly lived up to his billing and batted .475 in sixty-two games with twenty-five stolen bases, 112 hits, and sixty-four scored runs. Lloyd's teammates included some stellar names in black baseball: "Cannonball" Dick Redding, "Home Run" Johnson, Spot Poles, Luis Santop, and legendary pitcher "Smokey Joe" Williams. A 1952 poll of living ex-Negro League players rated "Smokey Joe" as the best pitcher of all time. Not bad coming from your peers.

This New York Lincoln Giants team played its games in Harlem at 135th Street and Fifth Avenue on Olympic Field. Their pay averaged $40 to $105 per month. The most famous pitcher of his time, Walter Johnson of the major league's Washington Senators, said when facing the Lincoln Giants, "It was the only time in my life that I was ever 2:1 to lose....I'll never forget the first hitter I faced... 'Home Run' Johnson. Up to the plate, he says to me 'Come on, Mr. Johnson, and throw the fast one in here and I'll knock it over the fence.' That's what he did too. But it was the only run they got off me."[26]

"Smokey Joe" was born near San Antonio on April 6, 1876. He got started late— at age thirty-four—when he was spotted by Arthur Hardy of the Kansas City Giants. "Rube" Foster grabbed him, and in 1914 he "was credited with 41 victories and only 3 defeats for the American Giants."[27] In the fall of 1916 in a game against the major league's Philadelphia Phillies, with the

bases loaded in the ninth inning with no outs, he struck out three straight batters.

Another twirler who deserves attention was John Donaldson, a left-hander who played for the All-Nations team during World War I. He began with the Tennessee Rats and later became a Chicago White Sox scout in 1947. "Cannonball" Redding was from Atlanta, Georgia, and had a blazing fastball. He won seventeen games as a rookie in 1911 and forty-three games in 1912. He finished in the mid-1930s with the Brooklyn Royal Giants. Frank Wickware hailed from Coffeeville, Kansas, and began with the Leland Giants. Wickware and Walter Johnson battled three times in 1913 and 1914, and Wickware won two and lost one. In their duel on October 5, 1913, Wickware defeated Johnson 1 to 0 after Johnson had won thirty-six games for the Washington Senators.

In Chicago, Foster's Chicago American Giants were busy building their own grounds. With the help of John Schorling, Connie Mack's nephew, Foster rebuilt the stands at Thirty-ninth and Shields for his team. Foster's nine was so popular that even the then-middle-class-oriented National Association for the Advancement of Colored People (NAACP) began reporting his team's comings and goings.

Black players and teams during the time of World War I were spectacular. It is a shame they could not share their talents with all Americans.

Military Baseball

Lest we forget, baseball was also the favorite sport among our black soldiers before World War I. Competition among the black units was keen, and being kept from playing was a tough punishment for rule infractions. Soldiers usually purchased their uniforms from unit funds; they were some of the best-equipped teams around. They took tremendous pride in their play.

The Spanish-American War offered them their first sustained exposure to Cuban players, most of whom were black as well. But they were most enthused about games against white units. When the 25th Infantry got to the Philippines in 1901, they immediately challenged any team to play "for money, marbles, or chalk, money preferred."[28] There were few takers.

Back in the United States at Fort Riley, Kansas, in 1903, the 25th Infantry again scored by winning the Regimental Tournament, which included several white teams. In May 1911 the Cuban Stars traveled to Fort Ethan Allen and defeated the 10th Cavalry 3 to 2 in freezing weather. The primary reason for the success of these squads is that they played together all the time. Black reenlistment was higher than for whites because of poor job possibilities in civilian life.

It is generally conceded that the 25th Infantry had the best of the Black teams through World War I. Wrote the *Army and Navy Journal* of September 12, 1914, "Every bit of wall space was covered with banners won by the companies, battalions, and the regiment in athletic contests during many years past." Their record in 1916 was 42-2, and some of these wins were over black professional nines.

Prelude to Unity

World War I brought tens of thousands of black southerners to the teeming northern cities. Most of the first wave were young and male, straight off the farms. There was a pressing need for entertainment, and movies, public parks, and the introduction of Daylight Savings Time in 1918 helped in this regard. But baseball brought more blacks together on a regular basis than any other endeavor. In the East, the popular teams were the Brooklyn Royal Giants and the Lincoln Giants. In the Midwest the Chicago American Giants and the Indianapolis ABC's held sway. At points in between and beyond, local teams brought out the fans on Saturdays and Sundays.

When the war ended and baseball resumed at full speed, more black stars on more teams were being touted by more black newspapers by a larger number of black sports writers than ever before. In Cuba, black American players were household names. But the squabbling continued among the teams. In 1916 the embarrassment was overwhelming when the Chicago American Giants and the Indianapolis ABC's quit a twelve-game season-ending playoff when they could not agree on a formula to decide the winner. They were deadlocked at four games each. A comprehensive league was now a must.

Within fifteen years of the end of the war, black baseball came together and produced the largest black-run business in America. The man who put the pieces together came from within their very own ranks.

Notes

1. John Blassingame, *Slave Testimony.* (Baton Rouge: Louisiana State University, 1977), p. 617.
2. Baker, op. cit., p. 139.
3. Quoted in Robert Peterson, *Only the Ball Was White*, p. 16.

4. Ibid, p. 17.
5. Ibid, p. 23.
6. Solomon White, *Sol White's Official Baseball Guide.* (Baltimore: Camden House, repr. of 1907 ed.), p. 17.
7. Ibid, p. 13.
8. Peterson, op. cit., p. 81.
9. White, op. cit., pp. 86-7.
10. Peterson, op. cit., p. 31.
11. Ibid.
12. Ibid, p. 39.
13. Ibid., p. 31.
14. White, op. cit., p. 25.
15. Peterson, op. cit., p. 57.
16. Telephone interview with the author, March 4, 1985.
17. Ocania Chalk, *Black College Sport,* p. 21.
18. Louis R. Harlan, *Booker T. Washington: The Wizard of Tuskegee.* (Oxford University Press, 1983), p. 282.
19. *ISAA Handbook* (1910), p. 52.
20. White, op. cit.
21. Peterson, op. cit., p. 54.
22. Quoted in ibid., p. 56.
23. Quoted in Peterson, op. cit., p. 77.
24. Quoted in ibid., p. 74.
25. Alexander, *Cobb,* p. 68.
26. Quoted in Henderson, op. cit., p. 182.
27. Peterson, op. cit., p. 217.
28. *Manila Times,* May 1, 1901.

Chapter
6

Football

Beginnings

Football has existed in some form for thousands of years. Team games involving round solid objects, later made of rubber or leather, have been played since ancient Egypt. The game evolved along with the urbanization of Western Europe. In rural medieval Europe, neighboring villages frequently held games with as many as a hundred players to a side. There were no uniforms, no standard set of rules, no referees, and no playing fields per se. The performers just felt a need to play some form of team competition where local pride was at stake.

Gradually, the playing of the various forms of the game became a nuisance as far as monarchies were concerned, and they passed laws to regulate it. During the Hundred Years' War between England and France in the 1300s, King Charles complained that the peasants were playing football, which did nothing to teach the arts of bearing arms. English King Edward III said football was useless and declared it unlawful. Edward then went even further and mandated that every man should use only bows, arrows, pellets, and bolts in sports. The Scottish Parliament in 1467 condemned both "futeball" and "golfe." Nevertheless, the games continued.

Nearly a century later, in 1555, Oxford University banned it for undergraduates. But schools formed natural teams, whether between classes of students or between different schools. The peasants continued playing their big games on Shrove Tuesday, and upper-class students played every day. In the 1700s some rudimentary rules were devised in England, which made their way to America almost intact. By 1800 variants of the sport were a staple of life in New England, with the kicking style predominating.

School Problems

One day in 1823, so the story goes, William W. Ellis, a student at the Rugby School in England, picked up the ball and ran with it during a game. His opponents gave chase and brought him down. Thus the sport rugby was born. This schoolboy version of football was much tamer than the cruder village games. Four years later at Harvard University in Boston, the freshmen-versus-sophomore-class annual games began—with twenty to thirty players to a side—on the first Monday of the school year. The day

89

became known as Bloody Monday because of the injuries. Officials called a halt in 1860.

In 1862, G. Smith Miller formed the first American club, the Oneida Football Club. They did not lose a game for three years. This aggregation played the soccer-style or kicking version, like their English counterparts. Five years later the first patent was granted for an air-filled canvas and rubber ball. But after the Civil War, American college football wound up as rugby style, which allowed the ball to be carried in the arms or hands. Yale University eventually prevailed with its "Boston" or rugby-style rules, partly because, from 1872 to 1909, it had a record of 324 wins, 17 losses, and 18 ties. Yale, in the interim, persuaded Princeton and Columbia Universities to play its style, and the game took off around the country.

By the 1880s the Thanksgiving Day game was already a tradition. Fans and sports writers began clamoring for rule changes to make it better. The most influential rule tinkerer and the man who is called "the father of football" was Walter Camp. Camp, a former Yale student, devised the "line of scrimmage," the position of quarterback, the team size of eleven, the field size of 110 yards by 53 yards, the concept of "downs," and the pattern of field stripes that gave the word gridiron to the playing area itself.

Black Players at White Colleges

Football was so popular at New England colleges that Walter Camp came up with a brilliant idea in 1889: the All-American Team. It was featured in *Collier's* magazine and later in *Harper's Weekly*. These my-thical eleven were Camp's and Caspar Whitney's opinions of the best players at every position. The first black All-American was William Henry Lewis of Amherst College.

Lewis was born in Berkeley, Virginia, on November 28, 1868, the son of free mulatto blacks before the Civil War. He finished Virginia Normal and Industrial (now Virginia State University) and enrolled at Amherst at the suggestion of Virginia Normal's president, John Langston. In the fall of 1889, the five-foot-seven-inch, 180-pound Virginian began five years at the center-rush position. (It was standard practice by then for some black colleges to establish relationships with certain white schools to accept their graduates.)

Lewis' black teammate on that Amherst squad was William Tecumseh Sherman Jackson of Alexandria, Virginia. Jackson was born on November 18, 1865, and attended the famed "M" Street School (now Dunbar High) in Washington, D.C. He also went to Virginia Normal before Amherst. As members of that first Amherst team, Lewis and Jackson, who played half-back, helped their school to a 3-5-2 record. The ease with which Lewis and Jackson seemed to make the Amherst squad suggests they had played before, for Ivy League colleges were using rather complex strategy by 1890.

In 1890, Amherst improved to a 5-6-1 showing, and Lewis was elected captain of the team. Said *The New York Times* of December 21, 1890, "The election of Lewis, '92, a colored man, to the football captaincy for next year does not cause much comment, owing, to the democratic spirit of Amherst. Lewis is undoubtedly the best man for the place, having played a very strong game at centre rush the last two years."

After the Harvard game in 1890, the Harvard *Crimson* noted, "For almost all his effectiveness rushing, though his tackles gained some ground with the ball, he, Captain Lewis, had to rely on halfback Jackson, whose play all around was as skillful as any on the field." In 1891 Amherst finished with a 6-4-3 record, for a three-year total of 14-15-6. After this season Jackson graduated and became an instructor in Greek and Latin. Lewis went to Harvard Law School and played on its football team.

In his first game for Harvard Law in 1892, he helped defeat Dartmouth 48-0 at Jarvis Field. But against archrival Yale before twenty-thousand fans—then the largest crowd ever to watch a black athlete in a team sport—Harvard lost to Yale 6-0. However, Walter Camp was in attendance and named Lewis to his All-America Team at center-rush for 1892, the first black player to be so honored. He was a repeat selection in 1893. After law school Lewis became an assistant district attorney in Boston. What a coincidence that the first recorded black player at a white college attained All-America status!

The third and fourth players made their debuts in 1890. George Jeweth was a punter, field-goal kicker, and halfback at the University of Michigan; William Arthur Johnson played halfback at the Massachusetts Institute of Technology (MIT). The black Indianapolis *Freeman* newspaper, in its November 8, 1890, edition noted of Jeweth, "the Afro-American 'phenomenon' of the University of Michigan football team, played a remarkable game last Saturday week in Detroit, and was very favorably spoken of by the daily press. He is an Ann Arbor [Michigan] boy and won applause by his wonderful runs and tackles." One week after this report Jeweth was ruled off the field in a game against Cornell for punching an opponent in the jaw. Jeweth obviously was not going to take any mischief from anyone.

Out in the Midwest, colleges were fewer in number and much farther apart, so club teams frequently appeared on the schedules. Many of these clubs had paid, semi-, or full professionals playing. In fact, the white colleges experienced their first recruiting scandals in the 1880s, well before the appearance of Lewis, Jackson, and Jeweth.

At the University of Nebraska, George A. Flippin starred at halfback from 1892 to 1894. After a game against the Denver Athletic Club on November 5, 1893, the Nebraska State *Journal* had this to say about Flippin's treatment: "Flippin went through the center like a cannonball and Denver had a special pick at him. He was kicked, slugged, and jumped on, but never knocked out, and gave as good as he received."[1] He later became a physician.

Another benchmark occurred in 1892. The University of Chicago hired Amos Alonzo Stagg as coach and awarded him professorial rank. He later went on to compile a record number of victories for a college coach. He and H. C. Williams wrote a book, *A Scientific and Practical Treatise on American Football for Schools and Colleges*, which became a bible for black college coaches down South.

As for their white counterparts in Dixie, football had become so complicated to schedule that the Southern Intercollegiate Association was formed in 1894 to regulate all athletics. A year later the Intercollegiate Conference of Faculty Representatives (later known as The Big Ten) was organized. In the late 1800s college football was the second most popular sport, after baseball. The Morrill Act of 1890, which created the large land-grant schools like Ohio State and Michigan Agricultural (later Michigan State), was of tremendous help in spreading the popularity of football. Texas and Texas A&M began their rivalry in 1894.

Following the rave notices given Lewis, Jackson, and Jeweth, a small but steady stream of black talent found its way into the northern white schools. Charles C. Cook played at Cornell and then became Howard University's first first-rate coach. Howard J. Lee played tackle at Harvard in 1896–97. George Chadwell was at the end position at Williams in 1897. William Washington lettered at Oberlin from 1895 to 1897. Charles Winterwood played at Beloit College and then became Tuskegee Institute's first nonstudent coach.

Blacks were just no longer a novelty by 1900. Yale's President Arthur Hadley implied that the sport did away with class distinctions altogether, although he did not mention racial distinctions. The rest of the cast of ebony players before 1900 included William N. Johnson at Nebraska, James Phillips at Northwestern, and William Clarence Matthews at Harvard.

When this century began, President Theodore Roosevelt was vocal in his support for football. His son even played in college. Crowds had increased, and with the increase in black participation came an increase in racial incidents. The black community was not surprised.

Earnie Marshall lettered at Williams in 1903. Robert Hamlin starred on the Springfield (Massachusetts) YMCA team. Strothers (his first name is unrecorded) played at Beloit the same year. Samuel Simon Gordon was involved in an incident that fall while playing for Wabash College. In a game against DePauw University, that school's manager and players refused to play after hearing Wabash had a black player. An Army officer, General Lew Wallace, and two ministers finally convinced DePauw to play. Wabash won so convincingly that *The New York Times* of November 22, 1903, wrote, "The team [DePauw] went into the game, and, as it turned out, Wabash had no need of Gordon's services."

William Craighead captained the side at Massachusetts State in 1905. His black teammates were William H. Williams and Charles E. Roberts. Samuel Ransom was at Beloit in 1904–08. Arthur D. Carr was at Ohio University in 1904. Henry Thomas was at Coe (Iowa). Ray Young played tackle at Illinois University in 1904–05 and was followed by H. H. Wheeler in 1906. Edward Gray was named to Camp's All-America Third Team in 1906 at Amherst. In the December 19, 1908, edition of *Collier's* magazine, Camp said after a game against Cornell, "Gray of Amherst, a colored star, showed good quality, and the whirlwind way in which he repeatedly went through the Cornell line when Amherst held them to a single score was worth noting."

College football was a violent endeavor in this first decade. The equipment was still cloth padding; leather helmets did little to protect against head injuries; and strategy formations invited mayhem. In 1905 alone eighteen players were killed on the field and 159 serious injuries were reported. Even President Roosevelt campaigned in *The New York Times* for reform. Partially in reply to the outcry, the Intercollegiate Athletic Association (later changed to the National Collegiate Athletic Association, or NCAA, in 1910) was formed in 1905 to change the rules. The stakes were enormous. In 1903 Yale reported receipts of $106,000 from its football operations.

Through all the violence and racial incidents, two players in particular were just stellar on the field—Robert "Bobby" Marshall at Minnesota and Matthew Bullock at Dartmouth. Marshall was born on March 12, 1880, and graduated at age twenty-two from high school. He entered the University of Minnesota in 1902 and began as a substitute end. The following year he was outstanding in a game against Michigan before ten thousand fans. In 1904 he was first-string as Minnesota racked up stupendous scores: over Carleton College, 65-0; over Iowa State, 32-0; over Grinnell College, 146-0; over Lawrence, 69-0; and over Northwestern, 17-0. In the win over Grinnell, Marshall scored seventy-two points—four touchdowns and thirteen field goals—a record that stands today.

In 1905 Marshall was equally brilliant at his defensive end position. For his play he was named to the All-Western Team by the Minnesota *Journal* and *The Chicago Tribune*. He was also an All-America Second Team selection. In 1906, his last season, he had a solid game against Amos A. Stagg's Chicago squad on November 11. Minnesota won 4-2 because of Marshall's accurate kicking. The Minnesota *Journal* described the difference: "Marshall dropped back, Larkin poised the ball for him and the player's feet sent the ball true between the posts."[2] He was again named to the All-America Second Team.

One player who deserved All-America status but never made it was Matthew Wash-ington Bullock of Dabney, North Carolina. He played at Dartmouth from 1901 to 1903 at the end position as well. He was outstanding in 1902, when Dartmouth compiled a 6-1-1 record. In 1903 he played in the first six games and then was seen no more—a mystery. He later joined the staff at Atlanta Baptist (later Morehouse College) as an instructor.

Bullock and Marshall played through some rough times as far as rule enforcement was concerned. What is now referred to as the Rules Revolution of 1906 was the answer. Camp and his advisers met and made wholesale changes. A second umpire was installed, the forward pass was legalized but penalized fifteen yards if incomplete, three downs to make five yards was changed to ten yards for a first down, games were divided into two thirty-minute halves, the neutral zones (the lines of scrimmage) were reestablished, and huddling was disallowed.

These rules certainly said nothing about a quota of blacks on the teams. But seldom were there more than two blacks on one team. If there were any at all, they were starters. Most white schools, though, had no black players at all. The most notable Ivy League school with no blacks was Princeton. A scan of the reports of the period show Fenwich H. Watkins at Vermont in 1907–08; John Pinkett at Amherst in 1908; Leslie Pollard at Dartmouth in 1908; Nathaniel Brown at Oberlin in 1908; Hale Parker at Illinois in 1909; Robert Johnson at Dartmouth in 1910; William Kindle at Springfield in 1911; Gerald Lew and Benjamin Hubert at Massachusetts State in 1911–12; A.A. Alexander at Iowa in 1911; Eugene Collins at Coe College in 1913; Joseph Trigg at Syracuse in 1914–16; Clinton

Ross at Nebraska in 1913; and Hugh Shipley at Brown in 1913.

In 1911 Iowa refused to leave William Kindle off their team in a game against Missouri. When Missouri refused to budge, Iowa canceled the game. Some schools did stand on principle.

Meanwhile, Harvard began an unbeaten streak in 1911 that lasted five seasons. They brought in a professional coach, Percy D. Haughton, who added unaccustomed consistency and dedication to the craft. He adapted quickly to the 1912 rule changes, which added a fourth down to make ten yards for a first down. A touchdown was also changed from five points to six points, where it remains today. A year later the rules about incomplete passes were relaxed. Purists felt passes were for sissies.

Though football was king of the campus in 1913, it became an absolute craze after World War I.

Black College Play

Every sport was intramural before 1890 at black colleges. Facilities were poor, coaches were few, leagues and conferences were nonexistent, and most important, administrators did not want to spend their funds on fun and games. They had books to buy, teachers to pay, and laboratories to build. Needless to say, the recruiting scandals that plagued the white institutions in the 1880s had no effect whatsoever on black schools.

The first black college football game was played between Biddle (now Johnson C. Smith University) and Livingstone College on December 27, 1892, in Salisbury, North Carolina, Livingstone's home base.

Biddle had begun its life as Biddle Memorial Institute in 1867 with the help of black ministers. Livingstone began as Zion Wesley College in 1879.

The Indianapolis *Freeman* of December 3 of that year printed a dispatch from its Biddle representative: "Our football eleven has received a challenge from one of Livingstone College to play a match game of ball....the challenge will most likely be accepted, and the boys are now kicking the leather bag over the field." The weather on the day of the game was awful. The Biddle team had occupied nearly half of one of the "colored" cars on the train to Salisbury, and it had snowed all the night before. Both teams played in homemade uniforms, but Livingstone team members had chipped in to buy a regulation football from the Spaulding Company especially for this game.

The team for Biddle included the following players: C. H. Shute, W. L. Metz (Edisto, South Carolina), H. L. Peterson, L. B. Ellerson (Newark, New Jersey), Bright Funderbunk, T. R. Veal, M. Prather, H. H. Muldrow, Calvin Radford, W. H. Haig, George E. Caesar (Little Rock, Arkansas), Will Morrow, J. H. Hutton (Omaha, Nebraska), and S. M. Plair (Rock Hill, North Carolina).

The Livingstone lineup included, as far as could be obtained, J. W. Whaler (Captain), R. J. Rencher, Henry Levis, C. N. Garland, J. R. Villard, J. B. A. Yelverton, Wade Hampton, Charles H. Patrick, J. J. Taylor, F. H. Cummings, and William T. Trent (who later became president of Livingstone).

The umpire was a Mr. Murphy, a white law student from the University of North Carolina. Biddle scored in the first half of this game, which consisted of two forty-five-minute halves. William Trent supposedly scored in the second half after recovering a fumble, but Murphy ruled the score null and void because he thought Trent was out of bounds. The line markings were covered by the snow. Biddle finally won 5-0.

Meanwhile, Howard University, America's premier black college at the time and still one of the best, began interclass games that same fall. Its coach was Charles C. Cook, who had played at Cornell. Cook, a black man, had an interesting lineage. He was a great-grandson of President Thomas Jefferson's good friend John Randolph. Cook's father, John, was appointed collector of taxes for Washington, D. C., by President Ulysses S. Grant and was also a Howard trustee for thirty-five years.

Howard was, and is, federally funded. Administrators were worried about the propriety of appropriating American tax dollars for recently freed blacks to play fun and games. But it did have a recreation field, which was the scene of many impromptu sports played under ad hoc rules. Still, the addition of Cook was a step forward. He assembled a powerful squad for the 1893 season that beat the colored YMCA team 40-6.

On New Year's Day 1894, Tuskegee and Atlanta University squared off. Atlanta won, 10-0. Tuskegee's student-coach was seventeen-year-old William Clarence Matthews, who later played at Harvard. By a coincidence, this game was played at the same time as a long-planned Emancipation Day celebration. Only a few people turned out, and Tuskegee's manager had to wire home for train fare because gate receipts were insufficient. Then the money wired was not

enough to get them all the way home, so they had to off-load five miles from Tuskegee and walk the rest of the way.

On November 29 of that year Lincoln (Pennsylvania) University and Howard began what became the most hotly contested rivalry in black college football. Lincoln won 6-5, but a Lincoln player broke a leg, and the rest of the Lincoln squad was put in isolation back at home because some of them had visited a house under quarantine. The two schools canceled their games for the next decade.

The Black press printed columns upon columns about those games. The white sporting press, however, early on adopted a cynical approach to them. They reported the "incidents" but almost never the scores. Even the normally responsible *New York Times* ran this account on November 25, 1897: "The first football game ever played by Negroes in Tennessee took place here this afternoon between local teams. The game was not finished on account of the fatal wounding of Fred Staples and the serious injury of half a dozen other players. A riot concluded the game, when several drunken white men attacked the players because they could not make a touchdown."

The fatality made the game newsworthy; it was also the *only* sort of notice ever given to games by black teams. However, the teams sometimes brought on their own problems from lack of trust in one another. In a game played in 1900 between Virginia Union and Virginia Normal and Industrial, the referee, a Mr. Estees, ruled that Virginia Normal had duly made a first down, and he put the ball on the Virginia Union one-yard line. Virginia Union players protested that no first down was attained. When Virginia

Union was overruled, they walked off the field with five minutes remaining. Fights and disagreements were common during these times.

A primary reason for these on-field problems was the lack of proper training in high school, which in many cases was a part of the college. Edwin B. Henderson made note of this deficiency: "The reason we can't use the Notre Dame system in many of our colleges is because the boys from our own high schools haven't sufficient knowledge of fundamentals and of 'inside' football to fit into an intricate system. Thus we must adapt a less intricate system to conform to the players."[3] But matters got better quickly.

Conferences in the Making

In the first decade of this century, while white schools were forming athletic conferences, black schools were still struggling with academic standards and inadequate facilities. But interest in football was so strong that administrators soon usurped the powers of the student-coaches and managers. This transition was unevenly accomplished, but nevertheless it happened.

If black schools had any hope of improving their own games, of avoiding unnecessary hassles over officiating, or of ceasing the forfeiting of games over disagreements, high school football had to be improved. Colored high schools in the Virginia-Washington, D. C.-Maryland area had banded together to coordinate their programs. The "M" Street School in Washington, D. C., started the game around 1900. Nearby Armstrong High was the first black secondary school to boast its own gymnasium. Charles Cook's brother, Victor, organized a team at Baltimore's Frederick Douglass High. There was a team at the preparatory department of Morgan State College. But as Henderson points out, "in no school system of these mentioned do the facilities for colored boys and girls equal or even approach those for the white children."[4]

They did manage to feature intercity competition. The initial roster of schools included Howard High of Wilmington, Delaware; Wiley Bates of Annapolis, Maryland; the Dunbar, Booker T. Washington, and Vocational Schools of Baltimore; and Manassas and Parker-Gray in Virginia. Local communities took enormous pride in these schools. They were to these communities what a big-time college squad was to a large city. Even so, Henderson warned that some educators were already trying to make these local teams into replicas of the collegiate versions. More than any other reason, the presence of these well-coached high schools in the mid-Atlantic area gave local colleges the edge in conference formation.

This first decade featured several memorable collegiate encounters that are still talked about today. The most famous was between Fisk and Talladega in 1903, at Westside Park in Birmingham, Alabama. Playing for Talladega was the most well-known player of the decade, Floyd Wellman "Terrible" Terry. The first half was scoreless, but Fisk lost the ball on a fumble on the opening kickoff of the second half at midfield. Talladega moved the ball to the Fisk eight-yard line. Fisk dug in, held, and took possession on their one-yard line.

In two plays, Fisk did not gain so much as an inch. On third down (the last in those days), Steele of Fisk punted from his own end zone. Terry broke through and blocked the punt attempt, and Dick Hubbard fell on it for a safety. Talladega led 2-0 with twelve minutes to play. Talladega's supporters began a victory dance as both teams exchanged aborted drives until Fisk had the ball on Talladega's twenty-five-yard line with two minutes left. After two downs Steele again dropped back to the thirty-five-yard line and drop-kicked the ball through the uprights. Fisk held on to win 4-2. All said it was the finest black college game ever seen but a loss for Terry and his teammates.

Milton Roberts, the sports historian, said Terry was clearly the best player yet seen on a black college squad. He later played at Howard and at Meharry Medical School in Tennessee.

The black elite who sent their offspring to these schools liked football, especially since William H. Lewis acquired his status as an All-America selectee. Typical schedules then had three to six games each season except for big institutions like Howard. Their main athletic rivals were always within a few hours' train ride away.

By the end of the first decade the chief rivalries included Howard-Lincoln (Pennsylvania), Fisk-Meharry, Alabama State-Tuskegee, Livingstone-Biddle, and Virginia Union-Virginia Normal. They all, however, flouted the rules when they could get away with it. They used ineligible players, and too many players played too many years. It got so bad that the *ISAA Handbook* of 1911 mentioned that "it is a lamentable fact that at some of our institutions of learning an athlete may represent his college for twelve years through preparatory, collegiate, and professional school courses."[5]

When observers look back now on the records of the schools between 1900 and 1912, most rate Howard and Meharry as having the best teams. For a time Howard had the coaching services of Edward Gray, who played at Amherst, and Samuel Ransom of Beloit, who later coached at Meharry. Atlanta Baptist (Morehouse) was coached by Matthew Washington Bullock, who played at Dartmouth. These teams drew crowds of five to six thousand on a Thanksgiving Day or some other special occasion. Of course, the Chicago *Defender* of January 22, 1910, saw other motives: "They [the players] are doing it all for the glory of the college and the admiring applause of the scores of well-dressed girls." Perhaps they were.

Inevitably, the black press followed Walter Camp in picking an All-America team for black schools. It first appeared in 1911 and was selected by Edwin B. Henderson and Matthew W. Bullock. Every name was from a school that would, in 1912, form a part of the first conference, the Colored (now Central) Intercollegiate Athletic Association (CIAA).

The players on that inaugural roster included (first names are simply unavailable): Oliver of Howard at left end; Aikens of Hampton at left tackle; Island Johns of Shaw at left guard; Warner of Hampton at center; John M. Clelland of Howard at right guard; Goss of Lincoln at right tackle; Fred M. Slaughter of Howard at right end; Leslie Pollard of Lincoln at left halfback; Edward B. Gray of Howard at right halfback; Henry Collins of Lincoln at quarterback; and

Joseph Brown of Shaw at fullback. Missing from this 1911 list but a noted player in this era was Henry E. Barco of Virginia Union, who was honored by a building in his name on that school's campus.

This first period of college football came to a close in 1912, when three key decisions were made that ushered in a new era. One, Dean George W. Hubbard persuaded Meharry's board to abolish football; two, the circumference of the football itself was reduced from twenty-seven inches to twenty-three; and three, the CIAA was formed. Meharry's decision was a wise choice. The smaller ball enhanced the passing game, and the formation of the CIAA forever changed the nature of black college sports.

The First Professionals

Professional football always suffered at the hands of the college game in its early years. The first teams were based in the Midwest, and crowds were seldom enthused about standing out in the cold to watch a game played by squads whose rosters changed from week to week. Black players were sparse but present nonetheless. Their participation is divided into four distinct eras: the early years before the formation of the National Football League (NFL); 1920 to 1933, the NFL's infancy; 1934 to 1945, when blacks were barred from the NFL; and 1946 to the present.

The college game was king, especially in the East, where there were plenty of schools and prep schools to feed the college squads. But precisely because there was a relative paucity of college teams, club teams had for years filled in schedules. The professional game took root in western

Pennsylvania and the Ohio Valley, starting on August 31, 1895, when the first game was played at Latrobe, Pennsylvania. No blacks played in this premier event.

Blacks began professional play in 1902, when Charles W. Follis of Cloverdale, Virginia, played for the Shelby Athletic Association. He was born on February 3, 1879, and moved to Wooster, Ohio, and played at Wooster High there. The Wooster *Republican* gave this assessment of his talents in secondary school in a victory over Alliance High: "The ball was kicked off and Follis brought it back half way across the field, plugging through the Alliance boys as if they were paper."[6]

He came by his spot on the Shelby Athletic Association eleven after he was wooed away from the Wooster Athletic Association amateur team by Frank C. Schiffer, the former's manager. In their first game with Follis, Shelby defeated Freemont 58-0. One of Follis' teammates was Branch Rickey, a student at Ohio Wesleyan and later the president of the Brooklyn Dodgers baseball team. Roberts added that "Rickey's first hand observation of Follis' unruffled handling of prejudice, on the field and off, influenced his decision to introduce Jackie Robinson to major league baseball."[7]

In 1904, Follis formally signed with Shelby and led them to an 8-1-1 season. Their only loss was to the Massillon Tigers, who won the professional title that year. In 1905 in a game against Toledo, fans became so unruly that a public announcement had to be made. Roberts quoted a source as saying of that game, "the Shelby halfback is a Negro and the crowd got after him early. . . . Toledo captain Jack Tattersoll addressed the crowd by saying 'Don't call Follis a nigger. He is a gentleman, and a

The first regimental baseball team of the Twenty-fifth Infantry Regiment is shown in 1894, when they were stationed at Fort Missoula, Montana. Bottom row, left to right: Freeman, Company H; Green, Company B; Smith, Company H; Gardner, Company F; and Foreman, Company H. Top row, left to right: Jackson, Company G; Thomas, Company H; Settlers, Company H; Baltimore, Company H; Swann, Company G; Coles, Company G; and Croffer, Company G. (History of the Twenty-fifth Regiment *by John H. Nankivell, Denver: Smith-Brooks Printing Company, 1927, page 50)*

Bud Fowler, back row on right, as a member of the 1900 Black Tourists. Perhaps only the second photo extant of the first black professional baseball player. The All-American Black Tourists were organized in 1899, and Fowler, then about fifty-seven, was one of the owners and the managers. *(From the* Cincinnati Enquirer, *courtesy of Jerry Malloy)*

The 1885 Cuban Giants. The first all-black professional baseball team. Top, left to right: Clarence Williams, catcher; George Parego, pitcher; John Fry, first base; and Arthur Thomas, infield. Middle row: Siki Govern, manager; Chase Lyons, pitcher; and William Malone, pitcher-outfielder. Bottom row: George Williams, infield; William Whyte, pitcher; Ben Holmes, infield; and Ben Boyd, outfield. *(Courtesy of the Schomburg Collection)*

Merton Paul Robinson entered Oberlin Academy in 1897—and the college division in 1898. He received an A.B. from Oberlin College in 1902. Robinson is shown in the back row on the 1902 Oberlin College baseball team. *(Courtesy of Oberlin College)*

Robert Higgins, pitcher for the Syracuse Stars, about 1887.
(Source unknown)

The 25th Infantry Regiment team at Fort Niobrara, Nebraska, poses with their baseball championship banner in 1903. (History of the Twenty-fifth Regiment, *page 55)*

John Henry "Pops" Lloyd in a Brooklyn Royal Giants uniform. *(Source unknown)*

John Henry "Pops" Lloyd, in Cuba as a member of the Havana Stars, 1909. (CP7 *(Source unknown)*

Charlie Lee Thomas, second row, third from left, on Ohio Wesleyan squad. Branch Rickey is in the top row left wearing a hat, 1903. *(Courtesy of Ohio Wesleyan)*

William Clarence Matthews, on the Harvard University squad, bottom row, left, 1903. *(Courtesy of Harvard University)*

James Francis Gregory, on 1898 Amherst team, second row, center. *(Courtesy of Amherst College)*

Virginia Union University baseball team, 1913. *(Courtesy of Virginia Union University)*

Bud Fowler, on Keokuk, Iowa, squad, back row, center, about 1885. *(Source unknown)*

Moses Fleetwood Walker, seated at left, and his brother Weldy, top row, second from right, on the 1881 Oberlin College team.
(Courtesy of Oberlin College)

Charley "Tokohama" Grant, whom major league manager John
McGraw tried to sign up as an "Indian," 1901. *(Source unknown)*

Atlanta Baptist College (now Morehouse College) team in 1897. *(Courtesy of Morehouse College)*

"Smokey" Joe Williams, pitcher of the Negro Leagues, about 1912. *(Source unknown)*

Henry Thomas, second row, far right, on the 1905 Coe College football team. *(Courtesy of Coe College)*

The veteran actor, Clarence Muse, fifty-nine, who appeared in over one hundred films (and is here "playing quarterback"), is shown with, from left to right: Paul Robeson, fifty-one; Fritz Pollard, fifty-five; Duke Slater, fifty-one; and Joe Lillard, forty-four in 1949. No all-time football team would be complete that excluded these football greats. *(Courtesy of Nina Eisenberg, Joe Lillard's daughter)*

Frederick Douglas "Fritz" Pollard, halfback, is seen as a member of the 1916 Brown University team. *(Courtesy of* Providence Journal)

Fritz Pollard, all-time Brown University football great, receives plaque as he is welcomed into the National Football Hall of Fame by Boston columnist Bill Cunningham during halftime ceremonies at the Brown – Springfield game in 1954. Cunningham holds the plaque. *(AP/Wide World Photos)*

Henry Freeman Coleman, top row, fourth from right, on Cornell University team, 1908. *(Courtesy of Cornell University)*

Ralph Metcalf (left), former Marquette track star and a member of the Illinois State Athletic Commission; Duke Slater (center), former University of Iowa gridder and a judge in Chicago; and Larry Doby, Cleveland Indians outfielder, get together at a luncheon in Chicago, February 22, 1950. They were guests of honor at the luncheon for sports people in the Chicago area. *(AP/Wide World Photos)*

Duke Slater, of the Chicago Cardinals, 1930. *(Courtesy of Saint Louis Cardinals)*

Duke Slater, of Iowa, opening a hole on the offensive line. He played without a helmet. *(Courtesy of the University of Iowa)*

The Howard University team in 1894. Coach Cecil C. Cook is on back row, center. Note size of the football under manager's right arm.
(Courtesy of Howard University)

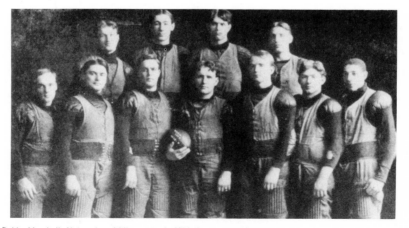

Bobby Marshall, University of Minnesota, in 1904, front row, right. *(Courtesy of the University of Minnesota)*

William Henry Lewis, front row, right, and William T. S. Jackson, second row, second from left, on 1889 Amherst team. *(Courtesy of Amherst College)*

Howard Joseph Lee, second row, left, on Harvard University team in 1896. *(Courtesy of Harvard University)*

Paul Leroy Robeson, center-forward of the 1919 Rutgers University
basketball team. *(Courtesy of Rutgers University)*

The 1902 Washington, D.C., 12th Street YMCA basketball team. Edwin B. Henderson is front row center. *(Source unknown)*

The Monticello Delaney Rifles basketball team in 1910. Cumberland Posey is front row, second from left. *(Source unknown)*

Cumberland Posey, top row, left, on the 1917 Duquesne University team. *(Courtesy of Duquesne University)*

clean player, and please don't call him that.'"[8] Good for Captain Tattersoll.

Follis stopped playing football in 1906 because even though he stood six feet tall and weighed two hundred pounds, he was constantly gang-tackled. Injuries forced his retirement. He died of pneumonia on April 5, 1910, at thirty-one—much too soon. In 1975, when Wooster was acclaimed an All-American city, the relatives of Charles Follis were accorded a place of honor in the festivities. He was buried in Wooster Cemetery.

In the year that Follis hung up his cleats, Charles "Doc" Baker played halfback for the Akron Indians. He was on the squad from 1906 to 1908, mysteriously left for two years, and then returned in 1911. He suffered, unfortunately, from the scandals that rocked professional football from 1906 to 1911 through no fault of his own.

After these scandals subsided, the first truly superior player surfaced. He was Haitian-born Henry McDonald, who came to the United States and settled in Canandaigua, New York. A running back for the Oxford Pros in 1911 and then for the Rochester Jeffersons, he earned twenty-five dollars per game for nearly six years. A quote of his has been found, attesting to the difficulty in getting around then: "We traveled trains in those days. Trains and steamboats....It was all steam trains...Very few cars."[9] In 1917, McDonald played against the incomparable Jim Thorpe, star of the 1912 Olympic Games in Stockholm. McDonald is quoted as saying Thorpe's team beat his squad 29-0, but the score was actually 49-0. Thorpe at the time was making $250 per game.

The last black star before the NFL was organized was Gideon E. "Charlie" Smith, a tackle who played only one game in 1915 for the Canton Bulldogs, Thorpe's team. He had graduated both from Hampton Institute and from Michigan Agricultural (now Michigan State).

Though not listed as a full professional, Robert Marshall, of the University of Minnesota fame, played semiprofessional ball from 1906 through 1921. He donned the uniforms of the Rock Island Independents, the Cleveland Panthers, the Minnesota Marines, and the Duluth Eskimos.

Blacks thus earned a toehold on the ground floor of football, the only major team sport that accepted them so early. The white college game was "it," and blacks were a part, even though a quota existed. The college game set the rules, and everyone else followed. It was thus no surprise that black club teams never formed. The expense of outfitting and renting stadiums was prohibitive.

As the Golden Decade of Sports—as the 1920s were called—played itself out, black gridders were gradually frozen out of the professional game altogether. Their brethren at some white colleges shared the same fate. Some institutions that had previously featured token blacks shut them out completely and offered no explanation. Blacks did excel, however, on black campuses, where rivalries were renewed and the crowds better than ever.

Pollard and Robeson

The year 1915 was a momentous one for black America. Jack Johnson lost his world heavyweight title; D. W. Griffith debuted the thoroughly racist movie *Birth of a Nation*; and the esteemed leader Booker T. Washington died. But that same year two black football players—Paul Leroy Robeson and Frederick Douglass "Fritz" Pollard—entered college and thoroughly changed the way blacks' positions were viewed.

William Drew Robeson, Paul's father, was born a slave in Martin County, North Carolina, on July 27, 1845. He escaped at age 15, joined the Union Army, and after the Civil War attended Lincoln University in Pennsylvania. There he met and married Maria Louisa Bustil. The couple moved to Princeton, New Jersey, in 1879, and their fifth child, Paul Leroy, was born on April 9, 1898. Their child became one of the most heralded citizens in the history of black America.

The young Robeson attended the segregated Jamison Elementary School and performed well, considering the premature death of his mother in 1904. At racially mixed Somerville High in Somerville, New Jersey, he played fullback on the football team. His thoughts of college centered on Lincoln because of his father, but he changed his mind when he scored the highest marks ever attained on the New Jersey High School Examination. He entered Rutgers University in the fall of 1915 on an academic scholarship.

Rutgers prided itself on its outstanding sports teams. Very few freshmen were good enough to play on varsity squads. Robeson began as a substitute tackle, and after not playing at all in the first two games, he played against Rensselaer Polytechnic on October 9, and Rutgers won 96-0. His second game was against Springfield, and his first starting assignment was at right guard on November 20 against Stevens Tech. Rutgers won 39-3. At the end of his fresh-

man season he had played in half the games, and Rutgers' record was 7-1.

In his sophomore year Robeson was already six feet, one and a half inches tall and weighed 210 pounds. He was upgraded to first-string at the tackle and guard positions and played in six of the seven games. Rutgers had a 3-2-2 record, but Robeson was involved in a shameful incident. On October 14, 1916, he was left off the team in a game against Washington and Lee (Virginia), which refused to play against blacks. On a more pleasant note, Robeson faced Fritz Pollard in a Rutgers-Brown game on October 28. Pollard scored twice—once on a forty-eight-yard run—and Brown won 21-3.

Robeson did not mention the benching against Washington and Lee in his later books, but it does not take a leap of faith to imagine the consternation he felt when told he could not play. Rutgers clearly had the option of canceling the game or insisting that all its varsity members take the field with no exceptions. Racial slights like this are never forgotten and form an indelible part of any person's social frame of reference in American life.

In 1917, Walter Camp did not make his usual All-America selections because of the war. Rutgers had a 7-1-1 season, and by all accounts Robeson would have been named to Camp's mythical eleven. *The New York Times* of October 14, 1917, said of Robeson, "the giant colored end from New Brunswick stood head and shoulders above his teammates in all around playing....He was a tower of strength on the Scarlet defense....He towered above every man on the field, and when he stretched his arms up in the air he pulled down forward passes that an ordinary player would have to use a stepladder to reach."

Later, the November 28, 1917, *New York Herald* was equally lavish in praise: "Paul Robeson, the big Negro end of the Rutgers eleven, is a football genius." This came as no surprise since by 1918 Robeson was six foot three and weighed 225 pounds. Walter Camp said he was the finest end that ever played the game—college or professional—and named him to his first-team All-America roster.

His senior year was again marred by a second benching against Washington and Lee, and Rutgers finished with a 5-2 record. One of the losses—54-14—was to the Great Lakes Naval Training Center, which featured George Halas at right end and Paddy Driscoll at quarterback. (Halas later coached and owned the Chicago Bears professional team.) Rutgers' record while Robeson was present was 22-6-3. He graduated Phi Beta Kappa with highest honors and later played professional football to help pay his tuition at Columbia University Law School.

He became one of the nation's most acclaimed opera performers and also immersed himself in the black Civil Rights Movement. He was present when the publishers of the country's leading black papers met with major league baseball officials during World War II to petition for admittance of Negro League players in Organized Ball. But in July 1949 he later had to defend himself before the Congressional House Un-American Activities Committee (HUAC). One of the government witnesses at the latter hearing for Robeson's supposed Communist Party sympathies was the first black player in the major leagues since the 1880s, Jackie Robinson. Robinson said of Robeson's statement that black Americans would not fight in a war against the Soviet Union: "I and many other Americans have too much invested in our country's welfare, for any of us to throw it away for a siren song in bass."[10]

The black press was critical of Robinson's comments. The Afro-American newspaper complained that Robinson had been invited to the HUAC hearings "to call Paul Robeson a liar" and that Robinson himself "cannot begin to fill Paul Robeson's shoes."[11] But in the October 1957 issue of *Ebony* magazine—the nation's leading black periodical—an article entitled "Has Paul Robeson Betrayed The Negro?" was penned by black journalist Carl T. Rowan. However, when all was said and done, black Americans generally agreed that Paul Robeson was a giant among men; on the football field, in concert, and on the battlefront for racial justice.

While Robeson was anchoring the Rutgers eleven, another black performer, Frederick Douglass "Fritz" Pollard of Brown University, positively was amazing his pursuers, although he almost failed to gain admittance. To be sure, Pollard was no Robeson: He was only five feet eight inches tall and barely tipped the scales at 155 pounds. But he was the most elusive running back yet seen in college play.

Pollard came out of Chicago's Lane Technical High School, where he learned firsthand about racial prejudice in his sophomore year. His coach acceded to a demand from an opposing team to leave him off the team, but Pollard was not told of it beforehand. As this was an away game, Pollard dutifully showed up at the train station at the appointed time, only to find out his teammates had left. Said Pollard later about the incident, "The coach didn't know how to tell me so he just had the entire squad take an earlier train."[12] The same thing had happened to his older brother, Leslie, while at Dartmouth in a game against Princeton. The Pollards had no illusions about racism.

Fritz Pollard had initially registered at Northwestern University in 1913 near his home but was told to leave when the dean found out that Pollard just wanted to play football. Then in February 1914 Pollard tried Brown, where he was three credits short of the entrance requirements after failing a Spanish exam. Then he tried Dartmouth, where his brother had played, but was tossed out once again for being less than candid about Brown University. On to Harvard, where he suited up but sat on the bench during a game against Bates College. Then he tried Bates but left because it was too cold. This scenario is reminiscent of the recruiting follies of the 1970s. Finally his friends persuaded him to earn the proper credits for graduation, which he did at Springfield, Massachusetts. He graduated at last and entered Brown in the fall of 1915 as a twenty-one-year-old freshman.

After the first day of practice he showered alone, but following his first game against Amherst everything changed: he returned a punt sixty yards. In his first start against Williams he scored twice and had a run of seventy yards. Against Vermont he had scamps of forty and thirty-two yards;

and against mighty Yale, before twelve thousand fans, he had runs of thirty-two and twenty-three yards. Brown had its first victory—3-0—over Yale since 1910. Following this Yale game, an opposing tackle named Sheldon paid Pollard a backhanded compliment: "You're a nigger, but you're the best goddamn football player I ever saw."[13]

Against Harvard before twenty-five thousand people, Pollard was brilliant. Runs of twenty-two, twenty, eighteen, nineteen, and seventeen yards were made. He scored three touchdowns against Carlisle Indian School in a 39-0 victory. In a losing effort against Syracuse and its black player, Joseph Trigg, Pollard and Brown University were scoreless. But more news was made on New Year's Day 1916, when Pollard became the first black player in the Rose Bowl. He was so popular by then that when a Pullman dining car attendant refused to serve him, his teammates got up and left *en masse*. He was later served. But Brown lost the game against Washington State 14-0, on a perfectly miserable day when it never stopped raining. He was, however, the most talked-about black man in America in January 1916.

In the 1916 season Pollard scored twice against Vermont; twice against Yale, for 307 total yards, to help Brown win 21-6; and twice against Harvard, for 254 yards in a 21-0 victory, Brown's first ever against that heralded school. His last game came in a losing effort against Colgate on Thanksgiving Day. One month later, in the December 30 *Collier's*, Camp named him to the All-America list—the first black running back to be so named. Camp said, "Pollard of

Brown was the most elusive back of the year, of any year. He is a good sprinter and once loose is a veritable will-o-the-wisp that no one can lay hands on."

Pollard must have been the shiftiest runner the game had ever seen. His diminutive size was not that much a hindrance, since the average weight of players then was less than two hundred pounds. With schedules cut down due to the war in 1917, Pollard left Brown and became the director of physical education at Camp Mead. Two years later he was one of the first blacks in the newly formed American Professional Football Association (APFA), that in 1921 changed its name to the National Football League (NFL).

Notes

1. Quoted in Chalk, op. cit., p. 146.
2. Quoted in Chalk, op. cit., p. 158.
3. Henderson, op. cit., p. 272.
4. Ibid., p. 272.
5. *ISAA Handbook* (1911), p. 67.
6. Milton Roberts, *First Black Pro Gridder*. (Monograph, 1975).
7. Ibid.
8. Quoted in ibid.
9. Quoted in Chalk, p. 213.
10. Quoted in Dorothy Butler Gilliam, *Paul Robeson: All-American*. (Washington, D. C.: New Republic Books, 1976), p. 141.
11. Quoted in ibid.
12. Quoted in *Ebony* (January 1972), p. 102.
13. Quoted in ibid., p. 106.

Chapter

7

Basketball

The Springfield YMCA

The game of basketball had to be invented sooner or later. In the late 1800s the nation's athletic calendar was filled in three of the four seasons: baseball in the summer; football in the fall; and track and field in the spring. A winter game was needed to keep the competitive juices flowing, and basketball was the answer.

James Naismith, a Canadian YMCA training instructor in Springfield, Massachusetts, hit upon the idea in 1891 of tossing a soccer-size ball through an elevated opening. He asked a janitor, so the story goes, for some containers that he could affix to the wall. The workman replied with peach baskets—with the bottoms intact. Soon the bottoms were removed and the baskets refined, and the sport was on its way. No indoor game ever caught on as fast, and the YMCA spread its virtues the world over.

Naismith's fellow instructors did not like his invention because too few people could play. The initial scoring system called for three points for a basket and three points for a free throw. In just five years it was changed to two points for a basket and one point for a free throw. This did not change until the introduction of the three-

point basket in the 1980s. In 1897 the team size was set at five, and that too has remained. This simplicity was central to the sports early appeal.

The influential *New York Times* on May 7, 1894, merely echoed the obvious in reporting that "Basketball is about the youngest of the athletic games, but it has gained great popularity...played with more enthusiasm than any other sport in the gymnasiums in this city." Girls played, too, according to a special set of rules formulated by Senda Berenson of Smith College. Other schools and clubs quickly added it to their roster of activities.

As with the other sports, it was not long—1896—before the first professional game was played at the Masonic Temple in Trenton, New Jersey. The professional National Basketball League (NBL) was formed in 1898. In 1897 the Amateur Athletic Union began competitions, and the final seal of approval came with an introduction at the 1904 Olympic Games. This first Olympic event was won by a team composed almost entirely of members of the Buffalo (New York) German YMCA.

First Black Participation

Black players began with the YMCAs and schools of the Ivy League. YMCA College

Student Associations at Clafflin, Straight, Tougaloo, Spelman, Alabama A&M, and Howard Universities introduced the game, and other Colored YMCAs with gymnasiums embraced it wholeheartedly. YMCAs and YWCAs formed the first black teams and continued to be the focal point for a decade until clubs offered stronger competition.

One gentleman who helped bridge the decade 1895–1905 was Edwin B. Henderson. He attended Harvard University as this century began and returned to his native Washington, D.C., to organize local teams in the public school system. He immediately included it in his Interscholastic Athletic Association (ISAA) program formed in 1905. At the same time the first club team was organized in Brooklyn, New York, calling themselves the Smart Set Club. They built their athletic programs around basketball and track. Within a year the St. Christopher Athletic Club and the Marathone Athletic Club joined Smart Set in forming the Olympian Athletic League (OAL), which became the first black club league outside the YMCA family.

In 1907 Smart Set won the first OAL title with the following members: Charles Scrotton, Chester Moore, Robert Lattimore, Robert Barnard, Harry Brown, Alfred Groves, George Trice, and manager George Lattimore. One year later, the OAL added the Alpha Physical Culture Club, the St. Cyprian Athletic Club, and the Jersey City YMCA to its membership. In spite of its distinct northeastern location, the OAL was a solid beginning for a sport eventually dominated by black players.

Similar clubs formed in the Washington, D.C., vicinity with Henderson's assistance, and interregional competition began on December 18, 1908, when that city's Crescent Athletic Club lost to Smart Set in "the first athletic contest between colored athletes of New York and Washington."[1] The success of this game was not lost on the segregated black public schools in Washington, D.C., and other cities.

Schools and clubs in Baltimore, Philadelphia, St. Louis, Wilmington (Delaware), and northern New Jersey soon had clubs of players. Philadelphia was a special case as its schools were integrated. As Henderson noted, their "colored athletes are thrown into competition with the whites."[2] Its clubs, however, were segregated. The Wissahickon School Club and the Stentonworth Athletic Club were the first black groups to form in that city.

With the exception of St. Louis and towns where black colleges were positioned, the sport in southern black communities was almost nonexistent before 1910. Warm weather the year round lessened the impetus for a winter game. There were no gymnasiums, equipment was poor, coaching was out of an A. G. Spaulding manual. The YMCAs had too few indoor facilities. Yet the YMCAs' outdoor play areas offered the only hope for a time.

The best YMCA squad was the Twelfth Street Branch in Washington, D.C., which was so good that when Howard University began varsity play in 1911, it inherited the YMCA team almost intact. Its members were Lewis S. Johnson, Hudson J. Oliver, Arthur L. Curtis, Henry T. Nixon, J. L. Chestnut, Robert Anderson, Maurice Clifford, Edward B. Gray, and Edwin B.

Henderson. They were undefeated in 1909–10 and had wins over school and club teams from Washington, D.C., to New York City. At Brooklyn's Manhattan Casino in 1910 they defeated Smart Set before 3,000 fans. In Alabama, Tuskegee's first game was also against a YMCA team from Columbus, Georgia, in 1908, which they crushed 33-0.

These YMCA teams remained central to the success of basketball among blacks. School attendance was not required for blacks in the south, and only a small minority of those between 15 and 20 years of age attended. Consequently, if the YMCAs did not have teams, there would have been no play at all. In addition, their strict code of amateurism kept most players from trying to form professional associations. But that too changed before World War I.

The Early Club Teams

After the YMCAs initial influence came the clubs that sprang up in the major cities in the Northeast. Because of the YMCAs amateur tradition, it could not hope to keep the best players permanently. Likewise, school teams were hampered by the availability of its students. Like other sports—baseball, track, and football—club fives (basketball teams are sometimes called fives) filled a vacuum in the black basketball world. Their quality of play was superior, and their Friday and Saturday night games—followed by a dance—became a staple in the social calendar.

Clubs like Smart Set and Wissahickon blossomed because of natural constituencies and access to facilities and coaching.

Smart Set and Alpha Physical Culture also fielded girls' teams. Dora Cole and her sisters dominated the first Smart Set team and soon had imitators who played their games in blousy knee-length bloomers and long-sleeved shirts. Most girls' games were played with six players on a side, and there was a limit to the number of bounces a girl could take before being forced to pass or shoot. The idea of performing in short pants—or for money—was simply out of the question for women.

Not so for the second wave of clubs that began operating around 1910. Two of the earliest were the Incorporators of New York City and the Monticello Delaney Rifles of Pittsburgh, Pennsylvania. Will Madden, who ran the St. Christopher five, formed the semiprofessional Incorporators in 1911, and they were the best team in the area until World War I. Their main rivals were the Independents and the Scholastics. They had no reservations whatever about the propriety of playing for pay. Monticello agreed.

Nearly every black team was aware of the inaugural World Professional Championship held in 1905 between Company E of Schenectady, New York, and the Kansas City Blue Diamonds. Cumberland Posey of Pittsburgh, the Monticello organizer, wanted to do the same. He formed his team in 1909 and set out to put the skills he learned while on Penn State's varsity to good use. Oddly enough, Posey left the Penn State squad because his grades made him ineligible for games.

Posey's premier team consisted of his brother Seward; Baker, the coach; Mahoney, the manager; Dorsey; Brown; Clark; Hall;

and Richmond. The second year he added the Bell brothers and Norris. (First names could not be found for most of Posey's team.) Their play was so spectacular that the New York *Age* of March 14, 1912, said, "[T]he colored basketball world will be forced to recognize Monticello as one of the fastest colored quints. The Monticello team is open to meet all comers. It has not met defeat in two years, playing all white teams."

Posey was an anomaly among black sports figures in the pre–World War I era. He was a scion of a solid, stable, upper-class black family. His father was the first black man granted a chief engineer's license to operate a steamboat on the Mississippi River. Few prosperous blacks bothered with sports beyond their school days then.

Club owners like Posey were more market-oriented than product-oriented. There was evident public demand for quality basketball, and they meant to supply it. Some of these teams even played against all-black army squads like the 10th Cavalry Regiment, billed as "The Championship Team of the United States Army." The January 10, 1911, New York *Age* reported a loss by this squad to a black all-star team, saying, "The boys in blue proved as tricky as the horses they ride, and whenever an all star player attempted to tackle a cavalryman by jumping on his back he was usually given a quick excursion through the air. Medical aid and sticking plaster were called into use several times...but no one was seriously injured." Sounds rather exciting.

Professional teams like Monticello and the Incorporators were bound to cause dissension, and they did. The black elite wanted to see a sharper line of demarcation from amateur play, but the play-for-pay fives were more entertaining than school squads or those from social clubs. Possibly the fear was loss of control, as may be inferred from this quote in a black periodical, *The Competitor Magazine,* of 1914: "There is...a place for the professional in basketball, but let him promote his own following.... There can be no middle ground...the duty of each is plain."[3] The formation of the Colored Intercollegiate Athletic Association (CIAA) in 1912 and the Southern Intercollegiate Athletic Conference (SIAC)—two black college conferences—helped address the amateur-vs-professional issue.

In 1913, the same year, that the SIAC was formed, Posey organized a new team that featured the first truly famous players. He called his new quintet The Loendi Big Five, and they played their home games at Pittsburgh's Labor Temple. The members were Posey, James "Stretch" Sessoms, William T. Young, William "Big Greasy" Betts, and James "Pappy" Ricks. They dominated the black basketball world until the coming of the New York Renaissance and Harlem Globetrotters squads a decade later. Loendi was the best-known black team in any sport in the Ohio Valley until the Homestead Grays baseball team formed.

The Loendi Five played very physical basketball that fit the image of their steelmaking hometown. For instance, most teams stalled when they had a sizable lead near the end of games because there was then no rule requiring the offense to move the ball beyond the midcourt line in ten seconds. Not Loendi. Posey realized that boredom meant lower profits, so his team was aggressive. Most of their results were carried in the white press, especially when they played the all-Jewish Coffey Club. Crowds of five thousand at the Labor Temple were not uncommon.

Sometimes the aggression got a little out of hand because the spectators were so close. Basketball players got their familiar nickname "cagers" because in these early days the teams were separated from the spectators by floor-to-ceiling netting, which made it look like they were playing in a cage. In one game between the Incorporators and Orange (New Jersey), the Incorporators' captain "was struck on the nose by one of the Orange rooters and incapacitated for the rest of the game."[4] The paper did not say which team won that night.

By World War I the black press began trying to anoint a Colored World Champion for basketball as baseball and boxing had (though in boxing, a white paper, *The Police Gazette*, named the Colored Champion). But depending on which paper was believed, the Loendi Big Five won most nods before and during the war. *The Competitor Magazine* thought Loendi so good that it told its readers it was hardly possible to pick a basketball team from all the colored players of the country that would have a ghost of a chance to beat that Pittsburgh five. It was probably correct.

Loendi's success inevitably spawned imitators. Soon the black papers were trumpeting the wins and losses of semiprofessional squads like Homestead Steel, the Spartans, Edgar Thompson Steel, the Vandals (Atlantic City), Athenian (Baltimore), and the Borough Athletic Club of Brooklyn. Most of their players were making around twenty-five dollars per game and working at their regular jobs. Within a decade their successors had quit their jobs and played basketball full time.

White College Stars

While black colleges struggled with their meager athletic facilities, some white schools fielded respectable squads, and black players were sprinkled here and there. But neither the enthusiasm nor the presence was like that of football, and no All-America lists were published. Samuel Ransom of Beloit College (1904–08) seems to have been among the earliest players.

Though no specific names could be found, other blacks must have been playing since this quote appeared in the December 24, 1904 Indianapolis *Freeman*: "For drawing the color line a basketball team in Massachusetts was fined $100 by the president of the New England League." The New England League was composed of Dartmouth, Holy Cross, Williams, Amherst, and Trinity, so some guesses could be made to determine the culprit.

Other blacks documented before World War I include Wilbur Wood at Nebraska in 1907–10; Fenwich H. Watkins at the University of Vermont in 1907–09; Cumberland Posey at Penn State in 1909; William Kindle at Springfield College in 1911; Cleveland Abbott at South Dakota

State in 1913; and Sol Butler at Dubuque (Iowa) in 1916.

After the war participation in basketball became a cause célèbre at some schools. Blacks were allowed on football teams but not on basketball teams at the same institution. Racism was becoming more selective, but protestors demanded explanations just the same.

Notes

1. *ISAA Handbook* (1910), p. 67.
2. Ibid., p. 41.
3. Quoted in Chalk, op. cit., p. 79.
4. New York *Age*, January 14, 1915.

Reference Section

BOXING
African-American World Boxing Champions   *113*
African-American World Boxing Championship Matches, Through 1919   *113*
Jack Johnson   *113*
Joe Walcott   *116*
Dixie Kid   *118*
Joe Gans   *119*
George Dixon   *121*
Molineaux and Richmond Boxing Records   *124*

HORSE RACING
African-American Jockeys   *125*
Isaac Murphy's Record   *125*
Willie Simm's Record   *126*
Jimmy Winkfield's Record   *126*
Jimmy Lee's Record   *126*
Key Races Stakes Won by African-American Jockeys   *127*

CYCLING
Major Taylor's Bicycle Racing Record, 1891-1908   *131*

TRACK & FIELD
African-American Olympic Medalists, 1904 and 1908   *135*
African-American AAU National Champions, Through 1919   *135*
African-American Stars on White College Teams, Through 1919   *136*
African-American World Record Holders, Through 1919   *136*

BASEBALL
All-Time Register of African-American Players, Managers, Umpires, and Officials,
    1872-1919   *137*

FOOTBALL
Milton Roberts' All-Time Black College Squad   *171*
Black Football Players at White Colleges, 1889-1919   *173*

BASKETBALL
African-American Stars on White College Basketball Teams, Through 1919   *175*

Key to Abbreviations:
D–Decision
Exh.–Exhibition Match
KO–Knockout
KO BY–Knockout by Opponent
L–Loss
LD–Loss by Decision
LF–Loss by Foul
NC–No Contest
ND–No Decision
TB–Total Bouts
W–Wins
WD–Win by Decision
WF–Win by Foul

BOXING

AFRICAN-AMERICAN WORLD BOXING CHAMPIONS

Weight Class	Name	Year
Heavyweight	Johnson, Jack	1908-15
Welterweight	Walcott, Joe (Barbadian)	1901-04
Welterweight	Brown, Aaron (aka The Dixie Kid)	1904-05
Lightweight	Gans, Joe	1902-08
Featherweight	Dixon, George (Canadian)	1892–1900

AFRICAN-AMERICAN WORLD BOXING CHAMPIONSHIP MATCHES, THROUGH 1919

Weight Class	Name	Ht.	Wgt.	Opponent	Result		Date	Site
Heavyweight	Johnson, Jack	6'1	195	Tommy Burns	KO	14	12/26/08	Sydney, Australia
Welterweight	Walcott, Joe ("Barbados")	5'1	145	Jim Rube Ferns	KO	5	12/18/01	Fort Erie, Ontario
	Walcott, Joe ("Barbados")			Joe Gans	D	20	9/30/03	San Francisco
	Brown, Aaron ("Dixie Kid")	5'8	145	Joe Walcott	WF	20	4/30/04	San Francisco
Lightweight	Gans, Joe	5'6	131-37	Frank Erne	KO	1	5/12/02	Ft. Erie, Ontario
	Gans, Joe			Battling Nelson	WF	42	9/03/06	Goldfield, Colo.
Featherweight	Dixon, George (Canadian)	5'3	105-22	Fred Johnson	KO	14	6/27/92	Coney Island, NY
	Dave Sullivan				WD	10	11/11/98	New York

JACK JOHNSON

(John Arthur Johnson)
(The Galveston Giant)

Born, March 31, 1878, Galveston, Texas. Weight, 195 lbs. Height, 6 ft. 1¼ in. Managed by Morris Hart, Johnny Connors, Alec McLean, Sam Fitzpatrick, Abe Arends, George Little, Tom Flanagan, Sig Hart.

1897

–Jim Rocks, Galveston . . . . KO 4
–Sam Smith, Galveston . . . . W 10

1898

–Reddy Bremer, Galveston . . . . KO 3
–Jim Cole, Galveston . . . . W 4
–Henry Smith, Galveston . . . . D 15

1899

Feb. 11–Jim McCormick, Galveston . . . . NC 7
Mar. 17–Jim McCormick, Galveston . . . . WF 7
May   6–John (Klondike)Haynes, Chicago . . . . KO by 5
Dec. 16–Pat Smith, Galveston . . . . D 12

1900

–Josh Mills, Memphis . . . . W 12

1901

Feb. 25–Joe Choynski, Galveston . . . . KO by 3
Mar.   7–John Lee, Galveston . . . . W 15
Apr. 12–Charley Brooks, Galveston . . . . KO   2
May   6–Jim McCormick, Galveston . . . . KO   2
May   28–Jim McCormick, Galveston . . . . KO   7
June 12–Horace Miles, Galveston. . . . . KO   3
June 20–George Lawler, Galveston. . . . . KO 10
June 28–John (Klondike) Haynes, Galveston . . . . D 20
       –Willie McNeal . . . . KO 15
Nov.   4–Hank Griffin, Bakersfield . . . . L 20
Dec. 27–Hank Griffin, Oakland. . . . . D 15

1902

Jan. 17–Frank Childs, Chicago. . . . . D   6
Feb.   7–Dan Murphy, Waterbury . . . . KO 10
Feb. 22–Ed Johnson, Galveston . . . . KO   4
Mar.   7–Joe Kennedy, Oakland . . . . KO   4
Apr.   6–Bob White. . . . . W 15
May   1–Jim Scanlan . . . . KO   7
May   16–Jack Jeffries, Los Angeles . . . . KO   5
May   28–John (Klondike) Haynes, Memphis . . . . KO 13
June   4–Billy Stift, Denver . . . . D 10
June 20–Hank Griffin, Los Angeles. . . . . D 20
Sept. 3–Mexican Pete Everett, Victor, Colo.. . . . . . . W 20
Oct. 21–Frank Childs, Los Angeles . . . . W 12
Oct. 31–George Gardner, San Francisco. . . . . W 20
Dec.   5–Fred Russell, Los Angeles . . . . WF   8

1903

Feb.   3–Denver Ed Martin, Los Angeles . . . . W 20
         (Won Negro Heavyweight Title)
Feb. 27–Sam McVey, Los Angeles . . . . W 20
         (Retained Negro Heavyweight Title)
Apr. 16–Sandy Ferguson, Boston. . . . . W 10
May   11–Joe Butler, Philadelphia . . . . KO   3
July 31–Sandy Ferguson, Philadelphia . . . . ND   6
Oct. 27–Sam McVey, Los Angeles . . . . W 20
         (Retained Negro Heavyweight Title)
Dec. 11–Sandy Ferguson, Colma, Calif . . . . W 20

1904

Feb. 16–Black Bill, Philadelphia. . . . . ND   6

Apr. 22–Sam McVey, San Francisco . . . . KO 20
         (Retained Negro Heavyweight Title)
June   2–Frank Childs, Chicago . . . . W   6
Oct. 18–Denver Ed Martin, Los Angeles. . . . . KO   2
         (Retained Negro Heavyweight Title)

1905

Mar. 28–Marvin Hart, San Francisco . . . . L 20
Apr. 25–Jim Jeffords, Philadelphia . . . . KO   4
May   3–Black Bill, Philadelphia . . . . KO   4
May   9–Walter Johnson, Philadelphia. . . . . KO   3
May   19–Joe Jeannette, Philadelphia . . . . ND   6
June 26–Jack Monroe, Philadelphia . . . . ND   6
July 13–Morris Harris, Philadelphia . . . . KO   3
July 13–Black Bill, Philadelphia. . . . . ND   6
July 18–Sandy Ferguson, Chelsea, Mass . . . . WF   7
July 24–Joe Grim, Philadelphia . . . . ND   6
Nov. 25–Joe Jeannette, Philadelphia . . . . LF   2
Dec.   1–Young Peter Jackson, Baltimore . . . . W 12
Dec.   2–Joe Jeannette, Philadelphia . . . . ND   6

1906

Jan. 16–Joe Jeannette, New York . . . . ND   3
Mar. 14–Joe Jeannette, Baltimore . . . . W 15
Apr. 19–Black Bill, Wilkes-Barre . . . . KO   7
Apr. 26–Sam Langford, Chelsea, Mass. . . . . W 15
June 18–Charlie Haghey, Gloucester, Mass.. . . . . KO   2
Sept. 3–Billy Dunning, Millinocket, Me. . . . . D 10
Sept. 20–Joe Jeannette, Philadelphia . . . . ND   6
Nov.   8–Jim Jeffords, Lancaster, Pa.. . . . . W   6
Nov. 26–Joe Jeannette, Portland, Me. . . . . D 10
Dec.   9–Joe Jeannette, New York . . . . W   3

1907

Feb. 19–Peter Felix, Sydney. . . . . KO   1
Mar   4–Jim Lang, Melbourne . . . . KO   9
July 17–Bob Fitzsimmons, Philadelphia . . . . KO   2
Aug. 28–Kid Cutler, Reading, Pa. . . . . KO   1
Sept. 12–Sailor Burke, Bridgeport . . . . W   6
Nov.   2–Fireman Jim Flynn, San Francisco . . . . KO 11

1908

Jan.   3–Joe Jeannette, New York. . . . . D   3
June 11–Al McNamara, Plymouth, England . . . . W   4
July 31–Ben Taylor, Plymouth, England . . . . KO   8
Dec. 26–Tommy Burns, Sydney. . . . . KO 14
         (Won World Heavyweight Title)

1909

Mar. 10–Victor McLaglen, Vancouver, B.C. . . . . ND 6
  (Retained World Heavyweight Title)
Apr. –Frank Moran, Pittsburgh. . . . . Exh. 4
May 19–Phila. Jack O'Brien, Philadelphia. . . . . ND 6
  (Retained World Heavyweight Title)
June 30–Tony Ross, Pittsburgh. . . . . ND 6
  (Retained World Heavyweight Title)
Sept. 9–Al Kaufman, San Francisco . . . . ND 10
  (Retained World Heavyweight Title)
Oct. 16–Stanley Ketchel, Colma, Calif. . . . . KO 12
  (Retained World Heavyweight Title)

1910

July 4–James J. Jeffries, Reno . . . . KO 15
  (Retained World Heavyweight Title)

1911

(Inactive)

1912

July 4–Fireman Jim Flynn, Las Vegas, N.M. . . . . . . KO 9
  (Retained World Heavyweight Title)

1913

Dec. 19–Battling Jim Johnson, Paris, France . . . . D 10
  (Retained World Heavyweight Title)

1914

June 27–Frank Moran, Paris, France . . . . W 20
  (Retained World Heavyweight Title)
Dec. –Enrique Wilkinson, Buenos Aires. . . . . Exh. KO
Dec. 15–Jack Murray, Buenos Aires . . . . Exh. KO 3

1915

Jan. –Vasco Guiralechea, Buenos Aires. . . . . Exh. KO
Apr. 3–Sam McVey, Havana, Cuba . . . . Exh. 6
Apr. 5–Jess Willard, Havana, Cuba . . . . KO by 26
  (Lost World Heavyweight Title)

1916

Mar. 10–Frank Crozier, Madrid, Spain . . . . W 10
July 10–Arthur Craven, Barcelona, Spain . . . . KO 1

1917

(Inactive)

1918

Apr. 3–Blink McCloskey, Madrid, Spain . . . . W 4

1919

Feb. 12–Bill Flint, Madrid, Spain . . . . KO 2
Apr. 7–Tom Cowler, Mexico City . . . . D 10
June 2–Tom Cowler, Mexico City . . . . KO 12
July 4–Paul Sampson, Mexico City . . . . KO 6
Aug. 10–Marty Cutler, Mexico City . . . . KO 4
Sept. 28–Capt. Bob Roper, Mexico City . . . . W 10

1920

Apr. 18–Bob Wilson, Mexicali . . . . KO 3
May 17–George Roberts, Tijuana . . . . KO 3
Nov. 25–Frank Owens, Leavenworth. . . . . KO 6
Nov. 25–Topeka Jack Johnson, Leavenworth . . . . W 5
Nov. 30–George Owens, Leavenworth . . . . KO 6

1921

Apr. 15–Jack Townsend, Leavenworth . . . . KO 6
May 28–John Allen, Leavenworth . . . . Exh. 2
May 28–Joe Boykin, Leavenworth . . . . KO 5

1922

(Inactive)

1923

May 6–Farmer Lodge, Havana, Cuba. . . . . KO 4
May 20–Jack Thompson, Havana, Cuba . . . . ND 15
Oct. 1–Battling Siki, Quebec . . . . Exh. 6

1924

Feb. 22–Homer Smith, Montreal . . . . W 10

1925

(Inactive)

1926

May 2–Pat Lester, Nogales, Mexico . . . . W 15
May 30–Bob Lawson, Juarez, Mexico. . . . . WF 8

1927

(Inactive)

1928

Apr. 16–Bearcat Wright, Topeka, Kansas . . . . KO by 5
May 15–Bill Hartwell, Kansas City, KS . . . . KO by 7

TB	KO	WD	WF	D	LD	LF	KO BY	ND	NC
112	45	29	4	12	2	1	5	14	0

Died, June 10, 1946, Raleigh, N.C.
Elected to Boxing Hall of Fame, 1954.

JOE WALCOTT

Born, March 13, 1873, Barbados, West Indies. Nationality, West Indian. Weight, 145 lbs. Height, 5 ft. 1½ in. Managed by Tom O'Rourke. Came to America in 1887 and lived in Boston. Boxed and wrestled as amateur 1887-1889

1890

Feb.   29–Tom Powers, So. Boston............... KO   2

1891

Jan.   30–J. Barrett, Providence .... KO   1
Mar.   26–Alex. Clark, Cambridge................. W   2
Dec.   12–G.V. Meakin, Boston .... W   4
Dec.   12–Teddy Kelly, Boston.................... L   3
Dec.   23–Alex. Clark, Boston .... W   3

1892

Mar.   28–T. Warren, Boston .... W   4
May   17–Tom Powers, Boston .... W   3
Aug.   4–Frank Carey, Walpole .... D   3
Aug.   29–J.J. Leahy, Cambridge................. KO   3
Oct.   22–Fred Morris, Philadelphia .... D   4
Oct.   22–Joe Larg, Philadelphia .... W   3
Oct.   29–Andy Watson, Philadelphia .... D   4
Nov.   4–Harry Tracey, Boston .... D   5
Nov.   11–Charley Jones, Philadelphia .... W   3
Nov.   12–Jack Lymon, Philadelphia .... KO   1
Dec.   5–Sam Boden .... D   4
Dec.   5–Jack Connors, New York .... KO   1
Dec.   8–Billy Harris, New York .... KO   2

1893

June   5–Paddy McGuiggan, Newark .... W 10
June   17–Mike Harris, New York L   4
Aug.   22–Jack Hall, New York .... KO   1
Dec.   22–Harry Tracey, Boston .... WF   1
Dec.   28–Danny Russell .... KO   2

1894

Jan.   11–Tommy West, So. Boston .... KO   3
Feb.   26–Mike Welsh, Boston .... KO   2
Apr.   19–Tom Tracey, Boston .... KO 16
June   22–Mike Harris, Boston.................. KO   6
July   6–Dick O'Brien, Boston .... KO 12
Oct.   15–Austin Gibbons, New York............. KO   4
Nov.   1–Frank Carpenter, Chicago .... KO   3
Nov.   3–Frank Neill, Chicago................. W   8
Nov.   3–Shorty Ahern, Chicago .... KO   8
Nov.   14–George Thomas, Louisville .... KO   1
Nov.   15–Billy Green, Louisville .... KO   2

1895

Mar.   1–Billy Smith, Boston.................... D 15
Apr.   3–Mick Dunn, Coney Island .... W   8
Aug.   28–O'Brien, Boston...................... KO   1
Dec.   2–Geo. Lavigne, Maspeth .... L 15

1896

Jan.   30–Jim Jackson, New York................. W   4
Mar.   16–Scott Collins, L.I.C. .... KO   7
May   10–Scaldy Bill Quinn, Woburn .... W 20
Oct.   12–Scaldy Bill Quinn, Maspeth........... W 17
Dec.   9–*Tommy West, New York................. D 19
*Timer's error ended bout in 19th round. Referee Charley White called it a draw.

1897

Mar.   3–Tommy West, New York................. L 20
Apr.   20–Jim Watts, New York.................. D   4
June   14–Tom Tracey, Philadelphia............. D   6
Sept. 16–George Green, San Francisco .... W 18
Oct.   29–Kid Lavigne, San Francisco .... L 12
          (World Lightweight Title)
Dec.   27–Tom Tracey, Chicago................... D   6

1898

Apr.   4–Mysterious Billy Smith, Bridgeport .... D 25
          (Welterweight Title Bout)
Apr.   22–Tommy West, Philadelphia .... ND   6
Apr.   28–Kid McPartland, Detroit .... D   8
Dec.   6–Mysterious Billy Smith, N.Y. .... L 20
          (Welterweight Title Bout)

1899

Feb.   4–Australian Jimmy Ryan, Cincinnati .... KO 14
Mar.   16–Billy Edwards, New York .... KO 13
Apr.   8–Jim Judge, Toronto.................... KO 11
Apr.   25–Dan Creedon, New York .... KO   1
May   8–Charley Johnson, Athens .... W 11
May   19–Dick O'Brien, New York .... KO 14
May   30–Jim Watts, Louisville .... KO   8
June   12–Harry Fisher, Baltimore .... W 11
June   23–Dan Creedon, New York .... W 20
Nov.   25–Dan Creedon, Chicago .... W   6
Nov.   29–Dan Creedon, Utica .... W 20
Dec.   5–Bobby Dobbs, New York .... KO   6

1900

Feb.   23–Joe Choynski, New York .... KO   7
Mar.   16–Andy Walsh, New York .... W 20

Apr.   10–Dick Moore, Baltimore . . . . KO 4
May   4–Mysterious Billy Smith, N.Y. . . . . W 25
May   11–Jack Bonner, Philadelphia . . . . ND 6
Aug. 27–*Tommy West, New York . . . . KO by 11
Sept. 24–Mysterious Billy Smith, Hartford . . . . WF 10
Dec. 13–Billy Hanrahan, Hartford . . . . KO 12
*Walcott quit at end of 11th round.

1901

Jan.   17–Kid Carter, Harford . . . . LF 10
Mar.   21–Chas. McKeever, Waterbury . . . . KO 6
July   26–Jack Bonner, Bridgeport . . . . W 15
Sept. 27–George Gardner, San Fran. . . . . W 20
Oct.   15–Kid Carter, San Fran. . . . . KO by 7
Nov. 28–Young Jackson, Baltimore . . . . W 20
Dec. 18–Jim Rube Ferns, Fort Erie . . . . KO 5
(Won Welterweight Title)

1902

Jan.   13–Young Peter, Jackson, Phila. . . . . ND 6
Feb.   14–Jimmy Handler, Philadelphia . . . . KO 2
Mar.   13–Young Peter, Jackson, Balti. . . . . D 10
Mar.   15–Billy Stift, Chicago . . . . W 6
Apr.   4–Fred Russell, Chicago . . . . D 6
Apr.   11–Phil. Jack O'Brien, Phila. . . . . ND 6
Apr.   25–George Gardner, San Fran. . . . . L 20
June 23–*Tommy West, London . . . . W 15
Oct.   7–George Cole, Philadelphia . . . . ND 4
Oct.   9–Frank Childs, Chicago . . . . L 3
*Title bout.

1903

Mar.   9–Mike Donovan, Pittsburgh. . . . . W 10
Mar.   11–Charley Haghey, Boston . . . . KO 5
Mar.   18–George Cole, Pittsburgh . . . . KO 4
Apr.   2–Billy Woods, Los Angeles . . . . D 20
Apr.   15–Mike Donovan, Boston . . . . W 10
Apr.   20–Phil. Jack O'Brien, Boston . . . . D 10
May   28–Mysterious Billy Smith, Portland . . . . W 4
June 18–Young Peter Jackson, Portland . . . . D 20
July   3–Mose La Fontise, Butte . . . . KO 3
Aug. 13–Tom Carey, Boston . . . . KO 8
Sept. 11–Joe Grimm, Philadelphia. . . . . ND 6
Sept. 21–Tom Carey, Boston . . . . KO 5
Oct.   13–Kid Carter, Boston . . . . W 15
Nov.   3–Kid Carter, Boston . . . . W 15
Nov. 10–Sandy Ferguson, Boston . . . . L 15
Dec. 29–Larry Temple, Boston . . . . D 15

1904

Jan.   18–Chas. Haghey, New Bedford . . . . KO 3
Feb.   26–Black Bill, Philadelphia . . . . ND 6
Apr.   30–Dixie Kid, San Francisco . . . . LF 20
(Lost welterweight title)
May   12–Dixie Kid, San Francisco. . . . . D 20
(Welterweight title bout)
May   23–Sandy Ferguson, Portland . . . . D 10
June 10–Young Peter Jackson, Baltimore. . . . . KO by 4
June 24–Mike Donovan, Baltimore . . . . W 5
July   1–Larry Temple, Baltimore . . . . D 10
Sept. 5–Sam Langford, Manchester . . . . D 15
Sept. 10–Dave Holly, Philadelphia . . . . ND 6
Sept. 30–Joe Gans, San Francisco . . . . D 20
(World Welterweight Title)
(Dixie Kid outgrew class; Walcott claimed title)

1906

July   10–Jack Dougherty, Chelsea . . . . KO 8
Sept. 30–Billy Rhodes, Kansas City . . . . D 20
Oct.   16–Honey Mellody, Chelsea . . . . L 15
(Lost welterweight title)
Nov. 29–Honey Mellody, Chelsea . . . . L 12

1907

Jan.   15–Mike Donovan, Providence . . . . L 10
June 18–Mike Donovan, Brazil, Ind. . . . . D 10
Oct.   17–Billy Payne, Rockland, Me . . . . KO 6
Oct.   25–Mike Donovan, Providence . . . . D 15
Dec. 26–George Cole, Philadelphia . . . . ND 6

1908

Jan.   7–Jimmy Gardner, Boston . . . . L 12
Jan.   14–George Cole, Troy, N.Y. . . . . ND 6
Jan.   15–Mike Donovan, Montreal . . . . D 10
Mar.   3–Mike Donovan, Canadagua, N.Y. . . . . D 10
Apr.   3–Charlie Hitte, Schenectady . . . . L 6
June 11–Charles Kemp, Springfield, O. . . . . KO 5
June 16–Mike Lansing, Rochester, N.Y. . . . . W 6
June 18–Russell Van Horne, Columbus. . . . . W 6
June 29–Billy Hurley, Schenectady . . . . ND 6
July   5–Jack Robinson, New York . . . . ND 6
Sept. 8–Bartley Connelly, Portland, Me. . . . . L 6
Nov. 17–Larry Temple, Boston . . . . KO by 10
Nov. 18–Jack Robinson, Easton, Pa. . . . . W 10

1909

May   10–Ed Smith, Columbus, O. . . . . ND 6
Sept. 6–Tom Sawyer, Portland, Me. . . . . ND 6
Dec.   3–Young Jack Johnson, Haverhill, Mass. . . . . . . D 6

1910

Mar.	7–Jimmy Potts, Minneapolis	D 10
Apr.	25–Bill McKinnon, Brockton, Mass..........	LF 6
May	13–Kyle Whitney, Brockton................	L 6

1911

Oct.	17–Bob Lee, Boston	KO 2
Nov.	2–Tom Sawyer, Lowell, Mass.	L 3
Nov.	13–Henry Hall, Eastport, Me.	ND 6

TB	KO	WD	WF	D	LD	LF	KO BY	ND	NC
150	34	45	2	30	17	3	4	15	0

Killed in automobile accident near Massillon, Ohio, October, 1935.

Elected to Boxing Hall of Fame 1955.

DIXIE KID
(Aaron L. Brown)
Born Dec. 23, 1883, Fulton, Mo. Weight, 145 lbs. Height 5 ft. 8 in.

1899

Knockouts: Tony Rivers, 1; Dan Ranger, 3: Clyde Burnham, 8. Draw: Kid Williams, 20; Billy Woods, 10.

1900

Knockouts: Mike McCure, 2; Tim Leonard, 1; Black Sharkey, 4; Bobby Dobbs, 4; Frank Dougherty, 2; Jack Dean, 10.

1901

Knockouts: Fresno Pete, 4; John Phillips, 2; Kid Ruggles, 6.

1902

Knockouts: Ben Hart, 4: Young McConnell, 4; Medal Dukelow, 1; Henry Lewis, 11; Guy Boros, 1; Medal Dukelow, 6. Won: Chas. Thurston, 20.

1903

Knockouts: Fred Mueller, 8; Soldier Green, 6; Eddie Cain, 2; Chas. Thurston, 1; Al Neil, 20; Mose La Fontise, 10.

1904

Apr.	30–Joe Walcott, San Francisco	WF 20
	(Won Welterweight Title)	
May	12–Joe Walcott, San Francisco	D 20
	(Title Bout)	
Sept.	21–Joe Grim, Saginaw...................	W 10

Oct.	3–Joe Grim, Mt. Clemens, Mich.	W 6
	(Dixie Kid outgrew class and gave up title)	
Nov.	12–Philadelphia Jack O'Brien Philadelphia.....	ND 6

Knockouts: Al Neil, 1; John Salomon, 11; Joe Mills, 9; John Dancer, 4; Chas. Thurston, 20; Young Peter Jackson, Draw, 15. No decisions: Dave Holly, 6; Larry Temple, 6; Dave Holly, 6.

1905

Jan.	2–Larry Temple, Baltimore................	D 15

Won: Joe Grim, 6, No decision: Geo. Cole, 6.

1908

Knockout: Fighting Ghost, 2. No decision: Cub White, 6; Fighting Ghost, 6; Geo. Cole, 6; Tommy Coleman, 6.

1909

Knockouts: Sailor Cunningham, 5; Bert Whirlwind, 3; Kid Williams, 4; Yg. Sam Langford, 1; Battling Johnson, 6; Sam Bolen, 6; Mike McDonough, 10; Al Grey, 8; Fighting Ghost 8, twice.

1910

Jan.	3–Chris Williams, Memphis	KO 3
Jan.	10–Sam Langford, Memphis.............	KO by 3
Jan.	26–Jack Ferrole, N.Y.C.	KO 9
Mar.	2–Jack Fitzgerald, N.Y.C.	ND 10
Mar.	14–Bill Hurley, Troy, N.Y.	KO 4
Mar.	15–Kyle Whitney, Boston	L 8
Mar.	21–Kid Henry, Troy, N.Y.	N.D. 8
Apr.	2–George Cole, N.Y.C.	KO 4
Apr.	5–Bill Hurley, Glen Falls, N.Y.C.	ND 10
May	5–Jimmy Clabby, N.Y.C.	ND 10
May	12–Fighting Kennedy, N.Y.C.	KO 8
July	16–Fighting Kennedy, N.Y.C.	ND 10
Aug.	1–Frank Mantell, N.Y.C.................	ND 10
Sept.	9–Willie Lewis, N.Y.C.	ND 10
Sept.	19–Fighting Dick Nelson, N.Y.C.............	ND 10
Aug.	19–Billy West, N.Y.C....................	KO 4
Oct.	2–Dennis Tighe, N.Y.C.	ND 10
Nov.	17–Willie Lewis, N.Y.C.	ND 10
Nov.	24–Frank Mantell, Waterbury	NC 5

1911

Jan.	17–Mike Twin Sullivan, Buffalo............	ND 10
Jan.	29–Joe Gaynor, N.Y.C.	KO 3
Feb.	10–Bob Moha, Buffalo..................	ND 10
Feb.	13–Kid Wilson, Harrison, N.J.	ND 10
Feb.	17–Bill Hurley, Glens Fls., N.Y.	W 8
Apr.	29–*Willie Lewis, Paris, France	L 20

May   20–Young Laughrey, Paris, Fr. . . . . WF 10
June 14–Fred Stuber, Reims, Fr. . . . . KO   3
July   3–Blink McCloskey, London . . . . LF   3
July 10–Harry Duncan, Dublin, Ire. . . . . ND   6
Aug. 29–Georges Carpentier, Tourville . . . . KO   5
Sept. 22–Seaman Brown, Plymouth, England . . . . KO   6
Nov.   9–Johnny Summers, Liverpool, England . . . . . . KO   2
*Referee's decision was reversed by jury of Parisian sportsmen in favor of Dixie.

1912

Jan. 18–Harry Lewis, Liverpool . . . . KO by 8
May   5–Dan Flynn, Glasgow, Scot. . . . . L 10
June   1–Jack Morris, London, England . . . . L 10
Oct.   4–Marcel Thomas, Paris, France . . . . L 15
Oct. 12–Johnny Mathieson, Birmingham, England . . . . L 20
Nov. 18–Johnny Mathieson, London . . . . D 10
Dec.   8–Bob Retson, London. . . . . KO   3
Dec. 20–Arthur Harman, London . . . . KO   9
Dec. 21–Arthur Evernden, Liverpool. . . . . KO   7

1913

Jan.   1–Arthur Harman, London . . . . KO   9
Jan.   2–Arthur Evernden, Liverpool. . . . . KO   9
Jan. 13–Johny Mathieson, Birmingham
Feb. 13–Jack Morris, Liverpool . . . . KO   4
Mar.   1–Seaman Hulls, Plymouth . . . . KO   3
Mar. 17–Louis Verger, London . . . . W 20
Mar. 26–Johnny Mathieson, Leicester, England . . . . . LF 12
Apr. 10–Jerry Thomson, Liverpool L   1
Sept. 22–Private Harris, London . . . . L 10
Oct. 11–Jack Goldswain, London . . . . KO   4
Oct. 27–Albert Scanlon, London . . . . W 20
Nov.   2–"Bat." Dick Nelson, London . . . . KO   5
Nov. 29–Demlen, Paris . . . . L 15
Dec.   –Dick Nelson, London . . . . W 20
Dec. 22–Fireman Anderson, London . . . . W 10

1914

Jan.   1–Bandsman Blake, London . . . . L 20
Jan. 12–Fireman Anderson, Birkenhead . . . . KO   2
Jan. 28–Con. Pluyette, Yarmouth . . . . W   4
Feb. 28–Tom Stokes, London . . . . W 10
Mar.   3–Fred Drummond, London . . . . KO   5
Mar.   9–Jim Rideout, Acton. . . . . KO   8
Mar. 16–Bill Bristowe, London . . . . L 20
Mar. 28–Dick Nelson, London . . . . L 20

Mar. 30–Bill Bristowe, London. . . . . KO   2
Dec.   7–Nicol Simpson, London . . . . L 20
Dec. 14–Dick Nelson, London . . . . W 20

TB	KO	WD	WF	D	LD	LF	KO BY	ND	NC
126	63	13	2	6	13	2	3	23	1

Died, October 3, 1935, Los Angeles, Calif.
Elected to Boxing Hall of Fame, 1975

JOE GANS

(Joseph Gaines)
(The Old Master)

Born, November 25, 1874, Baltimore, Md. Weight, 131-137 lbs. Height, 5 ft. 6¼ in. Managed by Al Herford.

1891-1894

–Dave Armstrong, Baltimore . . . . KO 12
–Arthur Coates, Baltimore . . . . KO 22
–Tommy Harden, Baltimore. . . . . KO   7
–George Evans, Baltimore . . . . KO   3
–Dave Armstrong, Baltimore . . . . KO   3
–Jack Daly, Pittsburgh . . . . KO 11
–Dave Horn, Baltimore. . . . . KO   2
–Bud Brown, Baltimore . . . . KO 10
–John Ball, Baltimore. . . . . KO   6
–Jack McDonald, Newark . . . . KO   7
–Dave Horn, Baltimore. . . . . KO 11
–Johnny Van Heest, Baltimore . . . . KO   9

1895

Feb.   6–Fred Sweigert, Baltimore . . . . W 10
Mar.   7–Sol English, Baltimore . . . . W 10
Mar. 16–Howard Wilson, Washington . . . . W 10
Apr.   2–Walter Edgerton, Baltimore. . . . . KO   7
Apr. 25–Walter Edgerton, Baltimore. . . . . KO   6
May   4–Frank Peabody, Baltimore . . . . KO   3
May   20–Benny Peterson, Baltimore . . . . KO 17
July 15–George Siddons, Baltimore . . . . D 20
Oct. 21–Joe Elliott, Baltimore . . . . KO   6
Nov. 18–Young Griffo, Baltimore . . . . D 10
Nov. 28–George Siddons, Baltimore . . . . KO   7

1896

Jan. 11–Benny Peterson, Philadelphia . . . . KO   3
Jan. 17–Joe Elliott, Baltimore, Md. . . . . KO   7
Jan. 28–Howard Wilson, Baltimore . . . . KO   8
Feb. 22–Jimmy Kennard, Boston . . . . KO   5
June   8–Jimmy Watson, Paterson . . . . KO   9

1896 (Cont'd.)

June	29–Tommy Butler, Brooklyn	W	12
Aug.	20–Jack Williams, Baltimore	KO	2
Aug.	31–Danny McBride, Baltimore	D	20
Sept.	28–Jack Ball, Philadelphia	W	4
Oct.	6–Dal Hawkins, New York	L	15
Oct.	19–Jack Williams, Baltimore	KO	2
Nov.	12–Jerry Marshall, Baltimore	W	20
Dec.	14–Charles Rochette, San Francisco	KO	12

1897

Apr.	3–Howard Wilson, New York	KO	9
May	19–Mike Leonard, San Francisco	W	10
Aug.	30–Isadore Strauss, Baltimore	KO	5
Sept.	21–Young Griffo, Philadelphia	D	15
Sept.	27–Bobby Dobbs, Brooklyn	L	20
Nov.	6–Jack Daly, Philadelphia	ND-W	6
Nov.	29–Stanton Abbott, Baltimore	KO	5

1898

Jan.	3–Billy Young, Baltimore	KO	2
Jan.	17–Frank Garrard, Cleveland	W	15
Mar.	11–Tom Shortell, Baltimore	ND-W	6
Apr.	11–Young Starlight, Baltimore	KO	3
Apr.	11–Young Smyrna, Baltimore	Exh.	4
May	11–Steve Crosby, Louisville	W	6
June	3–Kid Roberson, Chicago	W	6
Aug.	8–Billy Ernst, Coney Island	KO	11
Aug.	26–Young Smyrna, Baltimore	KO	15
Aug.	31–Tom Jackson, Easton	KO	3
Sept.	26–Herman Miller, Baltimore	KO	4
Nov.	4–Kid McPartland, New York	W	25
Dec.	27–Jack Daly, New York	W	25

1899

Jan.	13–Young Smyrna, Baltimore	KO	2
Jan.	28–Martin Judge, Toronto	W	20
Feb.	6–Billy Ernst, Buffalo	WF	10
Apr.	14–George McFadden, New York	KO by	23
July	24–Jack Dobbs, Ocean City	KO	4
July	28–George McFadden, New York	D	25
Sept.	1–Eugene Bezenah, New York	KO	10
Sept.	15–Martin Judge, Baltimore	W	12
Oct.	3–Spider Kelly, New York	W	25
Oct.	11–Martin Judge, Baltimore	W	20
Oct.	31–George McFadden, New York	W	25
Nov.	24–Steve Crosby, Chicago	W	6
Dec.	11–Kid Ashe, Cincinnati	W	15
Dec.	22–Kid McPartland, Chicago	D	6

1900

Feb.	9–Spike Sullivan, New York	KO	14
Mar.	23–Frank Erne, New York	KO by	12
	(For World Lightweight Title)		
Apr.	2–Chicago Jack Daly, Phila	KO	5
May	25–Dal Hawkins, New York	KO	2
June	26–Barney Furey, Cincinnati	KO	9
July	10–Young Griffo, New York	KO	8
July	12–Whitey Lester, Baltimore	KO	4
Aug.	31–Dal Hawkins, New York	KO	3
Sept.	7–George McFadden, Phila.	ND-D	6
Oct.	2–George McFadden, Denver	D	10
Oct.	6–Joe Young, Denver Colo.	W	10
Oct.	16–Otto Sieloff, Denver	KO	9
Oct.	19–Spider Kelly Denver	KO	8
Nov.	16–Kid Parker, Denver	KO	4
Dec.	13–Terry McGovern, Chicago	KO by	2

1901

Feb.	15–Jack Daly, Baltimore, Md.	WF	6
Apr.	1–Martin Flaherty, Baltimore	KO	4
May	31–Bobby Dobbs, Baltimore	KO	7
July	15–Harry Berger, Baltimore	ND-W	6
July	15–Jack Donahue, Baltimore	KO	2
July	15–Kid Thomas, Baltimore	ND-D	6
Aug.	23–Steve Crosby, Louisville	D	20
Sept.	20–Steve Crosby, Baltimore	W	12
Sept.	30–Joe Handler, Trenton	KO	1
Oct.	4–Dan McConnell, Baltimore	KO	3
Nov.	15–Jack Hanlon, Baltimore	KO	2
Nov.	22–Billy Moore, Baltimore	KO	3
Dec.	13–Bobby Dobbs, Baltimore	KO	14
Dec.	30–Joe Youngs, Philadelphia	KO	4

1902

Jan.	3–Tom Broderick, Baltimore	KO	6
Jan.	6–Eddie Connolly, Philadelphia	KO	5
Feb.	17–George McFadden, Philadelphia	ND-W	6
Mar.	7–Jack Ryan, Allentown, Pa.	KO	3
Mar.	27–Jack Bennett, Baltimore, Md.	KO	5
May	12–Frank Erne, Fort Erie, Ontario	KO	1
	(Won World Lightweight Title)		
June	27–George McFadden, San Francisco	KO	3
	(Retained World Lightweight Title)		
July	24–Ruge Turner, Oakland, Calif.	KO	15
	(Retained World Lightweight Title)		
Sept.	17–Gus Gardner, Baltimore, Md.	KO	5
	(Retained World Lightweight Title)		

Sept. 22–Jack Bennett, Philadelphia . . . . KO 2
Oct. 13–Kid McPartland, Fort Erie . . . . KO 5
    (Retained World Lightweight Title)
Oct. 14–Dave Holly, Lancaster, Pa. . . . . ND-W 10
Nov. 14–Charley Seiger, Baltimore . . . . KO 14
Dec. 19–Howard Wilson, Providence. . . . . KO 3
Dec. 31–Charley Seiger, Boston . . . . W 10

1903

Jan. 1–Gud Gardner, New Britain . . . . WF 11
    (Retained World Lightweight Title)
Mar. 11–Steve Crosby, Hot Springs. . . . . KO 11
    (Retained World Lightweight Title)
Mar. 23–Jack Bennett, Allegheny . . . . KO 5
May 13–Tom Tracy, Portland, Ore. . . . . KO 9
May 29–Willie Fitzgerald, San Fran. . . . . KO 10
    (Retained World Lightweight Title)
July 4–Buddy King, Butte, Montana . . . . KO 4
    (Retained World Lightweight Title)
Oct. 19–Joe Grim, Philadelphia . . . . ND-W 6
Oct. 20–Ed Kennedy, Philadelphia . . . . ND-W 6
Oct. 23–Dave Holly, Philadelphia. . . . . ND-L 6
Nov. 2–Jack Blackburn, Philadelphia . . . . ND-D 6
Dec. 7–Dave Holly, Philadelphia. . . . . ND-W 6
Dec. 8–San Langford, Boston, Mass. . . . . L 15

1904

Jan. 12–Willie Fitzgerald, Detroit . . . . W 10
Jan. 19–Clarence Connors, Mt. Clemens . . . . KO 2
Jan. 22–Joe Grim, Baltimore, Md. . . . . W 10
Feb. 2–Mike Ward, Detroit, Mich. . . . . W 10
Mar. 25–Jack Blackburn, Baltimore . . . . W 15
Mar. 28–Gus Gardner, Saginaw . . . . W 10
Apr. 21–Sam Bolen, Baltimore . . . . W 15
May 27–Jewey Cooks, Baltimore . . . . KO 8
June 3–Kid Griffo, Baltimore . . . . KO 7
June 13–Sammy Smith, Philadelphia . . . . KO 4
June 27–Dave Holly, Philadelphia . . . . ND-D 6
Sept. 30–Joe Walcott, San Francisco . . . . D 20
Oct. 31–Jimmy Britt, San Francisco . . . . WF 5
    (Retained World Lightweight Title)
Nov. –Relinquished World Lightweight Title.

1905

Mar. 27–Rufe Turner, Philadelphia . . . . ND-W 6
Sept. 16–Mike (Twin) Sullivan, Baltimore. . . . . D 15

1906

Jan. 19–Mike (Twin) Sullivan, San Fran. . . . . KO 15
    (Won Vacant World Welterweight Title)
Mar. 17–Mike (Twin) Sullivan, Los Angeles . . . . KO 10
May 18–Willie Lewis, New York . . . . ND-W 6
June 15–Harry Lewis, Philadelphia . . . . ND-W 6
June 29–Jack Blackburn, Philadelphia . . . . ND-D 6
July 23–Dave Holly, Seattle, Wash. . . . . W 20
Sept. 3–Battling Nelson, Goldfield . . . . WF 42
    (Regained World Lightweight Title)

1907

Jan. 1–Kid Herman, Tonopah, Nev. . . . . KO 8
    (Retained World Lightweight Title)
Sept. 9–Jimmy Britt, San Francisco . . . . KO 6
    (Retained World Lightweight Title)
Sept. 27–George Memsic, Los Angeles . . . . W 20
    (Retained World Lightweight Title)

1908

Jan. 3–Bart Blackburn, Baltimore. . . . . KO 3
Apr. 1–Spike Robson, Philadelphia . . . . KO 3
May 14–Rudy Unholz, San Francisco . . . . KO 11
    (Retained World Lightweight Title)
July 4–Battling Nelson, Colma. . . . . KO by 17
    (Lost World Lightweight Title)
Sept. 9–Battling Nelson, Colma. . . . . KO by 21
    (For World Lightweight Title)

1909

Mar. 12–Jabez White, New York . . . . ND-W 10

TB	KO	WD	WF	D	LD	LF	KO BY	ND	NC
156	85	42	5	15	4	0	5	0	0

Died, August 10, 1910, Baltimore, MD.
Elected to Boxing Hall of Fame, 1954.

GEORGE DIXON

(Little Chocolate)

Born, July 29, 1870, Halifax, Nova Scotia, Canada. Weight, 105-122 lbs. Height, 5 ft. 3½ in. managed by Tom O'Rourke.

1886

Nov. 1–Young Johnson, Halifax. . . . . KO 3

1887

Sept. 21–Elias Hamilton, Boston. . . . . W 8
    –Young Mack, Boston . . . . KO 3

1888

Jan.	2 – Jack Lyman, Boston	KO	5
Jan.	20 – Charley Parton, Boston	KO	6
Feb.	17 – Barney Finnegan, Boston	KO	7
Mar.	10 – Ned Morris, Boston	KO	3
Mar.	21 – Paddy Kelly, Boston	D	15
Apr.	27 – Tommy Doherty, Boston	D	8
May	10 – Tommy Kelly, Boston	NC	9
June	13 – Jimmy Brackett, Boston	KO	5
June	21 – Hank Brennen, Boston	NC	14
Dec.	14 – Hank Brennan, Boston	NC	9
Dec.	28 – Hank Brennan, Boston	D	15

1889

Jan.	27 – Paddy Kelly, Boston	W	10
	– Frank Maguire, Putnam, Conn.	D	10
May	– Billy James, Haverhill, Mass.	KO	3
Oct.	14 – Hank Brennan, Boston	NC	26
Dec.	11 – Mike Sullvan, New Bedford	W	6
Dec.	27 – Eugene Hornbacher, New York	KO	2

1890

Jan.	7 – Joe Murphy, Providence	Exh.	4
Feb.	7 – Cal McCarthy, Boston	NC	70
	(For American Bantamweight Title)		
Mar.	1 – Paddy Kearney, Paterson	Exh.	4
Mar.	3 – Joe Farrell, Jersey City	Exh. KO	2
Mar.	5 – Jack Carey, Hoboken	Exh. KO	3
Mar.	31 – Matt McCarthy, Philadelphia	Exh. KO	3
May	3 – Sailed for England on the *Catalonia*.		
May	12 – Arrived in Liverpool.		
June	27 – Nunc Wallace, London	KO	18
Oct.	23 – Johnny Murphy, Providence	KO	40
Nov.	5 – J. Allan, Baltimore	Exh. KO	2
Nov.	7 – Virginia Rosebud, Baltimore	Exh. KO	3
Nov.	11 – Lee Andrews, Washington	Exh. KO	4
Nov.	13 – W. Dyson, Washington, D.C.	Exh. KO	2
Dec.	3 – Nick Collins, New York	Exh.	4

1891

Mar.	31 – Cal McCarthy, Troy, New York	KO	22
	(Won American Bantamweight Title)		
Apr.	20 – Martin Flaherty, Chicago	W	6
May	19 – Bobby Burns, Providence	Exh.	4
July	28 – Abe Willis, San Francisco	KO	5
Sept	26 – Jimmy Hagen, Philadelphia	Exh.	4
Sept.	28 – Marcellus Baker, Montreal	Exh.	3
Oct.	1 – Dan Coakley, Montreal	Exh.	3

Oct.	2 – Jack Fitzpatrick, Montreal	Exh.	4
Nov.	3 – Eugene Hornbacher, New York	Exh.	4
Nov.	5 – Nick Collins, New York	Exh.	4
Nov.	6 – Frank Wall, New York	Exh. KO	2
Nov.	12 – Billy Ross	Exh.	4
Dec.	17 – Lee Damro, Washington, D.C.	Exh.	4

1892

Jan.	– Tom Warren, Philadelphia	Exh. KO	3
Jan.	11 – Elwood McCloskey, Philadelphia	Exh.	4
Jan.	16 – Young, Philadelphia	Exh.	4
Feb.	4 – Watson, Paterson	Exh. KO	1
May	6 – Billy Russell, New York	Exh. KO	2
June	27 – Fred Johnson, Coney Island	KO	14
	(Won Vacant World Featherweight Title)		
Sept.	6 – Jack Skelley, New Orleans	KO	8
	(Retained World Featherweight Title)		
Oct.	29 – Walter Edgerton, Philadelphia	D	4
Nov.	11 – Walter Edgerton, Philadelphia	D	4

1893

Jan.	25 – Eddie Eckhardt, Brooklyn	Exh.	4
Mar.	20 – George Siddons, Coney Island	D	12
Mar.	22 – Eddie Boerum, New York	Exh. KO	4
Apr.	16 – Mike Gillespie, Cincinnati	Exh.	4
Apr.	28 – Bill Young, Washington, D.C.	Exh.	4
June	17 – Jerry Barnett, New York	Exh.	4
June	30 – Walter Edgerton, Philadelphia	W	4
Aug.	7 – Eddie Pierce, Coney Island	KO	3
	(Retained World Featherweight Title)		
Aug.	22 – Billy Plimmer, New York	L	4
Sept.	25 – Solly Smith, Coney Island	KO	7
	(Retained World Featherweight Title)		
Nov.	16 – Jack Downey, New York	Exh. KO	2
Nov.	21 – P.J. Hennessy, Lawrence	Exh. KO	2
Dec.	15 – Billy Murphy, Paterson	Exh.	3

1894

Jan.	4 – Robert Heeny, Huntington	Exh. KO	2
Jan.	16 – Paddy Lemmons, Cleveland	Exh. KO	1
Mar.	4 – Ed Doyle, New York	Exh. KO	1
Mar.	22 – Walter Edgerton, Philadelphia	Exh.	3
June	29 – Young Griffo, Boston	D	20
Oct.	25 – Joe Flynn, Wilmington, Del.	Exh.	4

1895

Jan.	19 – Young Griffo, Coney Island	D	25
Jan.	28 – Walter Sanford, Dayton	Exh. KO	2

Mar. 6–John Conroy, New York . . . . Exh. KO 2
Mar. 7–Sam Bolen, New York . . . . Exh. 6
May 8–C. Slusher, Louisville . . . . Exh. 4
May –Charlestown, St. Louis . . . . Exh. KO 2
May –Frede, St. Louis . . . . Exh. KO 2
July 31–Tommy Connelly, Boston . . . . KO 4
Aug. 27–Johnny Griffin, Boston . . . . W 25
(Retained World Featherweight Title)
Oct. 28–Young Griffo, New York . . . . D 10
Dec. 5–Frank Erne, New York . . . . D 10

1896

Jan. 30–Pedlar Palmer, New York . . . . D 6
Mar. 17–Jerry Marshall, Boston . . . . KO 7
June 16–Martin Flaherty, Boston . . . . D 20
Sept. 25–Tommy White, New York . . . . D 20
Nov. 27–Frank Erne, New York . . . . L 20

1897

Jan. 22–Billy Murphy, New York . . . . KO 6
Feb. 15–Jack Downey, New York . . . . D 20
Mar. 24–Frank Erne, New York . . . . W 25
Apr. 26–Johnny Griffin, New York . . . . W 20
June 21–Walter Edgerton, Philadelphia . . . . ND 6
July 23–Dal Hawkins, San Francisco . . . . D 20
Oct. 4–Solly Smith, San Francisco . . . . L 20
(Lost World Featherweight Title)

1898

Mar. 31–Tommy White, Syracuse . . . . D 20
June 6–Eddie Santry, New York . . . . W 20
(Advertised for World Featherweight Title)
July 1–Ben Jordan, New York . . . . L 25
(Advertised for World Featherweight Title)
(Jordan won recognition as champion in Great Britain.)
Aug. 29–Jimmy Dunn, Fall River, Mass. . . . . ND- 6
Sept. 5–Joe Bernstein, Philadelphia . . . . ND- 6
Nov. 11–Dave Sullivan, New York . . . . W disq. 10
(Regained World Featherweight Title)
Nov. 29–Oscar Gardner, New York . . . . W 25
(Retained World Featherweight Title)

1899

Jan. 17–Young Pluto, New York . . . . KO 10
(Retained World Featherweight Title)
May 15–Kid Broad, Buffalo . . . . W 20
(Retained World Featherweight Title)

June 2–Joe Bernstein, New York . . . . W 25
(Retained World Featherweight Title)
July 3–Sam Bolen, Louisville . . . . KO 3
July 11–Tommy White, Denver . . . . W 20
(Retained World Featherweight Title)
July 14–Eddie Santry, Chicago . . . . W 6
Aug. 11–Eddie Santry, New York . . . . D 20
(Retained World Featherweight Title)
Oct. 13–Tim Callahan, Philadelphia . . . . ND- 6
Nov. 2–Will Curley, New York . . . . W 25
(Retained World Featherweight Title)
Nov. 21–Eddie Lenny, New York . . . . W 25
(Retained World Featherweight Title)

1900

Jan. 9–Terry McGovern, New York . . . . KO by 8
(Lost World Featherweight Title)
Feb. 21–Terry McGovern, New York . . . . Exh. 3
June 4–Tim Callahan, Philadelphia . . . . ND- 6
June 12–Benny Yanger, Chicago . . . . D 6
June 23–Terry McGovern, Chicago . . . . L 6
July 31–Tommy Sullivan, Coney Island . . . . KO by 7

1901

Feb. 8–Harry Lyons, Baltimore . . . . D 20
Aug. 16–Young Corbett, Denver . . . . L 10
Aug. 24–Abe Attell, Denver . . . . D 10
Sept. 26–Benny Yanger, St. Louis . . . . L 15
Oct. 20–Abe Attell, Cripple Creek . . . . D 20
Oct. 28–Abe Attell, St. Louis . . . . L 15
Dec. 19–Austin Rice, New London . . . . L 20

1902

Jan 17–Joe Tipman, Baltimore . . . . D 20
Jan. 24–Eddie Lenny, Baltimore . . . . KO by 9
Feb. 13–Chic Tucker, New Britain . . . . W 20
May 16–Billy Ryan, Ottawa . . . . D 15
May 27–Dan Dougherty, Philadelphia . . . . ND- 6
June 6–Eddie Lenny, Chester, Pa. . . . . D 6
June 10–Biz Mackey, Findlay, Ohio . . . . KO by 5
June 30–Tim Callahan, Philadelphia . . . . ND- 6
Sept. 8–Pedlar Palmer, Glasgow . . . . L 15
Sept. 29–Will Curley, Gateshead . . . . D 15

1903

Jan. 24–Jem Driscoll, London . . . . D 6
–Dave Wallace, Birmingham . . . . D 6

1903 (Cont'd.)

Mar.	7–Fred Delaney, Woolwich	L 6
Apr.	6–Jack Pearson, Liverpool	KO 8
Apr.	16–George Phalin, Liverpool	D 15
Apr.	25–Spike Robson, Newcastle	L 20
May	2–Ben Jordan, London	L 6
May	–Harry Paul	D 6
May	16–Spike Robson, Newcastle	L 20
May	25–George Phalin, Birmingham	D 15
June	27–Pedlar Palmer, London	L 8
Aug.	1–Digger Stanley, London	W 6
Aug.	29–Harry Ware, London	W 6
Sept.	13–Charlie Lampey, London	D 6
Sept.	24–Billy Barrett, Liverpool	D 10
Sept.	29–Charlie Lampey, London	D 6
Oct.	10–Jim Williams, London	KO 4
Oct.	12–Digger Stanley, London	L 6
Nov.	7–Harry Slough, West Hartlepool	Exh. 3
Nov.	9–Pedlar Palmer, Newcastle	W 20
Dec.	7–Cockney Cohen, Newcastle	W 15
Dec.	20–Dai Morgan, Newcastle	D 15

1904

Jan.	16–Cockney Cohen, Newcastle	W 20

Feb.	23–Harry Mansfield, Newcastle	D 20
Mar.	7–Cockney Cohen, Leeds	L 15
Mar.	19–Spike Robson, Newcastle	KO 11
Apr.	7–Billy Barrett, London	KO 12
Apr.	9–George Moore, London	D 6
Apr.	21–Tommy Burns, Liverpool	L 20
Aug.	22–Charlie Arrowsmith, New Brighton	Exh. 3
Oct.	17–Owen Moran, London	L 6
Nov.	24–Boss Edwards, London	D 15

1905

Jan.	6–Johnny Hughes, Ashford	D 8
Apr.	6–Jack Foy, London	D 15
Sept.	20–Tommy Murphy, Philadelphia	KO by 2
Dec.	28–Frankie Howe, New York	Exh. 3

1906

Jan.	4–Harry Shea, New York	KO 3
May	21–Billy Ryan, Gloucester	D 12
Dec.	10–Monk the Newsboy, Providence	L 15

TB	KO	WD	WF	D	LD	LF	KO BY	ND	NC
130	27	22	1	42	20	1	5	7	5

Died, January 6, 1909, New York City, N.Y.
Elected to Boxing Hall of Fame, 1956.

MOLINEAUX AND RICHMOND BOXING RECORDS

Thomas Molineaux 5'8", 185 lbs.
Born: Georgetown, D.C., 1784. Died:
Galway, Ireland, Aug. 4, 1818.

1810	July 14	Defeated Tom Blake	8 rounds
	Dec. 10	Lost to Tom Cribb	33 rounds
1811	May 21	Defeated Jim Rimmer	21 rounds
	Sept. 28	Lost to Tom Cribb	11 rounds
1813	April 2	Defeated Jack Carter	25 rounds
1814	May 27	Defeated Bill Fuller	2 rounds
1815	March 10	Lost to George Cooper	14 rounds

Bill Richmond 5'9", 175 lbs.
Born: Richmond, Staten Island, New York Aug. 5, 1793.
Died: London, Dec. 28, 1829.

1805	May 11	Defeated Youssep	6 rounds
	July 8	Defeated Jack Holmes	26 rounds
	Oct. 8	Lost to Tom Cribb	1 hr. 30 minutes
1809	April 11	Defeated Isaac Wood	23 rounds
	April 14	Defeated Jack Carter	25 minutes
	Aug. 9	Defeated George Maddox	52 minutes
1810	May 1	Defeated Young Powers	15 minutes
1814	April 7	Defeated Jack Davis	13 rounds
1815	Aug. 11	Defeated Tom Shelton	23 rounds

HORSE RACING

AFRICAN-AMERICAN JOCKEYS

Alonzo Allen	Dow Allen	"Spider" Anderson	Dan Austin
Joe Barnes	Shelby Barnes	Wayne Bennett	L. Blackburn
Tom Blevins	C. Bonner	J. Booker	Harry Boyce
Breckenridge	Thomas Britton	Al Brown	Edward D. Brown
T. Burns	Burrell	"Caesar"	Felix Carr
Jimmy Carter	M. Carter	"Cato"	Willie Chambers
Jerry Chorn	John Clay	Pete Clay	Alonzo Clayton
Rob Clayton	Willie Coburn	Raleigh Colston	Jesse Conley
H. Crowhurst	Clarence Dishman	W. Dodrich	T. Drake
Louis Durrousseau	Fisher	Leon J. Goines	Halloway
Andrew Hamilton	Abe Hawkins	Erskine Henderson	"Henry"
Noah Heywood	J. Hicks	Willie Hicks	G. Hightower
J. Houston	J. Huggins	Babe Hurd	Mitchell Hurd
Bob Isom	J. Jackson	"Jesse"	"Crescendo" John
Sam Johnson	Dick Jones	George Jones	Linc Jones
M. Jones	Monroe Kelso	Jimmy Knight	Tommy Knight
Jimmy Lee	George Lewis	Isaac Lewis	Oliver Lewis
James Long	Charley Macklin	Masterson	Willie Martin
Bob McCurdy	Emanuel Morris	G. Morris	Mike Mountjoy
Isaac Murphy	Q. Murphy	F. Nelson	Ben Oliver
Henry Overton	"Monk" Overton	Albert Peale	Willie Penn
Frank Perkins	James Perkins	L. Porter	Henry Ray
Clarence Reed	Hosea Richardson	Jim Ross	John Sample
"Scipio"	Willie Simms	Monkey Simon	James Simpson
Ralph Simpson	Robert Simpson	Stevenson	Coley Stone
John Stoval	Stradford	William Tally	Edward Taylor
Albert Thompson	J. Thompson	Louis Thompson	Tom Thompson
Billy Walker	George Weathers	Eddie West	Atkin Williams
Howard Williams	Leroy Williams	Robert Williams	William Williams
Jimmy Winkfield			

ISAAC MURPHY'S RECORD

Year	Race	Aboard	Year	Race	Aboard
1879	Travers Stakes	Falsetto		Latonia Cup	Harry Gilmore
	Kenner Stakes	Falsetto		Kentucky Oaks	Modesty
	Clark Handicap	Falsetto	1885	Alabama Stakes	Ida Hope
1881	Saratoga Cup	Checkmate		American Derby	Volante
1883	Latonia Cup	Leonatus		Clark Handicap	Bersan
1884	Clark Handicap	Buchanon	1886	American Derby	Silver Cloud
	American Derby	Modesty		Clipsetta Stakes	Jennie T.
	Kentucky Derby	Buchanon		Latonia Derby	Silver Cloud
	Latonia Derby	Bersan		Saratoga Cup	Volante

Year	Race	Aboard
1887	First Special	Volante
	Hyde Park Stakes	Emperor of Norfolk
	Latonia Derby	Libretto
	St. Louis Derby	Terra Cotta
1888	Dwyer Stakes	Emperor of Norfolk
	First Special	Kingston
	Kenner Stakes	Los Angeles
	Swift Stakes	Emperor of Norfolk
	Second Special	Kingston
1889	Alabama Stakes	Princess Bowling
	First Special	Kingston
1890	Clark Handicap	Riley
	Kentucky Derby	Riley
	Tidal Stakes	Burlington
	Suburban Handicap	Salvator
1891	Kentucky Derby	Kingman
	Latonia Derby	Kingman
1892	Gazelle Stakes	Yorkville Belle
	Ladies' Handicap	Yorkville Belle

WILLIE SIMM'S RECORD

Year	Race	Aboard
1891	Spinaway Stakes	Promenade
1892	Flatbush Stakes	Lady Violet
	Second Special	Lamplighter
	Tidal Stakes	Charade
	First Special	Lamplighter
1893	Belmont Stakes	Comanche
	Gazelle Stakes	Naptha
	Ladies' Handicap	Naptha
	Lawrence Realization	Daily America
1894	Belmont Stakes	Henry of Navarre
	Dwyer Stakes	Dobbins
	First Special	Banquet
	Juvenile Stakes	Prince of Monaco
	Lawrence Realization	Dobbins
	Second Special	Clifford
	Swift Stakes	Discount
	Tidal Stakes	Dobbins
1895	Champagne Stakes	Ben Brush
	Jerome Handicap	Counter Tenor
	Second Special	Clifford
1896	Clark Handicap	Ben Eder
	Kentucky Derby	Ben Brush

Year	Race	Aboard
	Latonia Derby	Ben Brush
	Wither Stakes	Handspring
1897	Brighton Handicap	Ben Brush
	First Special	Ben Brush
	Tidal Stakes	Buddha
	Tremont Stakes	Handball
	Suburban Handicap	Ben Brush
	Second Special	Ben Brush
	Wither Stakes	Octagon
1898	Brighton Handicap	Ornament
	Kentucky Derby	Plaudit
	Toboggan Handicap	Octagon
1901	Annual Champion Stakes	Maid of Harlem

JIMMY WINKFIELD'S RECORD

Year	Race	Aboard
1900	Great Western Handicap	Jolly Roger
1901	Clark Handicap	His Eminence
	Kentucky Derby	His Eminence
	Latonia Derby	Hernando
	Tennessee Derby	Royal Victor
1902	Bashford Manor Stakes	Von Rouse
	Crescent City Derby	Lord Quex
	Kentucky Derby	Alan-a-Dale
1903	Tennessee Oaks	Olefant

JIMMY LEE'S RECORD

Year	Race	Aboard
1907	Clipsetta Stakes	Grand Dame
	Latonia Oaks	Lillie Turner
	Kentucky Oaks	Wing Ting
	Latonia Derby	The Abbott
1908	Sheepshead-Double	Sir Martin
	Grand American Stakes	Sir Martin
	Grand Trial Stakes	Sir Martin
	National Stallion Stakes	Sir Martin
	Travers Stakes	Dorante
1909	California Derby	High Private

KEY RACES STAKES
WON BY AFRICAN-AMERICAN JOCKEYS

Year	Jockey	Horse
Alabama Stakes (originated Saratoga, 1872)		
1882	John Stoval	Belle of Runnymmede
1885	Issac Murphy	Ida Hope
1887	Ed West	Grisette
1889	Isaac Murphy	Princess Bowling
1890	Pike Barnes	Sinaloa
1891	Spider Anderson	Sallie McClelland
1892	Alonza Clayton	Ignite

Year	Jockey	Horse
American Derby (originated Washington Park, 1884)		
1884	Issac Murphy	Modesty
1885	Isaac Murphy	Volante
1886	Isaac Murphy	Silver Cloud
1887	Anthony Hamilton	C.H. Todd
1892	Tiny Anderson	Carlsbad

Year	Jockey	Horse
Annual Champion Stakes (originated at Sheepshead Bay, 1900)		
1901	Willie Simms	Maid of Harlem
1902	Jimmy Winkfield	Von Rouse
1918	R. Simpson	Billy Kelly

Year	Jockey	Horse
Belmont Stakes (originated Jerome Park, 1867)		
1890	Pike Barnes	Burlington
1893	Willie Simms	Comanche
1894	Willie Simms	Henry of Navarre

Year	Jockey	Horse
Brighton Handicap (originated Brighton Beach, 1896)		
1897	Willie Simms	Ben Brush
1898	Willie Simms	Ornament

Year	Jockey	Horse
Brooklyn Handicap (originated Gravesend, 1897)		
1889	Anthony Hamilton	Exile
1891	Pike Barnes	Tenny
1895	Anthony Hamilton	Hornpipe

Year	Jockey	Horse
Burns Handicap (originated Oakland, Cal., 1894)		
1894	Jerry Chorn	Lissak
1895	Felix Carr	Hawthorne

Year	Jockey	Horse
California Handicap (originated Oakland, Cal., 1897)		
1898	Alonzo Clayton	Traverser
1909	Jimmy Lee	High Private

Year	Jockey	Horse
Champagne Stakes (originated Jerome Park, 1867)		
1889	Pike Barnes	June Day
1891	Alonzo Clayton	Azra
1895	Willie Simms	Ben Brush
1903	Willie Hicks	Stalwart

Year	Jockey	Horse
Chicago Derby (originated Hawthorne, Ill., 1890)		
1890	Monk Overton	Prince Fonso
1892	Monk Overton	Lew Weir

Year	Jockey	Horse
Christmas Handicap (originated Jefferson Park, 1919)		
1920	H. King	Eddie Rickenbacker

Year	Jockey	Horse
Cincinnati Trophy (originated Latonia, Ky., 1902)		
1903	Tommy Knight	Paris
1909	Dale Austin	The Fad

Year	Jockey	Horse
Clark Handicap (originated Churchill Downs, 1875)		
1879	Isaac Murphy	Falsetto
1883	John Stoval	Ascender
1884	Isaac Murphy	Buchanon
1885	Isaac Murphy	Bersan
1887	Line Jones	Jim Gore
1890	Isaac Murphy	Riley
1891	Monk Overton	High Tariff
1892	Alonzo Clayton	Azra
1895	James Perkins	Halma
1896	Willie Simms	Ben Eder
1897	Alonzo Clayton	Ornament
1898	Tiny Williams	Plaudit
1901	Jimmy Winkfield	His Eminence

Year	Jockey	Horse
Clipsetta Stakes (originated Latonia, Ky., 1883)		
1883	John Stoval	Eva S.
1886	Isaac Murphy	Jennie T.
1888	Pike Barnes	Kee-Vee-Na
1889	John Stoval	Flyaway
1891	Monk Overton	Ignite
1892	Tom Britton	Issie O.
1894	Monk Overton	Kitty Olive
1895	Tiny Williams	Myrtle Harkness
1903	Tiny Williams	Stumpy
1906	Dale Austin	La Velta
1907	Jimmy Lee	Grand Dame

Year	Jockey	Horse
Crescent City Derby (originated New Orleans, 1898)		
1902	Jimmy Winkfield	Lord Quex

Year	Jockey	Horse

Dixie Handicap (originated Pimlico, Md., 1870)

Year	Jockey	Horse
1877	Billy Walker	King Fargo
1884	John Stoval	Loftin

Double Event—First Part
(originated Sheepshead Bay, N.Y., 1889)

Year	Jockey	Horse
1889	Spider Anderson	Torso
1896	Alonzo Clayton	Ornament

Double Event—Second Part
(originated Aqueduct, N.Y., 1887)

Year	Jockey	Horse
1908	Jimmy Lee	Sir Martin

Dwyer Stakes (originated Aqueduct, N.Y., 1887)

Year	Jockey	Horse
1888	Isaac Murphy	Emperor of Norfolk
1890	Pike Barnes	Burlington
1894	Willie Simms	Dobbins

Eclipse Stakes (originated Morris Park, 1889)

Year	Jockey	Horse
1890	Spider Anderson	Sallie McClelland

First Special (originated Gravesend, 1886)

Year	Jockey	Horse
1887	Isaac Murphy	— Volante
1888	Isaac Murphy	Kingston
1889	Isaac Murphy	Kingston
1891	Pike Barnes	Tenny
1892	Willie Simms	Lamplighter
1894	Willie Simms	Banquet
1897	Willie Simms	Ben Brush
1899	Pete Clay	Imp

Flash Stakes (originated Saratoga, 1869)

Year	Jockey	Horse
1888	Pike Barnes	Princess Bowling
1889	Don Allen	Protection
1895	Alonzo Clayton	Onaretto
1903	Willie Hicks	Tippacanoe
1918	R. Simpson	Billy Kelly

Flatbush Stakes (originated Sheepshead Bay, N.Y., 1884)

Year	Jockey	Horse
1885	Tiny Williams	Charity
1888	Pike Barnes	Salvator
1889	Anthony Hamilton	Torso
1890	Anthony Hamilton	Potomac
1892	Willie Simms	Lady Violet
1896	Alonzo Clayton	Ornament

Futurity Stakes (originated Sheepshead Bay, N.Y., 1888)

Year	Jockey	Horse
1888	Pike Barnes	Proctor Knott
1890	Anthony Hamilton	Potomac

Gazelle Stakes (originated Gravesend, 1887)

Year	Jockey	Horse
1887	Anthony Hamilton	Firenze
1890	Anthony Hamilton	Amazon
1892	Isaac Murphy	Yorkville Belle
1893	Willie Simms	Naptha

Great American Stakes (originated Aqueduct, 1889)

Year	Jockey	Horse
1908	Jimmy Lee	Sir Martin

Grand Trial Stakes (originated Sheepshead Bay, 1891)

Year	Jockey	Horse
1892	Anthony Hamilton	Chiswick
1908	Jimmy Lee	Sir Martin

Great Western Handicap
(originated Washington Park, 1884)

Year	Jockey	Horse
1884	George Withers	Boatman
1886	Ed West	Jim Guest
1888	Isaac Lewis	Montrose
1889	Pike Barnes	Elyton
1891	Tony Williams	Verge d'Or
1894	Alonzo Clayton	Sabin
1900	Jimmy Winkfield	Jolly Roger
1902	Tommy Knight	Six Shooter

Hyde Park Stakes (originated Washington Park, 1884)

Year	Jockey	Horse
1887	Isaac Murphy	Emperor of Norfolk
1888	Pike Barnes	Caliente
1891	Isaac Lewis	Curt Gunn
1901	Tommy Knight	Sir Oliver
1902	Tommy Knight	Dick Welles

Jerome Handicap (originated Jerome Park, 1866)

Year	Jockey	Horse
1866	Abe Hawkins	Watson
1889	Isaac Murphy	Longstreet
1891	Alonzo Clayton	Picknicker
1895	Willie Simms	Counter Tenor

Juvenile Stakes (originated Jerome Park, 1874)

Year	Jockey	Horse
1890	Anthony Hamilton	St. Charles
1894	Willie Simms	Prince of Monaco
1898	Willie Simms	Glenheim

Year	Jockey	Horse
Kenner Stakes (originated Saratoga, 1870)		
1870	Raleigh Colston	Enquirer
1879	Isaac Murphy	Falsetto
1882	Billy Walker	Boatman
1884	John Stovall	Powhatan III
1885	Ed West	Isish Pat
1887	Tiny Williams	Swarthmore
1888	Isaac Murphy	Los Angeles
1889	Pike Barnes	Long Dance
1891	Tiny Williams	Valera
Kentucky Derby (originated Churchill Downs, 1875)		
1875	Oliver Lewis	Aristides
1877	Billy Walker	Baden-Baden
1880	George Lewis	Fonso
1882	Babe Hurd	Apollo
1884	Isaac Murphy	Buchanon
1885	Erskine Henderson	Joe Cotton
1887	Isaac Lewis	Montrose
1890	Isaac Murphy	Riley
1891	Isaac Murphy	Kingman
1892	Alonzo Clayton	Azra
1895	James Perkins	Halma
1896	Willie Simms	Ben Brush
1898	Willie Simms	Plaudit
1901	Jimmy Winkfield	His Eminence
1902	Jimmy Winkfield	Alan-a-Dale
Kentucky Oaks (originated Churchill Downs, 1875)		
1882	John Stoval	Katie Creel
1883	John Stoval	Vera
1884	Isaac Murphy	Modesty
1889	John Stoval	Jewel Ben
1891	Tom Britton	Miss Hawkins
1892	Harry Ray	Miss Dixie
1894	Alonzo Clayton	Selika
1895	Alonzo Clayton	Voladora
1900	Monk Overton	Etta
1905	Dale Austin	Janetta
1907	Jimmy Lee	Wing Ting
Ladies' Handicap (originated Jerome Park, 1868)		
1890	Pike Barnes	Sinaloa II
1892	Isaac Murphy	Yorkville Belle
1893	Willie Simms	Naptha

Year	Jockey	Horse
Latonia Cup (originated Latonia, Ky., 1884)		
1884	Isaac Murphy	Harry Gilmore
1885	George Withers	Bob Miles
1887	John Stoval	Fosteral
Latonia Derby (originated Latonia, Ky., 1883)		
1883	Isaac Murphy	Leonatus
1884	Isaac Murphy	Bersan
1886	Isaac Murphy	Silver Cloud
1887	Isaac Murphy	Libretto
1888	Pike Barnes	White
1890	Don Allen	Bill Letcher
1891	Isaac Murphy	Kingman
1892	Alonzo Clayton	Newton
1896	Willie Simms	Ben Brush
1897	Alonzo Clayton	Ornament
1898	Jess Conley	Han d'Or
1901	Jimmy Winkfield	Hernando
1907	Jimmy Lee	The Abbott
Latonia Oaks (originated Latonia, Ky. 1887)		
1888	John Stoval	Lavinia Belle
1889	Pike Barnes	Retrieve
1891	Tiny Williams	Ida Pickwick
1892	Alonzo Clayton	Lake Breeze
1894	James Perkins	Orinda
1898	Alonzo Clayton	Sardonic
1900	Monk Overton	Anthracite
1906	Dale Austin	Content
1907	Jimmy Lee	Lillie Turner
Lawrence Realization (originated Sheepshead Bay, 1889)		
1891	Anthony Hamilton	Potomac
1893	Willie Simms	Daily America
1894	Willie Simms	Dobbins
1896	Alonzo Clayton	Requital
Louisville Cup (originated Douglas Park, Ky., 1913)		
1913	M. Dishmon	Clubs
Matron Stakes (originated Morris Park, 1892)		
1903	Willie Hicks	Armenia
Metropolitan Handicap (originated Morris Park, 1891)		
1896	Anthony Hamilton	Counter Tenor
1898	Pete Clay	Bowling Brook

Year	*Jockey*	*Horse*

National Stallion Stakes (originated Morris Park, 1898)

1908	Jimmy Lee	Sir Martin

Saratoga Cup (originated Saratoga, 1865)

1881	Isaac Murphy	Checkmate
1886	Issac Murphy	Volante
1891	Isaac Lewis	Los Angeles

Second Special (originated Gravesend, 1886)

1888	Isaac Murphy	Kingston
1890	Pike Barnes	Los Angeles
1892	Willie Simms	Lamplighter
1894	Willie Simms	Clifford
1895	Willie Simms	Clifford
1897	Willie Simms	Ben Brush
1899	Pete Clay	Imp

Spinaway Stakes (originated Saratoga, 1881)

1882	John Stoval	Miss Woodford
1887	Ed West	Los Angeles
1890	Don Allen	Sallie McClelland
1891	Willie Simms	Promenade
1903	Jimmy Hicks	Raglan

St. Louis Derby (originated St. Louis, 1882)

1882	Billy Walker	Monogram
1883	John Stoval	Bondholder
1887	Isaac Murphy	Terra Cotta
1888	Anthony Hamilton	Falcon
1890	Don Allen	Bill Letcher
1896	James Perkins	Prince Lief
1897	Alonzo Clayton	Ornament

Suburban Handicap (originated Sheepshead Bay, 1884)

1890	Isaac Murphy	Salvator
1895	Anthony Hamilton	Lazzarone
1897	Willie Simms	Ben Brush
1898	Alonzo Clayton	Tillo

Swift Stakes (originated Sheepshead Bay, 1885)

1888	Isaac Murphy	Emperor of Norfolk
1892	Anthony Hamilton	Vestibule
1893	Marlo Thompson	Ajax
1894	Willie Simms	Discount
1896	Alonzo Clayton	Requital

Year	*Jockey*	*Horse*

Tennessee Derby (originated Memphis, 1884)

1885	Erskine Henderson	Joe Cotton
1891	Tom Britton	Valera
1892	Tom Britton	Tom Elliot
1897	Tiny Williams	Buckvedere
1901	Jimmy Winkfield	Royal Victor

Tennessee Oaks (originated Memphis, 1884)

1885	Ed West	Ida Hope
1895	Alonzo Clayton	Handspun
1896	James Perkins	Lady Inez
1903	Jimmy Winkfield	Olefant

Tidal Stakes (originated Sheepshead Bay, 1880)

1890	Isaac Murphy	Burlington
1891	Anthony Hamilton	Portchester
1892	Willie Simms	Charade
1894	Willie Simms	Dobbins
1897	Willie Simms	Buddha
1898	Tiny Williams	Handball

Toboggan Handicap (originated Belmont Park, 1890)

1890	Anthony Hamilton	Fides
1898	Willie Simms	Octagon

Travers Stakes (originated Saratoga, 1864)

1866	Abe Hawkins	Merrill
1879	Isaac Murphy	Falsetto
1889	Pike Barnes	Long Dance
1891	Tiny Williams	Valera
1892	Alonzo Clayton	Azva
1908	Jimmy Lee	Dorante

Tremont Stakes (originated Gravesend, 1887)

1897	Willie Simms	Handball

United States Hotel Stakes (originated Saratoga, 1880)

1884	John Stoval	Kosciusko
1889	Isaac Lewis	Retrieve
1890	Pike Parnes	Sinaloa II
1891	Spider Anderson	Bermuda
1895	Alonzo Clayton	Axiom
1918	R. Simpson	Billy Kelly

Wither Stakes (originated Jerome Park, 1874)

1896	Willie Simms	Handspring
1897	Willie Simms	Octagon

CYCLING

MAJOR TAYLOR'S BICYCLE RACING RECORD, 1891–1908

Year	Race	Site	Place
	Amateur Record, 1891–1896		
1891	Ten-Mile, Road	Lexington, Ky.	1st
1893	Ten-Mile, Road	Lexington, Ky.	1st
1893	Quarter Mile	Lexington, Ky.	1st
1893	Half Mile	Lexington, Ky.	1st
1893	One Mile	Lexington, Ky.	1st
1894	75 Mile, Road	Matthews, Ind.	1st
1895	Ten-Mile, Road	Worcester, Mass.	1st
1896	Ten-Mile, Road	New Haven, Conn.	1st
1896	Half Mile, Open	Meriden, Conn	2nd
1896	25 Mile, Road	Irvington, N.J.	2nd
1896	25 Mile, Road	Jamaica, Long Island	1st
	Professional Record, 1896–1908		
1896	Half Mile	New York City	1st
1896	Six Day	New York City	8th
1897	One Mile, Open	Boston	1st
1897	One Mile, Open	Providence, R.I.	1st
1897	Half Mile, Open	Providence, R.I.	2nd
1898	Match Race vs. Jimmy Michael	Manhattan Beach, N.Y.	1st
1898	One Mile, Open	Asbury Park, N.J.	1st
1899	⅓ Mile, Open	Philadelphia, Pa.	1st
1899	One Mile, Open	Boston	1st
1899	Two-Mile Handicap	Boston	1st
1899	One-Mile Match vs. Tom Butler	Boston	Lost
1899	⅓ Mile, Open	Boston	1st
1899	25-Mile Match vs. Ed McDuffie	Boston	Won
1899	One-Mile Match vs. Tom Butler	Boston	Won
1899	One-Mile Championship	Chicago	1st
1899	One-Mile Championship	Janesville, Ill.	2nd
1899	Two-Mile Handicap	Janesville, Ill.	1st
1899	One-Mile Championship	St. Louis	1st
1899	Two-Mile Championship	Ottumwa, Ill.	2nd
1899	One Mile, Open	Ottumwa, Ill	1st
1899	One-Mile Championship	Ottumwa, Ill.	1st
1899	One-Mile Championship	Chicago, Ill.	1st
1899	Half Mile, Open	Montreal	2nd
1899	One-Mile World's Championship	Montreal	1st
1899	Two-Mile, Open	Montreal	1st
1899	Five-Mile Championship	Boston	5th

Year	Race	Site	Place
1899	Half-Mile Championship	Boston	1st
1899	One-Mile Championship	Brockton, Mass	1st
1899	Half Mile, Open	Worcester, Mass	1st
1899	Five-Mile Match vs. James Casey	Worcester, Mass	1st
1899	Fifty-Yard Match vs. Charles Raymond	Worcester, Mass	1st
1899	One Mile, Open	Taunton, Ill.	1st
1899	One Mile, Invitational	Peoria, Ill	1st
1899	Two Mile, Open	Peoria, Ill	1st
1899	Five Mile, Lap	Peoria, Ill	1st
1900	One Mile, Open	Manhattan Beach, N.Y.	3rd
1900	One-Mile match vs. Frank Kramer	Manhattan Beach, N.Y.	1st
1900	One-Mile match vs. Jay Eaton	Vailsburg, N.J.	1st
1900	Half Mile	Indianapolis	2nd
1900	Two-Mile Handicap	Indianapolis	1st
1900	Half Mile	Buffalo, N.Y.	1st
1900	Two-Mile, Handicap	Buffalo, N.Y.	3rd
1900	One Mile, Open	Hartford, Conn.	1st
1900	One-Mile Handicap	Hartford, Conn.	1st
1900	One Mile	New Bedford, Mass.	1st
1900	Half-Mile Handicap	New Bedford, Mass.	1st
1900	Quarter Mile	Newark, N.J.	1st
1900	⅓-Mile	Indianapolis	Tie 1st
1900	One-Mile Match vs. Owen Kimble	Indianapolis	1st
1900	Two-Mile Championship	Indianapolis	1st
1900	One-Mile International Professional	Montreal	2nd
1900	⅓-Mile Handicap	Montreal	1st
1900	One-Mile Match vs. Bill Fenn	Hartford, Conn.	1st
1900	One-Mile Match vs. Tom Cooper	New York City	1st
1900	One-Mile Match vs. Harry Elkes	Boston	1st
1901	One Kilometer	Berlin	3rd
1901	One Kilometer	Berlin	1st
1901	Match vs. Louis Grognia	Verviers, Belgium	1st
1901	Match vs. Edmond Jacquelin	Paris	2nd
1901	Match vs. Edmond Jacquelin	Paris	1st
1901	Match vs. Thorwald Ellegard	Copenhagen	2nd
1901	Match vs. Thorwald Ellegard	Agen, France	1st
1901	1000 Meters	Berlin	1st
1901	Match Tandem vs. Grognia/Prevost	Bordeaux, France	2nd
1901	Match Tandem vs. Arend/Huber	Leipzig, Poland	1st
1901	Match vs. Grognia/Momo/Protin	Antwerp, Belgium	1st
1901	Match vs. Van den Born/Cornelli	Toulouse, France	1st
1901	Match Tandem vs. Grognia/Provost	Bordeaux	2nd
1901	Match vs Lambrecht/Legarde	Lyons, France	1st
1901	1000–Meter Handicap	Lyons	1st
1901	Match vs. Gougoltz/Henneburn	Geneva, Switz.	1st
1901	Half-Mile Championship	New York City	1st
1901	⅓–Mile Championship	Providence, R.I.	1st

Year	Race	Site	Place
1901	One-Mile Championship	Springfield, Mass.	1st
1901	One-Mile Championship	Worcester, Mass.	1st
1901	One-Mile Match vs. Frank Kramer	New York	1st
1902	1,000 Meters	Paris	1st
1902	Match vs. Harri Meyers	Holland	1st
1902	Match vs. Louis Grognia	Belgium	1st
1902	Match vs. Thorwald Ellegard	Denmark	1st
1902	Match vs. Thorwald Ellegard	Denmark	1st
1902	Match vs. Walter Rutt	Germany	1st
1902	Match vs. Lembrecht	Paris	1st
1902	Match vs. Linton	Paris	1st
1902	Half-Mile Championship	New York City	2nd
1902	Match vs. Willie Fenn	Hartford, Conn.	1st
1902	Half-Mile Championship	Vailsburg, N.J.	2nd
1902	Match vs. Willie Fenn	Hartford	1st
1902	Quarter-Mile Championship	Ottawa, Canada	1st
1902	Half-Mile Championship	Ottawa, Canada	2nd
1902	⅓-Mile Team (With Willie Fenn)	Manhattan Beach, N.Y.	1st
1902	Two-Mile Circuit	Baltimore, Md.	1st
1902	⅓-Mile Championship	Manhattan Beach, N.Y.	2nd
1902	Five-Mile Handicap	Manhattan Beach, N.Y.	1st
1902	Match vs. Frank Kramer	Newark, N.J.	2nd
1902	Half-Mile Championship	Revere Beach	1st
1902	Two-Mile Circuit	Baltimore	1st
1902	⅓-Mile Championship	Hartford, Conn.	1st
1902	One-Mile Championship	Philadelphia	1st
1903	Wyalon Half-Mile Handicap	Sydney, Australia	1st
1903	Quarter-Mile International	Sydney	1st
1903	Five-Mile Walker Cup	Sydney	2nd
1903	Half-Mile Handicap	Sydney	1st
1903	Half-Mile Scratch	Sydney	1st
1903	Five-Mile Scratch	Sydney	1st
1903	Half-Mile Scratch	Sydney	1st
1903	Lap Dash Event	Sydney	1st
1903	Half-Mile Handicap	Sydney	3rd
1903	League Cup One-Mile Scratch	Sydney	1st
1903	First-Class Handicap, One Mile	Sydney	1st
1903	League Cup, One Mile	Sydney	2nd
1903	Centennial Mile	Sydney	1st
1903	Major Taylor Plate, Quarter-Mile Dash	Sydney	1st
1903	International Mile Scratch	Sydney	1st
1903	Quarter-Mile Scratch	Sydney	1st
1903	Federation Handicap Mile	Melbourne, Australia	4th
1903	Australian Cup Handicap, 1¼ Miles	Melbourne	3rd
1903	Grand Challenge Match vs. Don Walker	Melbourne	1st
1903	Match vs. George Morgan	Melbourne	1st
1903	International Scratch Race	Melbourne	2nd

Year	Race	Site	Place
1903	Great Sydney Thousand	Sydney, Australia	3rd
1903	Kent Plate	Sydney	1st
1903	Sydney Thousand	Sydney	1st
1903	Casterleigh Plate, Five Miles	Sydney	1st
1903	York Handicap, Half Mile	Sydney	1st
1903	Oxford Plate, Half-Mile Handicap	Sydney	3rd
1903	Sir Edwin Smith Stakes	South Australia	1st
1903	Adelaide Wheel Race	Adelaide, S. Australia	1st
1903	American Whirl	South Australia	2nd
1903	Morgan Stakes	South Australia	1st
1903	International Championship, One Mile	South Australia	1st
1903	International Championship, Five Miles	Melbourne	1st
1904	New Zealand Wheel Race, One Mile	Christchurch, Aus.	2nd
1904	International Test Mile	Sydney, Australia	1st
1904	International Test, Four Miles	Sydney	1st
1904	International Test, Five Miles	Sydney	2nd
1904	International Test, One-Mile Championship	Sydney	1st
1904	International Test, Half-Mile Championship	Sydney	3rd
1904	Commonwealth Stakes, Five Miles	Melbourne	2nd
1904	Brisbane Handicap, Half Mile	Melbourne	3rd
1904	First-Class Handicap	Melbourne	2nd
1904	Furracabod Handicap, One Mile	Sydney	4th
1904	Summer Wheel Race, One-Mile Handicap	Sydney	4th
1904	Melbourne Handicap, One Mile	Melbourne	2nd
1904	Commonwealth Stakes, Three Miles	Melbourne	DNQ
1904	McCullagh Plate, Five-Mile Scratch	Melbourne	2nd
1904	Australian Gold Stakes Mile Scratch	Melbourne	2nd
1904	Australian Gold Stakes, Ten-Mile Scratch	Melbourne	3rd
1904	Australian Gold Stakes, Three-Mile Scratch	Melbourne	2nd
1904	Australian Gold, Five-Mile Feature	Melbourne	1st
1904	National Fete Match vs. Iver Lawson	Melbourne	1st
1904	World's Championship Match vs. Iver Lawson	Melbourne	1st
1904	International, One-Mile Championship	Adelaide	1st
1904	Sydney Thousand	Sydney	2nd
1904	Kent Plate, One Mile	Sydney	2nd
1904	International Championship	Adelaide	1st
1904	Druids Plate, Half-Mile Handicap	Adelaide	1st
1904	Druids Wheel Race, Two-Mile Handicap	Adelaide	4th
1904	Norwood Handicap, Half-Mile	Adelaide	3rd
1904	Goodwin Stakes, One-Mile Handicap	Adelaide	3rd
1904	Fitzroy Stakes, One-Mile Scratch	Adelaide	1st
1904	Medindie Handicap, 1½-Mile Handicap	Adelaide	1st
1904	Autumn Handicap	Adelaide	5th
1904	International, Ten-Mile Scratch	Adelaide	1st

Year	*Race*	*Site*	*Place*
1908	Quarter Mile (World Record 0:25.4)	Paris	1st
1908	Half Mile (World Record 0:42.2)	Paris	1st
1908	Race of Nations (Buffalo Track Record)	Paris	1st
1908	Three Corners vs. Friol/Ellegarde	Paris	1st
1908	Three Corners vs. Ellegarde/Verri	Marseilles	1st
1908	Match vs. Friol	Paris	1st
1908	Match vs. Poulain	Paris	1st

Note: Taylor was inactive for much of the period 1905 to 1907.

TRACK & FIELD

AFRICAN-AMERICAN OLYMPIC MEDALISTS, 1904 and 1908

1904	George C. Poage	Bronze	400-meter hurdles	No time available	Olympics at St. Louis, Mo.
1908	John Baxter Taylor	Gold	4–by–400-meter relay[1]	3:29.4 min.	Olympics at London, England

[1]White teamates: William Hamilton, Nathaniel Cartmel, Melvin Sheppard

Non-medalist

1908	W. C. Holmes	Event—Standing Broad Jump		Olympics at London, England

AFRICAN-AMERICAN AAU NATIONAL CHAMPIONS, THROUGH 1919

100 Meter Dash	**Time**	**Affiliation**
1912 Howard Porter Drew	10.0 s.	Springfield H.S. (Mass.)
1913 Howard Porter Drew	10.4 s.	Springfield H.S. (Mass.)

200 Meter Dash		
1913 Howard Porter Drew	22.8 s.	Springfield H.S. (Mass.)
1914 I.T. Howe	22.2 s.	Unattached, Boston
1915 Roy Morse	21.2 s.	Salem Crescent A.C., N.Y.

400 Meter Run		
1907 John Baxter Taylor	51.0 s.	University of Pennsylvania

AFRICAN-AMERICAN STARS ON WHITE COLLEGE TEAMS, THROUGH 1919

Wm. T.S. Jackson	1890-92	Amherst
Napoleon Marshall	1895-97	Harvard
Spencer Dickerson	1896-97	U. of Chicago
G.C.H. Burleigh	1896-98	U. of Illinois
George Poage	1903	Wisconsin
John Baxter Taylor	1903–1908	Pennsylvania
Howard Smith	1907	Pennsylvania
Dewey Rogers	1907	Pennsylvania
Ted Cable	1909-13	Harvard
Alexander Louis Jackson	1913	Harvard
Binga Dismond	1913	U. of Chicago
Cecil Lewis	1915	U. of Chicago
Irving Howe	1915	Dartmouth
W. Randolph Granger	1916	Dartmouth
J. Ferguson	1916	Dartmouth
Sol Butler	1915-18	Dubuque (Iowa)
Paul Robeson	1915-18	Rutgers
Howard Martin	1917	U. of Cincinnati
Jim Ravenelle	1917	New York University
Fred "Duke" Slater	1918-21	U. of Iowa
Ben Johnson	1918	Springfield (Mass.)
Howard Porter Drew	1918	Drake U. Law and Univ. of Southern California

AFRICAN-AMERICAN WORLD RECORD HOLDERS, THROUGH 1919

400-Meter Dash	Time	Date	Site
Ted Meredith	47.4 s.	May 27, 1916	Cambridge, Mass
Binga Dismond	47.4 s.	June 3, 1916	Evanston, Illinois
800-Meter Dash			
Ted Meredith	1:51.9 m.	July 8, 1912	Stockholm, Sweden
1,600-Meter Relay[1]			
Ted Meredith	3:16.6 m.	June 21, 1912	Stockholm, Sweden

[1]White Teammates—M. Sheppard, E. Lindberg, C. Reidpath

BASEBALL

ALL-TIME REGISTER OF AFRICAN-AMERICAN PLAYERS, MANAGERS, UMPIRES, AND OFFICIALS, 1872-1919

Career	Last Name	First Name	Teams	Positions
1872–99	Fowler	J.W. (Bud) (John Jackson)	Evansville	Catcher
			New York Gorhams	Pitcher
			All-American Black Tourist	Shortstop
			Stillwater (Northwestern League)	Outfielder
			Sterling and Davenport (Illinois Iowa League)	Second Base
			Terre Haute and Galesburg (Central Interstate League)	Manager*
			Binghamton (International League)	
			Keokuk and Topeka (Western League)	
			Page Fence Giants	
1883–89	Walker	Moses Fleetwood (Fleet)	Waterbury (Southern New England and Eastern League)	Outfielder
				Catcher
			Toledo (North Western League and American Association	
			Newark and Syracuse (International League)	
			Cleveland (Western League)	
1884	Butler	J.	Philadelphia Mutual B.B.C.	Ball Blayer
	Carter	Ike	St. Louis Black Stockings	Second Base
	Cisco	J.	Philadelphia Mutual B.B.C.	Ball Player
	Cooper	C.	Philadelphia Mutual B.B.C.	Ball Player
	Fisher	A.	Philadelphia Mutual B.B.C.	Ball Player
	Fisher	F.	Philadelphia Mutual B.B.C.	Ball Player
	Fisher	W.	Philadelphia Mutual B.B.C.	Ball Player
	Harris	E.	Philadelphia Mutual B.B.C.	Ball Player
	Hart	Frank	St. Louis Black Stockings	Shortstop
	Jones	D.	Philadelphia Mutual B.B.C.	Ball Player
	Mitchell	A.	Philadelphia Mutual B.B.C.	Utility Player
	Paine	Henry	Brooklyn Remsens	Outfielder
1884–85	Burrell	George	Baltimore Atlantics	Catcher
				Pitcher
	Calhoun	F.	Baltimore Atlantics	Infielder
	Dorsey	F.T.	Baltimore Atlantics	Infielder
	Johnson	Joe	Baltimore Atlantics	Catcher
				Pitcher
	Raine	J.	Baltimore Atlantics	Outfielder
	Stuart	Joe	Brooklyn Atlantics	Catcher
				Pitcher
	Washington	L.	Baltimore Atlantics	Shortstop
	Williams	Sol	Baltimore Atlantics	Outfielder
1884–87	Gray	William	Baltimore Lord Baltimores	Outfielder
			Baltimore Atlantics	

*Managerial position

Career	Last Name	First Name	Teams	Positions
1884–87 *(Cont'd.)*	Harris	James	Baltimore Lord Baltimores Baltimore Atlantics	Outfielder
	Proctor	James (Cub)	Baltimore Lord Baltimores Baltimore Atlantics	Catcher Pitcher
	Walker	Weldy (Wilberforce)	Akron (Ohio State League) Toledo (American Association) Pittsburgh Keystones	Catcher Outfielder
1885	Batum	G.W.	Brooklyn Remsens	Second Base
	Bolden	L.W.	Brooklyn Remsens	Utility Player
	Coleman	John	Brooklyn Remsens	Outfielder
	Day	Guy	Argyle Hotel	Catcher
	Douglas	George	Brooklyn Remsens	Outfielder
	Eggleston	William	Argyle Hotel	Shortstop
	Hancock	W.	Brooklyn Remsens	Ball Player
	Harris	Frank	Argyle Hotel	Pitcher
	Jackson	F.	Brooklyn Remsens	Club Officer*
	Lang	John F.	Argyle Hotel	Manager*
	Martin	R.	Argyle Hotel	Pitcher
	Nichols	Charles	Argyle Hotel	Outfielder
	Oliver	John	Brooklyn Remsens	Third Base
	Peterson	L.	Brooklyn Remsens	First Base
	Randolph	A.	Argyle Hotel	First Base
	Smith	Hy	Brooklyn Remsens	Outfielder
	Smith	O.H.	Brooklyn Remsens	Pitcher
	Williams	James	Brooklyn Remsens	Catcher
	Williams	C.	Brooklyn Remsens	Manager*
1885–86	Trusty	Shep	Cuban Giants Philadelphia Orions	Pitcher
1885–1887	Boyd	–	Cuban Giants Argyle Hotel	
	Holmes	Ben	Cuban Giants Argyle Hotel	Third Base
1885–1893	Harrison	Abe	Argyle Hotel Philadelphia Orions Cuban Giants	Shortstop
1885–1896	Dabney	Milton	Argyle Hotel Cuban X Giants	Outfielder Pitcher
1885–1902	Williams	George	New York Gorhams Philadelphia Orions Cuban X-Giants Argyle Hotel Cuban X-Giants	First Base Second Base
1886–87	Cook	Walter	Cuban Giants	Officer*
1886–88	Johnson	Harry	Cuban Giants	Utility Player
1886–91	Thomas	Arthur	New York Cubans Cuban Giants	First Base Catcher

*Managerial position

Career	Last Name	First Name	Teams	Positions
1886–1896	Jackson	Andrew	Lansing Michigan, Colored Capital All-Americans New York Gorhams Cuban X-Giants Cuban Giants	Third Base
	Scovey	George W.	New York Gorhams Newark (International League) Cuban X-Giants Jersey City (Eastern League)	Pitcher
1886–1903	Grant	Frank	Cuban Giants Buffalo (International League) Harrisburg (Eastern Interstate League) Lansing Michigan Colored Capital All-Americans Meridien (Eastern League)	Shortstop Second Base
1886–1912	Williams	Clarence	Lansing Michigan Colored Capital All-Americans New York Gorhams Smart Set Cuban X-Giants Philadelphia Giants Cuban Giants	Catcher
1887	Allen	William	Cincinnati Browns	Utility Player
	Austin	John	Cincinnati Browns	Utility Player
	Aylor	James	Philadelphia Pythians Cincinnati Tigers	Utility Player Catcher
	Binga	Jess E.	Washington Capital Cities	Ball Player
	Blackstone	William	Cincinnati Browns	Utility Player
	Brady	John	Pittsburgh Keystones	Ball Player
	Brooks	James	Baltimore Lord Baltimores	Ball Player
	Brown	Walter	League of Colored Baseball Clubs	President*
	Brown	William H.	Pittsburgh Keystones	Ball Player
	Brown	—	Boston Resolutes	Utility Player
	Brown	Charles	Pittsburgh Keystones	Ball Player
	Card	Al	Pittsburgh Keystones	Ball Player
	Carroll	Hal	Cincinnati Browns	Ball Player
	Chapman	J.W.	Cincinnati Browns	Ball Player
	Chapman	John	Cincinnati Browns	Ball Player
	Condon	Lafayette	Louisville Falls Cities	Ball Player
	Crain	A.C.	Baltimore Lord Baltimores	Ball Player
	Cummy	Hugh S.	Baltimore Lord Baltimores	Ball Player
	Downs	Ellsworth	Cincinnati Browns	Ball Player
	Erye	John	New York Gorhams	Ball Player
	Evans	George	New York Gorhams	Ball Player
	Evans	John	New York Gorhams	Ball Player

*Managerial position

Career	Last Name	First Name	Teams	Positions
1887	Eyers	Henry	Pittsburgh Keystones	Ball Player
(Cont'd.)	Findell	Thomas	Washington Capital Citys	Ball Player
	Garrett	Frank	Louisville Falls Citys	Ball Player
	Gillespie	H.	Louisville Falls Citys	Ball Player
	Gross	Ben, Jr.	Pittsburgh Keystones	Ball Player
	Hargett	Yook	Philadelphia Pytians	Ball Player
	Harris	—	Boston Resolutes	Ball Player
	Hoods	William	Philadelphia Pythians	Ball Player
	Hordy	J.H.	Baltimore Lord Baltimores	Ball Player
	Jackson	Sam	Pittsburgh Keystones	Ball Player
	Jackson	George	Phialdelphia Pythians	Ball Player
	James	William	Philadelphia Pythians	Ball Player
	Jessie	W.	Louisville Falls Citys	Ball Player
	Kindeide	John	Louisville Falls Citys	Ball Player
	Lettlers	George	Washington Capital Citys	Utility Player
	Lewis	—	Boston Resolutes	Utility Player
	Lindsey	James	Pittsburgh Keystones	Ball Player
	Loving	J.G.	Washington Capital Citys	Ball Player
	Maison	J.	Pittsburgh Keystones	Utility Player
	Mayfield	Fred	Louisville Falls Citys	Utility Player
	Norwood	C.H.	Philadelphia Pythians	Utility Player
	Owens	W.E.	Cincinnati Browns	Utility Player
	Paine	John	Philadelphia Pythians	Utility Player
	Palmer	James	New York Gorhams	Utility Player
	Payne	James	Baltimore Lord Baltimores	Utility Player
	Perry	Ed	Washington Capital Citys	Utility Player
	Rankin	George	Cincinnati Browns	Ball Player
	Ray	Thomas	New York Gorhams	Ball Player
	Ricks	Napoleon	Louisville Falls Citys	Ball Player
	Rogers	Sid	Cincinnati Browns	Ball Player
	Smith	—	Boston Resolutes	Ball Player
	Smith	B.	New York Gorhams	Ball Player
	Stark	L.	Cincinnati Browns	Ball Player
	Still	Bobby	Philadelphia Pythians	Ball Player
	Still	Joe	Philadelphia Pythians	Ball Player
	Stinson	C.P.	Philadelphia Pythians	Ball Player
	Thomas	J.	Louisville Falls Citys	Ball Player
	Thomas	Jerome	Washington Capital Citys	Ball Player
	Thornton	Charles	Pittsburgh Keystones	Ball Player
	Turner	J.O.	Philadelphia Pythians	Ball Player
	Walker	—	Boston Resolutes	Ball Player
	Weyman	J.B.	Baltimore Lord Baltimores	Ball Player
	White	M.	New York Gorhams	Ball Player
	White	R.W.	Washington Capital Citys	Ball Player
	Willas	S.	New York Gorhams	Ball Player

Career	Last Name	First Name	Teams	Positions
	Williams	E.J.	Washington Capital Cities	Ball Player
	Williams	—	Boston Resolutes	Ball Player
	Wilson	William H.	Pittsburgh Keystones	Ball Player
	Wilson	J.H.	Baltimore Lord Baltimores	Ball Player
	Wilson	Joseph	Washington Capital Cities	Ball Player
	Zimmerman	George	Pittsburgh Keystones	Ball Player
1887–88	Higgins	Robert (Bob)	Syracuse (International League)	Pitcher
	Vactor	John	New York Gorhams	Ball Player
			Philadelphia Pythians	
1887–90	Johnson	Richard	Springfield and Peoria	Outfielder
			(Central Interstate League)	Catcher
			Zanesville (Ohio State League,	
			Tri-State League)	
1887–91	Davis	A.	New York Gorhams	Manager*
			Boston Resolutes	Ball Player
1887–95	Malone	William H.	Pittsburgh Keystones	Pitcher
			Page Fence Giants	
			Cuban Giants	
			New York Gorhams	
1887–96	Jackson	Bob	Cuban X-Giants	First Base
			New York Gorhams	Catcher
	Jackson	Oscar	Cuban X-Giants	First Base
			New York Gorhams	Outfielder
			Cuban Giants	
	Terrill	W.W.	Cuban X-Giants	Shortstop
			Boston Resolutes	
1887–97	Miller	Frank	Cuban Giants	Pitcher
			Pittsburgh Keystones	
			Cuban X-Giants	
1887–1900	Thompson	William	Genuine Cuban Giants	Catcher
			Louisville Falls Citys	
1887–1903	Nelson	John	Cuban X-Giants	Pitcher
			New York Gorhams	
			Philadelphia Giants	
			Cuban Giants	
1887–1912	Leland	Frank C.	Leland Giants	Manger*
			Washington Capital Cities	Ball Player
			Chicago Giants	
			Chicago Unions	
			Chicago Union Giants	
1887–1926	White	Sol	Philadelphia Giants	Third Base
			New York Monarchs (Eastern Interstate	First Base
			League)	Outfielder
			Cleveland Browns	Coach*
			Newark Stars	Second Base

*Managerial position

Career	Last Name	First Name	Teams	Positions
1887–1926 (Cont'd.)			Genuine Cuban Giants	Business Manager*
			Page Fence Giants	Manager*
			Fort Wayne (Western Interstate League)	
			Cuban X-Giants	
			Lincoln Giants	
			Pittsburgh Keystones	
			Wheeling (Ohio State League)	
			Washington Capital Citys	
			Columbia Giants and Quaker Giants	
1888	Bell	Frank	New York Gorhams	Ball Player
	Collins	Nat	New York Gorhams	Ball Player
	Bright	John M.	Cuban Giants	Manager*
1889–91	Kelley	Richard A.	Jamestown (Pennsylvania–New York League)	Shortstop
			Danville (Illinois–Indiana League)	Second Base
1890–1906	Patterson	John (Pat)	Cuban X-Giants	Manger*
			Brooklyn Royal Giants	Second Base
			Quaker Giants of New York	
			Lincoln Nebraska Giants	
			Page Fence Giants	
			Columbia Giants of Chicago	
			Philadelphia Giants	
1893	Whyte	(Billy)	Cuban Giants	Outfielder
				Pitcher
1893–96	Cato	Harry	Cuban Giants	Outfielder
			Cuban X-Giants	Second Base
				Pitcher
1893–1903	Jackson	William	Cuban X-Giants	Catcher
			Cuban Giants	Outfielder
1895	Brooks	Gus	Page Fence Giants	Outfielder
	Hackley	Al	Chicago Unions	Ball Player
1895–96	Graham	Vasco	Page Fence Giants	Outfielder
			Lansing Chicago Colored Capital All-Americans	Catcher
1895–97	Taylor	George	Page Fence Giants	First Base
	Vandyke	Fred	Page Fence Giants	Outfielder
				Pitcher
1895–99	Burns	Pete	Columbia Giants	Outfielder
			Page Fence Giants	Catcher
	Miller	Joe	Columbia Giants	Pitcher
			Pace Elite Giants	
1895–1903	Binga	William	Philadelphia Giants	Third Base
			Columbia Giants	
			St. Paul Gophers	
			Page Fence Giants	
1895–1904	Robinson	James (Black Rusie)	Lansing Chicago Colored Capital All-Americans	Pitcher
			Cuban Giants	

*Managerial position

Career	Last Name	First Name	Teams	Positions
1895–1921	Johnson	Grant (Home Run)	Pittsburgh Colored Stars	Manager*
			Lincoln Giants	Second Base
			Pittsburgh Stars of Buffalo	Shortstop
			Brooklyn Royal Giants	
			Philadelphia Giants	
			Page Fence Giants	
			Cuban X-Giants	
			Lincoln Stars	
1896	Banks	—	Cuban X-Giants	Pitcher
	Chavous	—	Page Fence Giants	Pitcher
	Cole	William	Cuban Giants	Catcher
	Hinson	Frank	Cuban Giants	Pitcher
	Southall	John	Celeron Acme Colored Giants (Iron & Oil League)	Catcher
	Taylor	Jim	Cuban Giants	Outfielder
	Trusty	Job	Cuban Giants	Third Base
	Williams	T.	Cuban X-Giants	Outfielder Catcher
1986–99	Hopkins	—	Chicago Unions	Pitcher
	Hyde	Harry	Chicago Unions	Ball Player
1896–1903	Wilson	Ed	Lansing Michigan Colored Capital All-Americans Cuban X-Giants	First Base
1896–1904	Horn	Will	Philadelphia Giants Chicago Unions	Pitcher
	Jordan	Robert	Cuban X-Giants	First Base
			Cuban Giants	Catcher
1896-1905	Holland	William (Billy)	Chicago Unions	Pitcher
			Page Fence Giants	
			Brooklyn Royal Giants	
	Wilson	George	Columbia Giants	Outfielder
			Chicago Union Giants	Pitcher
			Page Fence Giants	
1896–1910	Grant	Charles	Philadelphia Giants	Second Base
			Page Fence Giants	
			Columbia Giants	
			Cuban X-Giants	
			New York Black Sox	
1896–1911	Barton	Sherman	Cuban X-Giants	Outfielder
			Quaker Giants of New York	
			Columbia Giants	
			Chicago Unions	
			Chicago Giants	
			St. Paul Gophers	

*Managerial position

Career	Last Name	First Name	Teams	Positions
1896–1911 *(Cont'd.)*	Moore	Harry (Mike)	Philadelphia Giants Chicago Unions Lincoln Giants Algona Brownies Leland Giants Cuban X-Giants Chicago Giants	First Base Outfielder
1896–1914	Monroe	William (Bill)	Brooklyn Royal Giants Philadelphia Giants Chicago Unions Chicago American Giants	Second Base
1896–1918	Buckner	Harry	Smart Set Brooklyn Royal Giants Chicago Giants Philadelphia Giants Chicago Unions Columbia Giants Quaker Giants Cuban X-Giants Lincoln Giants	Outfielder Pitcher
1896–1920	Wyatt	David (Dave)	Constitution of Negro National League Chicago Union Giants Chicago Union	Co-drafter* Outfielder
1896–1923	Peters	W.S.	Peters Union Giants Chicago Union Giants	Manager* Owner*
1897	Parson	A.S.	Page Fence Giants	Manager*
1897–1932	Williams	Joe (Cyclone, Smokey)	Lincoln Giants Hemestead Grays San Antoio Bronchos Brooklyn Royal Giants Leland Giants Bacharach Giants Chicago Giants Chicago American Giants	Pitcher Manager*
1898	Baxter	Al	Celeron Acme Colored Giants (Iron & Oil League)	Outfielder
	Booker	Billy	Celeron Acme Colored Giants (Iron & Oil League)	Second Base
	Curtis	Harry	Celeron Acme Colored Giants (Iron & Oil League)	Manager*
	Day	Eddie	Celeron Acme Colored Giants (Iron & Oil League)	Shortstop
	Edsall	George	Celeron Acme Colored Giants (Iron & Oil League)	Outfielder

*Managerial position

Career	Last Name	First Name	Teams	Positions
	Kelly	William	Celeron Acme Colored Giants (Iron & Oil League)	Third Base
	Mickey	John	Celeron Acme Colored Giants (Iron & Oil League)	Pitcher
	Payne	William (Doc)	Celeron Acme Colored Giants (Iron & Oil League)	Outfielder
	Williams	Walter	Celeron Acme Colored Giants (Iron & Oil League)	Pitcher
	Wilson	Edward	Celeron Acme Colored Giants (Iron & Oil League)	Pitcher
	Wright	Clarence (Buggy)	Celeron Acme Colored Giants (Iron & Oil League)	First Base
1899	Howard	—	Cuban X-Giants	Ball Player
	Jackson	Robert	Chicago Unions	Catcher
	Jones	Bert	Chicago Unions	Ball Player
	Jordan	William F.	Baltimore Giants	Manager*
	Lyons	Chase	Genuine Cuban Giants	Pitcher
	Reynolds	—	Chicago Columbia Giants	Outfielder
1899–1906	Johnson	Junior	Quaker Giants	Catcher
			Brooklyn Royal Giants	First Base
			Columbia Giants	
			Philadelphia Giants	
1899–1909	Foots	Robert	Philadelphia Giants	Catcher
			Chicago Unions	
			Brooklyn Royal Giants	
1899–1921	Johnson	George (Chappie)	St. Louis Giants	
			Brooklyn Royal Giants	
			Norfolk Stars	
			Chicago Giants	
			Columbia Giants	
			Dayton Chappie's	
			Philadelphia Royal Stars	
			Leland Giants	
			Custer's Baseball Club of Columbus	
1900	Brown	Ben	Genuine Cuban Giants	Outfielder Pitcher
	Kelly	—	Genuine Cuban Giants	Shortstop
	Parker	—	Genuine Cuban Giants	Outfielder
	Rogers	—	Genuine Cuban Giants	Pitcher
	Williams	Bill	Genuine Cuban Giants	Pitcher
1900–04	Hill	John	Philadelphia Giants	Shortstop
			Cuban X-Giants	Third Base
			Genuine Cuban Giants	
1900–11	Smith	William T.	Philadelphia Giants	Outfielder
			Cuban X-Giants	Catcher
			Genuine Cuban Giants	
			Brooklyn Royal Giants	

Career	Last Name	First Name	Teams	Positions
1900–19	Watkins	Pop	Havana Red Sox	Catcher
			Genuine Cuban Giants	Manager*
1900–28	Duncan	Frank	Leland Giants	Outfielder
			Detroit Stars	Manager*
			Cleveland Tigers	
			Cleveland Hornets	
			Philadelphia Giants	
			Cleveland Elites	
			Chicago American Giants	
1900–37	Thomas	Clinton (Clint)	Bacharach Giants	Second Base
			Brooklyn Royal Giants	Outfielder
			Philadelphia Stars	
			Hilldale	
			Newark Eagles	
			Darby Daisies	
			New York Black Yankees	
			Lincoln Giants	
			Columbia Buckeyes	
1902	Manning	John	Philadelphia Giants	Outfielder
	Smith	Harry	Philadelphia Giants	First Base
1902–1904	Bell	William	Philadelphia Giants	Outfielder
				Pitcher
1902–1906	Carter	Charles (Kid)	Brooklyn Royal Giants	Pitcher
			Philadelphia Giants	
			Wilmington Giants	
1902–1909	Wilson	Ray	Philadelphia Giants	First Base
			Cuban X-Giants	
1902–1926	Foster	Andrew (Rube)	Negro National League	Founder*, President*
			Chicago American Giants	Treasurer*, Manager*,
				Pitcher
			Leland Giants	
			Cuban X-Giants	
			Chicago Union Giants	
			Philadelphia Giants	
1903	Evans	William	Philadelphia Giants	Ball Player
1903–1904	Johnson	Jack	Philadelphia Giants	First Base
1903–1923	Ball	Walter	Brooklyn Royal Giants	Pitcher
			Philadelphia Giants	
			Chicago Union Giants	
			Leland Giants	
			Mohawk Giants	
			Chicago American Giants	
			St. Louis Giants	
1904	Smith	J.	Cuban X-Giants	Third Base

*Managerial position

Career	Last Name	First Name	Teams	Positions
1904–1905	Ball	George W. (Ga. Rabbit)	Augusta Georgia Cuban X-Giants	Pitcher
1904–1922	Taylor	Charles I. (C.I.)	West Baden, Indiana Sprudels Birmingham Giants Negro National League Indianapolis ABC's	Manager* Vice-President*
1904–1925	Hill	J. Preston (Peter)	Leland Giants Detroit Stars Baltimore Black Sox Chicago American Giants Philadelphia Giants	Business Manager* Outfielder Manager* Second Base
1904–1948	Taylor	James (Candy, Jim)	Memphis Red Sox Baltimore Elite Giants Birmingham Giants Indianapolis ABC's Leland Giants Dayton Marcos Detroit Stars Columbia Elite Giants Cleveland Tate Stars St. Paul Gophers St. Louis Stars Homestead Grays Chicago American Giants & St. Louis Giants	Second Base Third Base Manager*
1905	Sampson	—	Genuine Cuban Giants	Pitcher
1905–1910	Davis	John	Philadelphia Giants Leland Giants Cuban Giants	Pitcher
	Matthews	William Clarence	New York Black Sox	Burlington (Vermont League)
Catcher		Washington	Tom	Pittsburgh Giants Philadelphia Giants Chicago Giants
1905–1912	Bowman	Emmett (Scotty)	Leland Giants Brooklyn Royal Giants Philadelphia Giants	Catcher Third Base Shortstop Pitcher
1905–1917	Booker	James (Peter)	Chicago Giants Philadelphia Giants Chicago American Giants Lincoln Giants Leland Giants	First Base Catcher
	Merritte	—	Lincoln Giants Brooklyn Royal Giants	Utility Player

*Managerial position

Career	Last Name	First Name	Teams	Positions
1905–1922	Connors	John W.	Bacharach Giants	Club Officer*
			Brooklyn Royal Giants	Club Officer*
1905–1928	Gatewood	Bill	Chicago Giants	Pitcher
			Leland Giants	Manager*
			Detroit Stars	
			Toledo Tigers	
			Birmingham Black Barons	
			Cuban X-Giants	
			Brooklyn Royal Giants	
			Chicago American Giants	
			Philadelphia Giants	
			Albany, Georgia Giants	
			St. Louis Stars	
	Lloyd	John Henry	Brooklyn Royal Giants	First Base
			Leland Giants	Second Base
			Lincoln Giants	Shortstop
			New York Black Yankees	Catcher
			Bacharach Giants	Manager*
			Cuban X-Giants	
			Hilldale	
			Macon Ames	
			Philadelphia Giants	
	DeMoss	Elwood (Bingo)	Detroit Stars	Shortstop
			Cleveland Giants	Second Base
			Indianapolis ABC's	Manager*
			Oklahoma Giants	
			Topeka Giants	
			Chicago Brown Bombers	
			Kansas City, Kansas Giants	
1906	Brown	William	Leland Giants	Assistant Manager*
	Gordon	—	Genuine Cuban Giants	Shortstop
	Harris	Nathan (Nate)	Leland Giants	Outfielder
			Chicago Giants	Second Base
			Philadelphia Giants	
	Hardy	Arthur W.	Kansas City Kansas Giants	Pitcher
			Topeka Giants	
	Wright	George	Leland Giants	Second Base
			Chicago Giants	Shortstop
			Quaker Giants	
			Brooklyn Royal Giants	
			Lincoln Giants	
	Earle	—	Lincoln Giants	Pitcher
			Bacharach Giants	Outfielder
			Philadelphia Giants	

*Managerial position

Career	Last Name	First Name	Teams	Positions
			Wilmington Giants	
			Cuban Giants	
			Brooklyn Royal Giants	
	Winston	Clarencce (Bobby)	Chicago Giants	Outfielder
			Leland Giants	
			Philadelphia Giants	
	Francis	William (Billy)	Chicago American Giants	Shortstop
			Hilldale	Third Base
			Cleveland Browns	
			Chicago Giants	
			Cuban Giants	
			Wilmington Giants	
			Philadelphia Giants	
			Lincoln Giants	
			Bacharach Giants	
	Petway	Bruce	Detroit Stars	Outfielder
			Brooklyn Royal Giants	Catcher
			Leland Giants	Manager*
			Chicago American Giants	
			Philadelphia Giants	
	McAdoo	Tully	St. Louis Giants	First Base
			Cleveland Browns	
			Kansas City, Kansas Giants	
			Topeka Giants	
			St. Louis Stars	
	Toney	Albert	Chicago American Giants	Second Base
			Chicago Giants	Shortstop
			Leland Giants	
			Chicago Union Giants	
	Gardner	James	Havana Red Sox	Ball Player
			Brooklyn Royal Giants	
			Cuban Giants	
	Veney	Jerome	Homestead Grays	Outfielder
				Manager*
	McClellan	Dan	Philadelphia Giants	Pitcher
			Lincoln Giants	Manager*
			Cuban X-Giants	
			Quaker Giants	
			Smart Set	
	Strong	Nat C.	New York Black Yankees	Booking Agent*
			Brooklyn Royal Giants	
1909	Batson	—	Philadelphia Giants	Outfielder
	Croxton	—	Cuban Giants	Pitcher
	Fisher	—	Philadelphia Giants	Pitcher

*Managerial position

Career	Last Name	First Name	Teams	Positions
1909 (Cont'd.)	Garrison	Robert	St. Paul Gophers	Ball Player
	Hannon	—	Philadelphia Giants	Outfielder
	Johnson	(Pat)	St. Paul Gophers	Ball Player
	Londo	Julius	St. Paul Gophers	Utility Player
	Miller	Eugene	St. Paul Gophers	Outfielder
	Norman	Jim	Kansas City Kansas Giants	Infielder
	Pate	Archie	St. Paul Gophers	Utility Player
	Patton	—	Philadelphia Giants	Pitcher Outfielder
	William	L.	Cuban Giants	Outfielder
	Norman	William (Shin)	Leland Giants)	Pitcher
	Wade	Lee	St. Louis Giants	Pitcher
			Philadelphia Giants	First Base
			Chicago American Giants	Pitcher
			Lincoln Giants	Outfielder
	James	(Gus)	Brooklyn Royal Giants	Outfielder Catcher
	Marshall	Bobby	Leland Giants	First Base
			Twin City Gophers	Manager*
	McMurray	William	St. Louis Giants	Catcher
			St Paul Gophers	
	Talbert	Danger	Chicago Giants	Third Base
			Leland Giants	
	Thomas	—	Brooklyn Royal Giants	Outfielder Pitcher
	Land	—	Smart Set	Outfielder
			Cuban Giants	
	Robinson	Al	Brooklyn Royal Giants	First Base
	Taylor	John (Steel Arm Johnny)	Chicago Giants	Pitcher
			Lincoln Giants	
			St. Paul Gophers	
			St. Louis Giants	
	Dougherty	Charles (Pat)	Chicago Giants	Pitcher
			Chicago-American Giants	
			Leland Giants	
	Emery	Jack	Smart Set	Outfielder
			Pittsburgh Colored Stars	Pitcher
			Philadelphia Giants	
	Hayman	Charles (Bugs)	Philadelphia Giants	First Base Pitcher
	James	W. (Nux)	Lincoln Giants	Second Base
			Smart Set	
			Bacharach Giants	
			Mohawk Giants	
			Philadelphia Giants	

*Managerial position

Career Last Name	First Name	Teams	Positions
Bragg	—	Brooklyn Royal Giants	Second Base
		Philadelphia Giants	Third Base
		Cuban Giants	Shortstop
		Mohawk Giants	
		Lincoln Giants	
Strothers	Tim Samuel (Sam)	Chicago Giants	First Base
		Leland Giants	Catcher
		Chicago Union Giants	Second Base
		Chicago American Giants	
Bradley	Phil	Smart Set	First Base
		Pittsburgh Stars of Buffalo	Catcher
		Pittsburgh Royal Giants	
		Pittsburgh Colored Stars	
		Lincoln Giants	
Dunbar	Ashby	Indianapolis ABC's	Outfielder
		Pennsylvania Red Caps of New York	
		Brooklyn Royal Giants	
		Lincoln Stars	
		Lincoln Giants	
Parks	Joseph	Pennsylvania Red Caps of New York	Shortstop
		Brooklyn Royal Giants	Outfielder
		Philadelphia Giants	Catcher
		Cuban Giants	
Mongin	Sam	Bacharach Giants	Second Base
		Brooklyn Royal Giants	Third Base
		St. Louis Giants	
		Lincoln Giants	
		Lincoln Stars	
Wallace	Felix	St. Louis Giants	Third Base
		St. Paul Gophers	Shortstop
		Lincoln Giants	Second Base Manager*
		Chicago Giants	
		Leland Giants	
		Bacharach Giants	
Payne	Andrew H. (Jap)	New York Central Red Caps	
		Cuban X-Giants	
		Chicago Union Giants	
		Philadelphia Giants	
		Leland Giants	
Pettus	William T. (Zack)	Richmond Giants	Second Base
		Kansas City Giants	Catcher
		Lincoln Stars	First Base
		Hilldale	Manager*
		Chicago Giants	
		Leland Giants	

*Managerial position

Career	Last Name	First Name	Teams	Positions
1909 (Cont'd.)			Bacharach Giants	
			Harrisburg Giants	
			Lincoln Giants	
	Poles	Spottswood (Spot)	Lincoln Stars	Outfielder
			Philadelphia Giants	
			Hilldale	
			Philadelphia Giants	
			Brooklyn Royal Giants	
			Lincoln Giants	
	Padrone	J.	Cuban Stars Negro National League	Second Base
			Cuban Stars Eastern Colored League	Outfielder
			Smart Set	Pitcher
			Long Branch Cubans	
			Chicago American Giants	
			Indianapolis ABC's	
			Lincoln Giants	
	Santop	Louis (Top)	Brooklyn Royal Giants	Outfielder
			Lincoln Stars	Catcher
			Chicago American Giants	Manager*
			Fort Worth Wonders	
			Lincoln Giants	
			Hilldale	
			Oklahoma Monarchs	
	Johnson	George (Dibo)	Hilldale	Outfielder
			Philadelphia Tigers	
			Forth Worth Wonders	
			Kansas City, Kansas Giants	
			Lincoln Giants	
			Brooklyn Royal Giants	
	Green	Charles (Joe)	Chicago Giants	Outfielder
			Leland Giants	Manager*
			Chicago American Giants	
	Wilkinson	J.L.	Negro National League	Secretary*
			Kansas City Monarchs	Club Officer*
			Negro American League	Treasurer*
			All Nations	Club Officer*
1910	Addison	—	Philadelphia Giants	Catcher
				Shortstop
	Baker	Howard (Home Run)	Leland Giants	Ball Player
	Bolden	Otto	Leland Giants	Catcher
	Green	P.	Pittsburgh Giants	Outfielder
	Green	W.	Pittsburgh Giants	Catcher
	Jackson	William (Ashes)	Kansas City, Kansas Giants	Third Base
	Lindsay	Robert (Frog)	Kansas City, Kansas Giants	Shortstop
	Myers	—	Brooklyn Royal Giants	Shortstop

*Managerial position

Career	Last Name	First Name	Teams	Positions
	Reese	—	Cuban Giants	Pitcher
	Tenney	William	Kansas City, Kansas Giants	Catcher
	Webb	James (Baby)	Leland Giants	Catcher
	Wilkins	Wesley	Kansas City Kansas Giants	Outfielder
	Brown	—	Brooklyn Royal Giants	Outfielder
	Pryor	Wes	Chicago Giants	Third Base
			Leland Giants	
			St. Louis Giants	
			American Giants	
	Brown	—	Mohawk Giants	First Base
			Cuban Giants	
	Lindsay	Bill	Chicago American Giants	Pitcher
			Kansas City, Kansas Giants	
			Leland Giants	
	Collins	—	Brooklyn Royal Giants	Catcher
			Lincoln Giants	
			New York Black Sox	
			Pennsylvania Red Caps of New York	
	Andrews	Pop	Pittsburgh Stars of Buffalo	Outfielder
			Brooklyn Royal Giants	Pitcher
	Handy	Bill	St. Louis Giants	Shortstop
			New York Black Sox	Third Base
			Bacharach Giants	Second Base
			Philadelphia Royal Giants	
			Brooklyn Royal Giants	
1910–25	Hutchinson	Fred (Butch)	Indianapolis ABC's	Third Base
			Bacharach Giants	Shortstop
			Chicago American Giants	
			Leland Giants	
	Wickware	Frank	Brooklyn Royal Giants	Pitcher
			Detroit Stars	
			Mohawk Giants	
			Leland Giants	
			Philadelphia Giants	
			Lincoln Giants	
			Norfolk Stars	
			Chicago American Giants	
			Lincoln Stars	
1910–26	Barbour	Jess	Detroit Stars	Third Base
			Harrisburg Giants	First Base
			Pittsburgh Keystones	
			Chicago American Giants	
	Bradford	Charles	Lincoln Giants	Coach*
			Pittsburgh Giants	Pitcher

*Managerial position

Career	Last Name	First Name	Teams	Positions
1910–31	Hewitt	Joe	Brooklyn Royal Giants	Manager*
			Cleveland Cubs	Second Base
			St. Louis Stars	Shortstop
			Philadelphia Giants	Outfielder
			St. Louis Giants	
			Detroit Stars	
			Chicago American Giants	
1910–32	Pierce	William H. (Bill)	East-West League	Outfielder
			Lincoln Stars	First Base
			Pennsylvania Red Caps of New York	Catcher
			Philadelphia Giants	
			Bacharach Giants	
			Detroit Stars	
			Norfolk Giants	
1910–37	Crawford	Sam	Indianapolis Athletics	Pitcher
			Detroit Stars	Manager*
			Kansas City Monarchs	
			New York Black Sox	
			Chicago American Giants	
			Chicago Union Giants	
			Brooklyn Royal Giants	
			Birmingham Black Barons	
			Chicago Columbia Giants	
1910–38	Gans	Robert Edward (Jude)	East-West League	Umpire*
			Negro National League	Pitcher
			Smart Set	Outfielder
			Chicago Giants	Manager*
			Lincoln Stars	
			Cuban Giants	
			Chicago American Giants	
			Lincoln Giants	
1910–50	Bolden	Edward (Ed)	Darby Phantoms	Club Officer*
			Philadelphica Stars	
			Hilldale	
1911	Brown	Theo	Chicago Union Giants	Third Base
	Lain	William	Chicago Giants	Third Base
	Neal	George	Chicago Giants	Second Base
	Redmon	Tom	Leland Giants	Ball Player
	Rolls	Charles	Leland Giants	Ball Player
	Thurston	Bobby	Chicago Giants	Outfielder
1911–12	Gillard	(Hamp)	St. Louis Giants	Pitcher
1911–14	Mcmahon	Jess	Lincoln Giants	Club Officer*
	McMahon	Rod	Lincoln Giants	Club Officer*
1911–15	Bernard	—	Pittsburgh Giants	Catcher
			Lincoln Stars	Outfielder

*Managerial position

Career	Last Name	First Name	Teams	Positions
1911–17	Mayo	—	Pittsburgh Colored Stars	Outfielder
			Pittsburgh Giants	First Base
			Hilldale	
1911–19	Parks	William	American Giants	Outfielder
			Pennsylvania Red Caps of New York	Second Base
			Lincoln Giants	Shortstop
			Lincoln Stars	
			Chicago Giants	
1911–20	Kindle	William (Bill)	Lincoln Stars	Second Base
			Indianapolis ABC's	
			Lincoln Giants	
			Brooklyn Royal Giants	
			Chicago American Giants	
	Moore	—	St. Louis Giants	Outfielder
1911–23	Wiley	Washeba (Doc)	Lincoln Giants	First Base
			Brooklyn Royal Giants	Catcher
			Philadelphia Giants	
1911–24	Mills	Charles A.	St. Louis Black Sox	Club Officer*
1911–25	Bennett	Sam	St. Louis Giants	Catcher
			St. Louis Stars	
	Grant	Leroy	Lincoln Giants	First Base
			Chicago American Giants	
	Johnson	Louis (Dicta)	Indianapolic ABC's	Coach*
			Pittsburgh Keystones	Manager*
			Detroit Stars	Pitcher
			Milwaukee Bears	
			Twin City Gophers	
			Chicago American Giants	
1911–32	Lyons	James (Jimmie)	Indianapolis ABC's	Outfielder
			St. Louis Giants	Manager*
			Brooklyn Royal Giants	
			Chicago American Giants	
			Louisville Black Caps	
			Chicago Giants	
1911–38	Redding	Richard (Cannon Ball)	Bacharach Giants	Outfielder
			Indianapolis ABC's	Pitcher
			Lincoln Stars	Manager*
			Lincoln Giants	
			Brooklyn Royal Giants	
			Chicago American Giants	
1911–46	Posey	Cumberland Willis (Cum)	East-West League	Founder*
			Negro–National League	Secretary*
			Detroit Wolves	Club Officer*
			Homestead Grays	Outfielder
1911–48	Posey	Seward H.	Homestead Grays	Business Manager*

*Managerial position

Career	Last Name	First Name	Teams	Positions
1912	Alexander	Freyl	Homestead Grays	President*
	Green	Willie	St. Louis Stars	Catcher
	James	J.	Smart Set	First Base
	Lindsey	—	Lincoln Giants	Outfielder
	Taylor	E.	St. Louis Giants	Pitcher
1912–15	Smith	—	Lincoln Giants	Outfielder
				Pitcher
1912–1919	Langford	(A.D.)	Brooklyn Royal Giants	Outfielder
			St. Louis Giants	Pitcher
			Pennsylvania Red Caps of New York	
			Lincoln Stars	
1912-21	Harvey	—	Lincoln Stars	Pitcher
			Brooklyn Royal Giants	
			Lincoln Giants	
			Bacharach Giants	
			St. Louis Giants	
	Miller	—	Brooklyn Royal Giants	Second Base
			Lincoln Giants	Third Base
			Smart Set	
			Lincoln Stars	
1912–22	Jones	Lee	Dallas Giants	Outfielder
			Brooklyn Royal Giants	
1912–26	Webster	William (Speck)	Hilldale	First Base
			Chicago Giants	Catcher
			Mohawk Giants	
			Brooklyn Cuban Giants	
			Detroit Stars	
			Dayton Marcos	
			Lincoln Giants	
			Brooklyn Royal Giants	
1912–31	Taylor	S.	Little Rock Black Travelers	Pitcher
			St. Louis Giants	Manager*
1912–34	Carpenter	George (Tank)	Bacharach Giants	Catcher
			Hilldale	Third Base
			Los Angeles White Sox	First Base
			Kansas City Monarchs	Outfielder
1912-42	McNair	Hurley	Negro American League	Outfielder
			Detroit Stars	
			Kansas City Monarchs	
			Chicago Union Giants	
			Gilkerson's Union Giants	
			Chicago American Giants	
1913	Alexander	Hub	Chicago Giants	Catcher
	Bennett	Frank	Bacharach Giants	Manager*
	Cornett	Harry	Indianapolis ABC's	Catcher

*Managerial position

Career	Last Name	First Name	Teams	Positions
	Davis	(Quack)	Indianapolis ABC's	Outfielder
	Miller	Pleas (Hub)	St. Louis Giants	Pitcher
			West Baden Indianapolis Sprudels	
1913–19	Coleman	Clarence	Cleveland Tate Stars	Catcher
			Chicago Union Giants	Pitcher
			Chicago Giants	
			Indianapolis ABC's	
	Watts	Jack	Indianapolis ABC's	Catcher
			Dayton Marcos	
			Louisville Cubs	
			Chicago American Giants	
1913–20	Russell	Aaron A.	Homestead Grays	Third Base
1913–25	Bartlett	H.	Kansas City Monarchs	Pitcher
			Indianapolis ABC's	
1913–30	Owens	W. Oscar	Indianapolis ABC's	Outfielder
			Homestead Grays	Pitcher
				First Base
1913–40	Taylor	Benjamin H. (Ben)	Washington Black Senators	Manager*
			Indianapolis ABC's	First Base
			Chicago American Giants	
			Baltimore Black Sox	
			Harrisburg Giants	
			St. Louis Giants	
			Washington Potomacs	
			Bacharach Giants	
			New York Cubans	
			Brooklyn Eagles	
1913–46	Cockrell	Philip (Phil)	Lincoln Giants	Umpire*
			Havana Red Sox	
			Philadelphia Stars	
			Darby Daisies	
			Hilldale	
			Bacharach Giants	
			Negro National League	
1913–50	Dismukes	William (Dizzy)	Negro National League	Pitcher, Secretary*
			Philadelphia Giants	Manager
			Cincinnati Dismukes	
			Detroit Wolves	
			Birmingham Black Barons	
			Mohawk Giants	
			Memphis Red Sox	
			Chicago American Giants	
			Columbus Blue Birds	
			Brooklyn Royal Giants	
			Indianapolis ABC's	

*Managerial position

Career	Last Name	First Name	Teams	Positions
1914	Banton	—	Chicago American Giants	Pitcher
1914–23	Clark	Dell	Washington Potomacs	Shortstop
			Brooklyn Royal Giants	
			Lincoln Giants	
			Indianapolis ABC's	
1914–25	Jenkins	Horace	Chicago Giants	Pitcher
			Chicago Union Giants	Outfielder
			Chicago American Giants	
	Patterson	William	Austin Tecas Senators	Manager*
			Birmingam Black Barons	
			Houston Black Buffaloes	
	Thomas	Jules	Lincoln Giants	Outfielder
			Brooklyn Royal Giants	
1914–26	Allen	Toussaint (Tom)	Wilmington Potomacs	First Base
			Newark Stars	
			Hilldale	
			Havana Red Sox	
1914–34	Briggs	Otto	Hilldale	Manager*
			Bacharach Giants	Outfielder
			West Baden Indiana Sprudels	
			Quaker Giants	
			Dayton Marcos	
1915	Banks	G.	Lincoln Giants	Pitcher
	Banks	S.	Lincoln Giants	Catcher
	Clarkson	—	Chicago Giants	Catcher
	Gordon	—	Indianapolis ABC's	
	Henderson	Armour	Mohawk Giants	Pitcher
	Jackson	—	Chicago Giants	Shortstop
	Leblanc	—	Lincoln Giants	Shortstop
	Washington	Ed	Chicago American Giants	Pitcher
1915–16	Despert	—	Brooklyn Royal Giants	Outfielder
			Lincoln Giants	
	Dixon	—	Chicago American Giants	Pitcher
1915–17	Kimbro	Arthur	Lincoln Giants	Second Base
			St. Louis Giants	Third Base
1915–19	Forbes	Joe	Bacharach Giants	Third Base
			Pennsylvania Red Caps of New York	Shortstop
			Lincoln Giants	
1915–20	Cobb	W.	Lincoln Giants	Catcher
			St. Louis Giants	
	Powell	Russell	Indianapolis ABC's	Second Base
				Catcher
1915–23	Bauchman	Harry	Chicago Giants	Second Base
			Chicago American Giants	
			Chicago Union Giants	

*Managerial position

Career	Last Name	First Name	Teams	Positions
	Clark	Morten	Baltimore Black Sox Indianapolis ABC's	Shortstop
	Green	William	Chicago Union Giants Chicago Giants	Outfielder Third Base
1915–24	Hill	C.	Detroit Stars Chicago Union Giants St. Louis Giants Dayton Marcos	Pitcher Outfielder
	Whitworth	Richard	Hilldale Chicago American Giants Chicago Giants	Pitcher
1915–25	Allen	Todd	Chicago American Giants Lincoln Giants Indianapolis ABC's	Manager* Third Base
	Anderson	Robert (Bobby)	Chicago American Giants Gilkerson's Union Giants Peters' Union Giants Chicago Giants Philadelphia Giants	Second Base Shortstop
	Hall	—	Philadelphia Giants Baltimore Black Sox Lincoln Giants	Outfielder
	Johnson	Thomas (Tommy)	Chicago American Giants Pittsburgh Keystones Indianapolis ABC's	Pitcher
1915–26	Sykes	Melvin (Doc)	Hilldale Baltimore Black Sox Lincoln Stars	Pitcher
1915–27	Gatewood	Ernst	Bacharach Giants Lincoln Giants Brooklyn Royal Giants Harrisburg Giants	Catcher First Base
	Jennings	Thurman	Chicago Giants	Shortstop Second Base Outfielder
1915–29	Jones	Edward	Bacharach Giants Chicago American Giants Chicago Giants	Catcher
1915–30	Jones	William (Fox)	Bacharach Giants Hilldale Chicago Giants Chicago American Giants	Pitcher Catcher
	Ryan	Merven J. (Red)	Baltimore Black Sox Lincoln Stars Pittsburgh Stars of Buffalo	Pitcher

*Managerial position

Career	Last Name	First Name	Teams	Positions
1915–30 (Cont'd.)			Brooklyn Royal Giants	
			Hilldale	
			Lincoln Giants	
			Bacharach Giants	
			Harrisburg Giants	
1915–34	Williams	Charles (Lefty)	Homestead Grays	Pitcher
1915–42	White	Burlin	Cuban Stars	Catcher
			Lincoln Giants	Manager*
			West Baden, Indiana Sprudels	
			Philadelphia Royal Stars	
			Bacharach Giants	
			Boston Royal Giants	
			Harrisburg Giants	
			Philadelphia Giants	
1915–50	Charleston	Oscar	Pittsburgh Crawfords	First Base
			Brooklyn Brown Dodgers	Outfielder
			Indianapolis ABC's	Manager*
			Lincoln Stars	
			Chicago American Giants	
			Harrisburg Giants	
			St. Louis Giants	
			Philadelphia Stars	
			Toledo Crawfords	
			Hilldale	
			Homestead Grays	
			Indianapolis Crawfords	
1916	Brazelton	—	Chicago American Giants	Catcher
	Green	—	Lincoln Stars	Outfielder
	Hooker	—	Lincoln Stars	Outfielder
	Johnston	—	Lincoln Stars	Second Base
	McReynolds	—	Indianapolis ABC's	Outfielder
	Melton	—	St. Louis Giants	Pitcher
	Nolan	—	St. Louis Giants	Catcher
	Pryor	—	St. Louis Giants	Pitcher
			Indianapolis ABC's	
	Turner	—	Chicago Union Giants	First Base
	Waters	Dick	St. Louis Giants	Manager*
1916-17	Edwards	—	Pennsylvania Red Caps of New York	Outfielder
			Lincoln Stars	Pitcher
	Hannibal	—	Indianapolis ABC's	Outfielder
	Mack	Paul	Jersey City Colored Giants	Third Base
			Bacharach Giants	Outfielder
1916-18	Bluett	—	Chicago Union Giants	Second Base
	Dilworth	Lincoln Giants	Catcher	

*Managerial position

Career	Last Name	First Name	Teams	Positions
	Arthur		Bacharach Giants	Outfielder
			Hilldale	Pitcher
	Johnson	Dan (Shang)	Brooklyn Royal Giants	Pitcher
			Bacharach Giants	
	Kelly	—	Chicago Union Giants	Pitcher
			Chicago Giants	
	Williams	S.	Philadelphia Giants	Pitcher
			Brooklyn Royal Giants	
	Williams	A.	Brooklyn Royal Giants	Second Base
1916–19	Bailey	D.	Pennsylvania Red Caps of New York	Third Base
			Lincoln Stars	Outfielder
	Fuller	W.W.	Pennsylvania Giants	Second Base
			Cuban Giants	Shortstop
			Cleveland Tate Stars	
			Bacharach Giants	
	Johnson	—	Brooklyn Royal Giants	Shortstop
				Outfielder
	Thompson	—	Pittsburgh Stars of Buffalo	Pitcher
			Lincoln Stars	
1916–1920	Hall	Seller Mckee (Sell)	Homestead Grays	Pitcher
			Pittsburgh Colored Giants	
			Chicago American Giants	
	Roberts	Elihu	Hilldale	Outfielder
			Bacharach Giants	
1916–22	Johnson	A.	Pennsylvania Giants	Catcher
			Homestead Grays	
			Bacharach Giants	
	Meade	Chick	Baltimore Black Sox	Shortstop
			Pittsburgh Stars of Buffalo	Third Base
			Pittsburgh Colored Stars	
			Harrisburg Giants	
			Hilldale	
	Pugh	Johnny	Bacharach Giants	Outfielder
			Brooklyn Royal Giants	Second Base
			Harrisburg Giants	Third Base
			Philadelphia Giants	
	Tucker	Henry	Bacharach Giants	Club Officer
1916–23	Crocket	—	Bacharach Giants	Outfielder
	Crump	Willis	Bacharach Giants	Outfielder
				Second Base
	Deas	James (Yank)	Pennsylvania Giants	Catcher
			Lincoln Giants	
			Bacharach Giants	
			Hilldale	
	Johnson	Ben	Bacharach Giants	Pitcher
	Peters	Frank	Peters Union Giants	Shortstop
			Chicago Union Giants	

Career	Last Name	First Name	Teams	Positions
1916-24	Hayes	Buddy	Pittsburgh Keystones Chicago American Giants Cleveland Browns Indianapolis ABC's	Catcher
	Tyree	Ruby	Chicago American Giants All Nations Cleveland Browns	Pitcher
1916-25	Kennard	Dan	St. Louis Giants St. Louis Stars Indianapolis ABC's Detroit Stars Chicago American Giants	Catcher
	Williams	Thomas (Tom)	Brooklyn Royal Giants Bacharach Giants Chicago Giants Chicago American Giants Hilldale Lincoln Giants	Pitcher
1916-27	Drake	William (Plunk)	Indianapolis ABC's Kansas City Monarchs St. Louis Stars St. Louis Giants Detroit Stars	Pitcher
1916-28	Brown	George	Detroit Stars Indianapolis ABC's Dayton Marcos	Manager* Outfielder
	Jackson	Thomas	Bacharach Giants	Club Officer*
1916-29	Blackwell	Charles	Indianapolis ABC's St. Louis Stars Birmingham Black Barons Nashville Elite Giants St. Louis Giants	Outfielder
	Cummings	Napoleon (Chance)	Hilldale Bacharach Giants	Second Base First Base
	Roberts	Leroy (Roy)	Columbus Buckeyes Bacharach Giants	Pitcher
1916-31	Jeffries	James C.	Baltimore Black Sox Birmingham Black Barons Indianapolis ABC's	Outfielder Pitcher
1916-32	Donaldson	John	Los Angeles White Sox Detroit Stars Donaldson All-Stars Indianapolis ABC's All Nations Brooklyn Royal Giants	Outfielder Pitcher

*Managerial position

Career	Last Name	First Name	Teams	Positions
	Warfield	Frank	Detroit Stars	Shortstop
			St. Louis Giants	Third Base
			Washington Pilots	Second Base
			Baltimore Black Sox	Manager*
			Indianapolis ABC's	
			Hilldale	
			Kansas City Monarchs	
1916-34	Malarcher	David J. (Gentleman Dave)	Chicago American Giants	Outfielder
			Indianapolis ABC's	Second Base
			Cole's American Giants	Third Base
			Detroit Stars	Manager*
1916–43	Downs	McKinley (Bunny)	Philadelphia Tigers	Shortstop
			Cincinnati Clowns	Second Base
			Brooklyn Roysl Giants	Third Base
			Brooklyn Cuban Giants	Manager*
			Hilldale	
			St. Louis Giants	
	Harris	M. (Mo)	East-West League	Umpire
			Negro National League	
			Homestead Grays	Outfielder
1916–48	Lundy	Richard (Dick)	Newark Eagles	Third Base
			Baltimore Black Sox	Shortstop
			Newark Dodgers	Second Base
			Bacharach Giants	Manager*
			Hilldale	
			Jacksonville Eagles	
			Philadelphia Stars	
1917	Allison	—	Chicago Union Giants	First Base
	Carry	—	St. Louis Giants	Second Base
	Dandy	—	Lincoln Giants	Pitcher
	Francis	Del	Indianapolis ABC's	Second Base
	Goodgame	John	Chicago Giants	Pitcher
	Lewis	—	Lincoln Giants	Pitcher
	Lynch	Thomas	Indianapolis ABC's	Outfielder
	Lyons	Bennie	Jewell's ABC's of Indianapolis	First Base
	Madert	—	Chicago Giants	Second Base
	Miller	L.	Bacharach Giants	Third Base
	Pinder	—	Hilldale	Shortstop
	Rhodes	—	Hilldale	Catcher
	Town	—	Bacharach Giants	Outfielder
	Wilson	—	Bacharach Giants	Shortstop
1917–18	Lee	Dick	Chicago Union Giants	Outfielder
1917–19	Maywood	—	Lincoln Giants	Pitcher
	McLaughlin	—	Lincoln Giants	Pitcher

*Managerial position

Career	Last Name	First Name	Teams	Positions
1917-20	Cunningham	—	Dayton Marcos St. Louis Stars	Shortstop
	Fuller	Jimmy	Bacharach Giants Cubans Giants	Catcher
	McDougal	LeMuel (Lem)	Indianapolis ABC's Chicago Giants Chicago American Giants	Pitcher
	Wilson	—	Dayton Marcos Dayton Giants	Outfielder Pitcher
1917-21	Bingham	Bingo	Chicago Giants Chicago Union Giants	Outfielder
1917-22	Lane	I.S.	Dayton Marcos Detroit Stars Dayton Giants Columbus Buckeyes	Pitcher Outfielder Third Base
1917-25	Jackson	—	Lincoln Giants Pennsylvania Red Caps of New York	Catcher
	Jewell	Warner	Indianapolis ABC's Jewell's ABC's	Owner* Owner*
	Johnson	B.	Lincoln Giants Pennsylvania Red Caps of New York	Pitcher First Base Outfielder Second Base
1917-26	Harris	Andy	Newark Stars Hilldale Pennsylvania Red Caps of New York Pennsylvania Giants	Third Base
1917-27	Dewitt	—	Toledo Tigers Cleveland Tigers Dayton Giants Dayton Marcos Indianapolis ABC's Columbus Buckeyes Kansas City Monarchs	Third Base
1917-28	Dixon	George	Birmingham Black Barons Cleveland Tigers Chicago American Giants Indianapolis ABC's	Catcher
1917-34	Eggleston	Mack	Washington Pilots Homestead Grays Bacharach Giants Baltimore Black Sox Wilmington Potomacs Harrisburgh Giants	Third Base Catcher Outfielder

*Managerial position

Career	Last Name	First Name	Teams	Positions
			New York Black Yankees	
			Columbus Buckeyes	
			Washington Potomacs	
			Dayton Marcos	
			Detroit Stars	
			Dayton Giants	
			Indianapolis ABC's	
1917–40	Burgin	Ralph	Philadelphia Stars	Outfielder
			Hilldale	Second Base
			Brooklyn Royal Giants	Third Base
			New York Black Yankees	Shortstop
1917–46	Rogan	Wilbur (Bullet)	Negro American League	Outfielder
			Kansas City Monarchs	Third Base
			Los Angeles White Sox	Shortstop
				Pitcher
				Manager*
1918	Brown	Tute	Washington Red Caps	Third Base
	Brown	B.	Washington Red Caps	Outfielder
	Brown	E.	Chicago Union Giants	Third Base
	Brown	F.	Chicago Union Giants	Second Base
	Devoe	—	Chicago Giants	Catcher
	Ferrell	W.E.	Pennsylvania Giants	First Base
	Ford	C.	Pennsylvania Giants	Pitcher
	Ford	F.	Pennsylvania Giants	Catcher
	Fuller	(Chick)	Hilldale	Second Base
	Hendricks	—	Lincoln Giants	Outfielder
				Pitcher
	Mann	—	Chicago Union Giants	First Base
	Robinson	George (Sis)	Bacharach Giants	Pitcher
	Sullivan	—	Chicago Union Giants	Outfielder
	Tomm	—	Philadelphia Giants	Outfielder
			Brooklyn Royal Giants	
	Wells	—	Pennsylvania Giants	Catcher
			Lincoln Giants	Second Base
1918–19	Palmer	Earl	Lincoln Giants	Outfielder
			Chicago Union Giants	
	Reed	—	Detroit Stars	Third Base
			Chicago Union Giants	
	Roberts	J.D.	Hilldale	Third Base
			Pennsylvania Giants	Shortstop
				Second Base
1918–20	McNeil	—	Dayton Marcos	Catcher
				First Base

*Managerial position

Career	Last Name	First Name	Teams	Positions
1918–21	Alexander	—	Culumbus Buckeyes	Second Base
			Dayton Marcos	Outfielder
	Brewer	Luther	Chicago Giants	Outfielder
				First Base
	Brooks	Beattle	Brooklyn Royal Giants	Catcher
			Philadelphia Giants	Infielder
			Lincoln Giants	
	Graham	—	Bacharach Giants	Outfielder
			Washington Red Caps	
	Howell	Henry	Brooklyn Royal Giants	Pitcher
			Pennsylvania Giants	
			Pennsylvania Red Caps of New York	
			Bacharach Giants	
	Malloy	—	Nashville Elite Giants	Outfielder
			Pennsylvania Red Caps of New York	
1918–22	Tate	George	Negro National League	Vice-President*
			Cleveland Tate Stars	Club Officer*
1918–23	Hampton	Wade	Hilldale	Pitcher
			Pennsylvania Giants	
	Weeks	—	Harrisburg Giants	Third Base
			Pennsylvania Giants	Second Base
1918–24	Brown	David (Dave, Lefty)	Lincoln Giants	Pitcher
			Chicago American Giants	
1918–25	Baynard	—	Pennsylvania Red Caps of New York	Outfielder
	Fiall	Tom	Lincoln Giants	Pitcher
			Brooklyn Royal Giants	
	Fields	—	Cleveland Browns	Pitcher
			Chicago American Giants	
1918–26	Reese	John E.	St. Louis Stars	Outfielder
			Bacharach Giants	
			Detroit Stars	
			Hilldale	
			Toledo Tigers	
1918–29	Douglass	Edward (Eddie)	Lincoln Giants	Manager*
			Brooklyn Royal Giants	First Base
1918–30	Brown	(Scrappy)	Baltimore Black Sox	Shortstop
			Brooklyn Royal Giants	
			Washington Red Caps	
			Lincoln Giants	
	Gardner	(Ping)	Hilldale	Pitcher
			Philadelphia Royal Stars	
			Washington Red Caps	
			Cleveland Tigers	
			Harrisburg Giants	
			Bacharach Giants	
			Brooklyn Royal Giants	

*Managerial position

Career	Last Name	First Name	Teams	Positions
	Marcelle	Oliver H. (Ghost)	Detroit Stars	Shortstop
			Brooklyn Royal Giants	Third Base
			Baltimore Black Sox	
			Lincoln Giants	
			Bacharach Giants	
1918–31	Cunningham	(Rounder)	Montgomery Grey Sox	Shortstop
1918–32	Cason	John	Baltimore Black Sox	Shortstop
			Norfolk Stars	Catcher
			Lincoln Giants	Second Base
			Bacharach Giants	Outfielder
			Brooklyn Royal Giants	
			Hilldale	
1918–33	Brooks	Chester	Brooklyn Royal Giants	Outfielder
	Brown	Country	Brooklyn Royal Giants	Outfielder
	Field	—	Cleveland Browns	Pitcher
			Chicago American Giants	
1918–34	Gillespie	Henry	Bacharach Giants	Outfielder
			Hilldale	Pitcher
			Lincoln Giants	
			Philadelphia Tigers	
			Quaker Giants	
			Pennsylvania Giants	
1918–1942	Brown	James	Cole's American Giants	Firstbase
			Mineapolis–St. Paul Gophers	Manager*
			Chicago American Giants	Catcher
			Louisville Black Caps	
1918–45	McDonald	Webster	Hilldale	Pitcher
			Philadelphia Stars	Manager*
			Richmond Giants	
			Washington Pilots	
			Darby Daisies	
			Philadelphia Giants	
	Williams	Robert L. (Bobby)	Indianapolis ABC's	Third Base
			Pittsburgh Crawfords	Second Base
			Chicago American Giants	Shortstop
			Homestead Grays	Manager*
			Cleveland Red Sox	
1918–47	Mackey	Raleigh (Biz)	Hilldale	Shortstop
			Newark Eagles	Catcher
			Darby Daisies	Manager*
			San Antonio Giants	
			Baltimore Elite Giants	
			Indianapolis ABC's	
	Wilson	Thomas T. (Tom)	The Negro National League	Vice Chairman, Treasurer, President*
			Negro Southern League	Secretary*

*Managerial position

Career	Last Name	First Name	Teams	Positions
1918–47			Nashville Standard Giants	Club Officer*
(Cont'd.)			Cleveland Cubs	Club Officer*
			Baltimore Elite Giants	Club Officer*
			Nashville Elite Giants	Club Officer*
1918–48	Suttles	George (Mule)	Washington Pilots	Outfielder
			St. Louis Stars	First Base
			Newark Eagles	
			Chicago American Giants	
			Detroit Wolves	
			Birmingham Black Barons	
			Cole's American Giants	
1918–49	Jones	Reuben	Birmingham Black Barons	Manager*
			Houston Eagles	Outfielder
			Dallas Giants	
			Indianapolis ABC's	
			Memphis Red Sox	
			Chicago American Giants	
1919	Allen	(M.)	Lincoln Giants	Second Base
	Brown	Tom	Chicago American Giants	Pitcher
	Coleman	—	St. Louis Giants	Second Base
	Cowan	Eddie	Cleveland Tate Stars	Player
	Edwards	—	Bacharach Giants	Catcher
	Flood	Jess	Cleveland Tate Stars	Catcher
	Green	—	Brooklyn Royal Giants	Outfielder
	Harris	H.B.	Brooklyn Royal Giants	Business Manager*
	Harris	—	Lincoln Giants	Outfielder
	Irvin	Bill	Cleveland Tate Stars	Manager*
	Johnson	O.	Bacharach Giants	Pitcher
	Jones	—	St. Louis Giants	Third Base
	Parker	—	Lincoln Giants	Pitcher
	Reddon	Bob	Cleveland Tate Stars	Pitcher
	Turner	Tuck	Chicago American Giants	Pitcher
	Wikes	Barron	New York Bacharach Giants	Club Officer*
1919–20	Dandridge	(Ping)	St. Louis Giants	Shortstop
			Lincoln Giants	
	Jeffreys	Frank	Chicago Giants	Outfielder
	Lucas	—	Cuban Stars (East)	Outfielder
			Cuban Stars of Havana	Pitcher
	Victory	George M.	Pennsylvania Giants	Club Officer*
1919–23	Clark	—	Indianapolis ABC's	Pitcher
			Cleveland Tate Stars	
			Pittsburgh Keystones	
1919–24	Brooks	Charles	St. Louis Stars	Pitcher
			St. Louis Giants	Second Base
	Brooks	Irvin	Brooklyn Royal Giants	Pitcher

*Managerial position

Career	Last Name	First Name	Teams	Positions
	Starks	Otis (Lefty)	Chicago American Giants	Pitcher
			Lincoln Giants	
			Brooklyn Royal Giants	
			Hilldale	
1919–25	Finner	John	Milwaukee Bears	Pitcher
			St. Louis Stars	
			Birmingham Black Barons	
			St. Louis Giants	
	Leonard	James	Cleveland Browns	Outfielder
			Cleveland Tate Stars	Pitcher
1919–26	Treadwell	Harold	Indianapolis ABC's	Pitcher
			Bacharach Giants	
			Brooklyn Royal Giants	
			Dayton Marcos	
			Chicago American Giants	
			Harrisburg Giants	
	Woods	—	Bacharach Giants	Outfielder
			Columbus Buckeyes	
			Brooklyn Royal Giants	
			Indianapolis ABC's	
			Washington Potomacs	
1919–27	Daniels	Fred	Hilldale	Pitcher
			Birmingham Black Barons	
			St. Louis Giants	
	Hawkins	Lemuel (Hawk)	Kansas City Monarchs	Outfielder
			Los Angeles White Sox	First Base
1919–31	Spearman	Charles	Homestead Grays	Third Base
			Pennsylvania Red Caps of New York	Catcher
			Brooklyn Royal Giants	Second Base
			Lincoln Giants	Shortstop
			Cleveland Elites	
	Wesley	Edgar	Bacharach Giants	First Base
			Detroit Stars	
			Cleveland Hornets	
1919–32	Currie	Reuben (Rube)	Detroit Stars	Pitcher
			Chicago Unions	
			Hilldale	
			Chicago American Giants	
			Kansas City Monarchs	
1919–1933	Blount	John T. Terry	Detroit Stars	Club Officer*
			Negro National League	Vice President*
	Flournoy	(Pud)	Baltimore Black Sox	Pitcher
			Hilldale	
			Brooklyn Royal Giants	
			Bacharach Giants	

*Managerial position

Career	Last Name	First Name	Teams	Positions
1919–33 (Cont'd.)	Gardner	Floyd (Jelly)	Homestead Grays Lincoln Giants Detroit Stars Chicago American Giants	First Base Outfielder
	Matthews	John	Dayton Marcos	Club Officer*
	Winters	Jesse (Nip)	Lincoln Giants Bacharach Giants Darby Daisies Norfolk Giants Harrisburg Giants Norfolk Stars Philadelphia Stars	Pitcher
1919–1934	Hubbard	Jesse (Mountain)	Hilldale Baltimore Black Sox Bacharach Giants Homestead Grays Brooklyn Royal Giants	Outfielder Pitcher
	Lewis	Joseph (Sleepy)	Quaker Giants Norfolk-Newport News Royals Darby Daisies Baltimore Black Sox Hilldale Homestead Grays Washington Potomacs Bacharach Giants	Third Base Catcher
	Young	William P. (Pep)	Homestead Grays	Catcher
1919–1938	Beckwith	John	New York Black Yankees Brooklyn Royal Giants Harrisburg Giants Chicago American Giants Chicago Giants Baltimore Black Sox Homestead Grays Newark Dodgers Bacharach Giants Lincoln Giants	Outfielder Third Base Catcher Shortstop Manager*
1919–1949	Brown	Larry	Memphis Red Sox Philadelphia Stars New York Black Yankees Lincoln Giants Birmingham Black Barons Indianapolis ABC's Pittsburgh Key Stones Detroit Stars Cole's American Giants Chicago American Giants	Manager* Catcher

*Managerial position

FOOTBALL

MILTON ROBERTS' ALL-TIME BLACK COLLEGE SQUAD

1892–1900

Name	*Position*	*School*
George F. Porter	end	Atlanta University
Walter L. Smith	end	Howard University
L.W. Baldwin	guard	Tuskegee, Meharry Medical
Lawrence B. Ellerson	guard	Biddle University (J.C. Smith)
James Phillips	guard	Lincoln University
Pulaski O. Holt	quarterback	Fisk University
Frank. W. Avant	quarterback	Howard, Lincoln University
Dwight O.W. Holmes	quarterback	Howard University
John W. Work	halfback	Fisk University
Cain P. Cole	halfback	Lincoln University
Elmer C. Campbell	halfback	Howard University
Robert L. Jones	halfback	Howard University
Robert H. Scott	halfback	Lincoln University
William J. Trent	fullback	Livingstone College
John H. Love	fullback	Shaw University
William C. Matthews	fullback	Tuskegee University

1900–1910

Augustus M. Fisher	end	Lincoln University
Richard "EPH" Morris	end	Lincoln University
Harry Matanga	end	Lincoln University
Livingstone Mzimba	end	Lincoln University
William H. Washington	tackle	Howard University
Benjamin B. Church	tackle	Livingstone College
Benjamin S. Jackson	guard, halfback	Howard University
Victor C. Turner	guard, tackle	Atlanta Baptist (Morehouse)
Frederick D. Smith	guard	Atlanta University, Howard U.
Sandy M. Jackson	center	Atlanta Baptist (Morehouse)
Tom Williams	center	Alabama State
Manuel Taylor	quarterback	Shaw University
Henry E. Barco	quarterback	Virginia Union, Howard University

Name	Position	School
Charles H. Wesley	quarterback	Fisk University
Edwin A. Harleston	quarterback	Atlanta University
Augustus A. Marquess	quarterback	Fisk University
Paul V. Smith	quarterback	Hampton University
Floyd "Terrible" Terry	halfback	Talladega, Meharry, Howard
Edward B. Gray	halfback	Howard University
John L. McGriff	halfback	Shaw, Meharry, Howard
Emory Peterson	halfback	Virginia State University
Luke Lowdog	halfback	Hampton University
Clarence "Gene" Allen	halfback	Roger Williams, Howard, Atlanta Baptist
Robert M. Turner	halfback	Atlanta Baptist (Morehouse)
George M. King	halfback	Tuskegee, Fisk University
William H. Craighead	halfback	Howard University
Jubie B. Bragg	fullback	Tuskegee University

1910—1920

Name	Position	School
Fred M. Slaughter	end	Howard University
Ulysses "Lyss" Young	end	Lincoln University
George Gilmore	end	Howard University
James "Pop" Gayle	end	Hampton University
Sam Holland	end	W. Virginia State
Edward P. Hurt	end	Lincoln, Howard University
George D. Brock	end	Morehouse University
Henry A. Kean	end	Fisk University
Samuel B. Taylor	end	Virginia Union University
Booker T. Washington, Jr.	end	Fisk University
John M. Clelland	tackle	Howard University
C.B. Dowdell	tackle	Howard University
James Meeks	tackle	Livingstone College
Zanas Tantsi	tackle	Shaw University
Andrew Savage	tackle	Talladega, Atlanta Baptist
Dick Richardson	tackle	Morehouse College
Island Johns	guard	Shaw University
John Goodgame	guard	Talladega, Atlanta Baptist
Reggie Beamon	guard	Howard University
Edward L. Dabney	center	Hampton University
Zeal Dillon	center	Tuskegee, Prairie View

Name	Position	School
L.N. Bass	center	Walden, Meharry Medical
Samuel Coles	center	Talladega University
Arthur Hendley	quarterback	Tuskegee University
Tom L. Zuber	quarterback	Atlanta Baptist, Meharry
Henry Hucles	quarterback	Virginia Union University
Henry Collins	quarterback	Lincoln University
George Brice	quarterback	Howard University
Jimmy Webster	quarterback	Wiley College
Fred Bender	quarterback	Hampton University
William Ziegler	halfback	Fisk University
Charles Lewis	halfback	Fisk University
Leigh Maxwell	halfback	Atlanta University
Henry A. Merchant	halfback	Howard, Fisk University
Charleston B. Cox	halfback	Talladega University
William H. Kindle	halfback	Fisk University
Hannibal Howell	halfback	Virginia Union University
Charles Pinderhughes	halfback	Howard University
Benjamin C. Gregory	halfback	Virginia Union University
Joseph Brown	fullback	Shaw University
James S. "Big" Bullock	fullback	Lincoln University

BLACK FOOTBALL PLAYERS AT WHITE COLLEGES, 1889-1919

Wm. Henry Lewis	Center-Rush	1889–92	Amherst, Harvard Law
Wm. T.S. Jackson	Halfback	1889–91	Amherst
George Jewett	Halfback	1893	Northwestern
Albert Flippin	HB	1894	Nebraska
Wm. Lee Washington	HB	1897	Oberlin
Alton Washington	HB, QB	1898–1901	Northwestern
W.N. Johnson	HB	1900–04	Nebraska
Sam Morrell	HB	1901–02	Oberlin
Robert Taylor	HB	1901	Nebraska
Matthew Bullock	End	1902	Dartmouth
James Johnson	QB	1903	Carlisle Indian
Samuel Gordon		1903	Wabash
Robert Marshall	End	1903–06	Minnesota
Samuel Ransom	HB	1904–08	Beloit

Henry Thomas		1904	Coe
Arthur Davis Carr	QB	1904	Ohio University
Roy M. Young		1904–05	University of Illinois
Wm. Craighead	HB (Captain)	1905	Mass. State
Willie Williams	HB	1905–06	Mass. State
Charles Roberts		1906	Mass. State
Henry Beckett		1906	Springfield (Mass.)
H.H. Wheeler		1906	University of Illinois
Ernest Marshall		1906–07	Williams
Fenwich H. Watkins	HB	1907–08	Williams
John Pinkett	Center	1908	Amherst
Edward B. Gray	HB, End	1906–08	Amherst
Leslie L. Pollard	HB	1908	Dartmouth
Nathaniel Brown	HB	1908	Oberlin
Hale Parker	Center	1909–10	Illinois, Northwestern
Robert Johnson	End	1910	Dartmouth
William Kindle	HB	1911	Springfield (Mass.)
Gerald Lew	HB	1911	Mass. State
A.A. Alexander	HB	1911	University of Iowa
Benjamin Hubert	HB	1912	Mass. State
Eugene Collins	HB	1913	Coe
Joseph Trigg	Tackle	1914–16	Syracuse
Clinton Ross	Tackle	1913	Nebraska
Hugh Shippley	Tackle	1913	Brown
Gideon Smith		1913–16	Michigan State
Edward Morrison		1914–16	Tufts
William F. Brown		1914–16	Tufts
Paul Robeson	End	1915–18	Rutgers
Frederick Pollard, Sr.	Halfback	1915–16	Brown
Adolph Hamblin	Halfback	1916	Knox (Ill.)
Edward Sol Butler	Quarterback	1916–18	Dubuque (Iowa)
Everett Cunningham	QB	1916	Springfield (Mass.)
Fred "Duke" Slater	Tackle	1918–21	University of Iowa
Harry Graves		1918–1922	Michigan State
George Collins		1918	Coe
Otis Galloway	Tackle	1918–23	Tufts
John Shelburne	HB	1919	Dartmouth
Edward Niles	HB	1919	Colby

BASKETBALL

AFRICAN-AMERICAN STARS ON WHITE COLLEGE BASKETBALL TEAMS, THROUGH 1919

Samuel Ransom	1904–08	Beloit College
Wilbur Wood	1907–10	Nebraska
Fenwich Watkins	1909	Vermont
Cumberland Posey	1909, 1916	Penn State, Duquesne
Sol Butler	1910	Dubuque (Iowa)
William Kindle	1911	Springfield (Mass.)
Cleve Abbott	1913	South Dakota State
Paul Robeson	1915–18	Rutgers

Sources

BOOKS

Aaron, Henry. *Aaron.* New York: Thomas Y. Crowell Publishers, 1974.

Abdul-Jabbar, Kareem, and Knobler, Peter. *Giant Steps.* New York: Bantam Books, 1983.

Achebe, Chinua. *Things Fall Apart.* New York: McDowell Obolensky, 1959.

Adelman, Bob, and Hall, Susan. *Out of Left Field: Willie Stargell and the Pittsburgh Pirates.* Boston: Little, Brown and Company 1974.

Adelman, Melvin L. *A Sporting Time: New York City and the Rise of Modern Athletics 1820–70.* Urbana, Illinois: University of Illinois Press, 1986.

Adu Boahen, Clark; Desmond, Clarke; John H., Curtin, Philip; Davidson, Basil; Samkange, Stanlake; Schaar, Stuart; Shepperson, George; Shinnie, Margaret; Vansina, Jan; Wallerstein, Immanuel; Willis, John R. *The Horizon History of Africa.* New York: American Heritage Publishing Company, 1971.

Alexander, Charles C. *Ty Cobb.* New York: Oxford University Press, 1984.

Ali, Muhammad. *The Greatest: My Own Story.* New York: Random House, 1975.

Allen, Maury. *Mr. October: The Reggie Jackson Story.* New York: New American Library, 1982.

Anderson, Dave. *Sports of Our Times.* New York: Random House, 1979.

Aptheker, Herbert. *A Documentary History of the Negro People in the United States: 1910–1932.* Secaucus, New Jersey: Citadel Press, 1973.

Ashe, Arthur. *Off the Court.* New York: New American Library, 1981.

——————*Portrait in Motion.* Boston, Massachusetts: Houghton Mifflin Company, 1975.

Astor, Gerald. *And a Credit to His Race: The Hard Life and Times of Joseph Louis Barrow.* New York: Saturday Review Press, 1974.

Baker, William J. *Jesse Owens: An American Life.* New York: The Free Press, 1986.

Barber, Red. *1947: When All Hell Broke Loose in Baseball.* Garden Clty, New York: Doubleday and Company, 1982.

Beart, Charles. *"Jeux et Jouets de L'Ouest Africain"* (a monograph). Tome 1. Number 42.

Behee, John. *Hail to the Victors!* Ann Arbor, Michigan: Ulrich's Books, 1974.

Bell, Marty. *The Legend of Dr. J.* New York: New American Library, 1975.

Bennett, Lerone, Jr. *Wade in the Water: Great Moments in Black History.* Chicago: Johnson Publishing Company, 1979.

Berkow, Ira. *Oscar Robertson: The Golden Year 1964.* Englewood Cliffs, New Jersey: Prentice Hall, 1971.

——————. *The DuSable Panthers.* New York: Atheneum Publishers, 1978.

Blassingame, John W. *Black New Orleans: 1860–1880.* Chicago: University of Chicago Press, 1973.

——————. *Slave Testimony: Two Centuries of Letters, Speeches, Interviews and Autobiographies.* Baton Rouge, Louisiana: Louisiana State University Press, 1977.

Boss, David. *The Pro-Football Experience.* New York: Harry N. Abrams, Inc., 1973.

Broderick, Francis L., and Meier, August. *Negro Protest Thought in the Twentieth Century.* Indianapolis: Bobbs-Merrill Company, 1965.

Brondfield, Jerry. *Kareem Abdul-Jabbar, Magic Johnson and the Los Angeles Lakers.* New York: Scholastic Book Services, 1981.

Brown, Gene. *The Complete Book of Basketball.* New York: Arno Press, 1980.

Brown, Jimmy. *Off My Chest.* New York: Doubleday and Company, 1964.

Brown, Larry. *I'll Always Get Up.* New York: Simon and Schuster, 1973.

Brown, Paul. *PB: The Paul Brown Story.* New York: Atheneum Publishers, 1979.

Butler, Hal. *The Willie Horton Story.* New York: Julian Messner Company, 1970.

Campanella, Roy. *It's Good to Be Alive.* Boston: Little, Brown and Company, 1959.

Carter, Rubin "Hurricane." *The Sixteenth Round.* New York: Viking Press, 1974.

Cashmore, Ernest. *Black Sportsmen.* London: Routledge and Kegan Paul, 1982.

Chalk, Ocania. *Black College Sport.* New York: Dodd, Mead and Company, 1976.

——————. *Pioneers of Black Sport.* New York: Dodd, Mead and Company, 1975.

Chamberlain, Wilt, and Shaw, David. *Wilt: Just Like Any Other 7-Foot Black Millionaire Who Lives Next Door.* New York: Macmillan Publishing Company, 1973.

Chambers, Lucille Arcola. *America's Tenth Men.* New York: Twayne Publishers, 1957.

Chambers, Ted. *The History of Athletics and Physical Education at Howard University.* Washington, D.C.: Vantage Press, 1986.

Chew, Peter. *The Kentucky Derby: The First 100 Years.* Boston: Houghton Mifflin and Company, 1974.

Chisholm, J. Francis. *Brewery Gulch: Frontier Days of Old Arizona, Last Outpost of the Great Southwest.* San Antonio: Naylor Company, 1949.

Cohen, Joel H. *Hammerin' Hank of the Braves.* New York: Scholastic Book Services, 1971.

Considine, Tim. *The Language of Sport.* New York: World Almanac Publications, 1982.

Corbett, J. James. *The Roar of the Crowd: The True Tale of the Rise and Fall of a Champion.* Garden City, New York: Garden City Publishing Company, 1926.

Cottrell, John. *Man of Destiny: The Story of Muhammed Ali.* London: Frederick Muller Press, 1967.

Cummings, John. *Negro Population in the United States, 1790–1915.* New York: Arno Press, 1968.

Cunard, Nancy. *Negro Anthology 1913–1933.* London: Wishart and Company, 1934.

Davies, Marianna W. *Contributions of Black Women to America.* Columbia, South Carolina: Kenday Press, Inc., 1982.

Davis, Edwin Adams, and Hogan, William Ranson. *The Barber of Natchez.* Baton Rouge, Louisiana: Louisiana State University Press, 1973.

Diamond, Wilfred. *How Great Was Joe Louis?* New York: Paebar Company, 1950.

Dolan, Edward F., Jr., and Lyttle, Richard B. *Jimmy Young: Heavyweight Challenge.* Garden City; New York: Doubleday and Company, 1979.

Donaldson, Thomas. *Idaho of Yesterday.* Westport, Connecticut: Greenwood Press, 1970.

Douglass, Frederick. *The Life and Times of Frederick Douglass.* New York: Bonanza Books, 1962.

Drake, St. Clair, and Cayton, Horace R. *Black Metropolis: A Study of Negro Life in a Northern City.* New York: Harcourt, Brace and Company, 1945.

Du Bois, W. E. Burghardt. *The Souls of Black Folk.* New York: Washington Square Press, 1970.

Duncan, Otis Dudley, and Duncan, Beverly. *The Negro Population of Chicago.* Chicago: University of Chicago Press, 1957.

Durant, John, and Bettman, Otto. *Pictorial History of American Sports from Colonial Times to the Present.* Cranberry, New Jersey: A.S. Barnes and Company, 1973.

Durham, Philip, and Jones, Everette L. *The Negro Cowboys.* New York: Dodd, Mead and Company, 1965.

Eaton, Hubert A. *Every Man Should Try.* Wilmington, North Carolina: Bonaparte Press, 1984.

Edwards, Audrey, and Wohl, Gary. *Muhammad Ali: The People's Champ.* Boston: 1977.

Edwards, Harry. *Sociology of Sport.* Homewood, Illinois: The Dorsey Press, 1973.

——————. *The Revolt of the Black Athlete.* New York: The Free Press, 1970.

——————. *The Struggle That Must Be: An Autobiography.* New York: Macmillan Publishing, 1980.

Egan, Pierce. *Boxiana.* London: G. Smeeton Publishers, 1812.

Ehre, Edward, and *The Sporting News. Best Sport Stories 1982.* New York: E. P. Dutton, 1982.

Einstein, Charles. *Willie Mays: Born to Play Ball.* New York: G. P. Putnam's Sons, 1955.

Eisenstadt, Murray. *The Negro in American Life.* New York: Oxford Book Company, 1968.

Farr, Finis. *Black Champion: The Life and Times of Jack Johnson.* London: Macmillan and Company, 1964.

——————. *Black Champions: The Life and Times of Jack Johnson.* New York: Charles Scribner's Sons, 1964.

Figler, Stephen, and Figler, Howard. *The Athlete's Game Plan for College and Career.* Princeton, New Jersey: Peterson's Guide, 1984.

Fisher, Galen M. *John R. Mott: Architect of Cooperation and Unity.* New York: Associated Press, 1962.

——————. *Public Affairs and the YMCA: 1844–1944.* New York: Association Press, 1948.

Fitzgerald, Ray. *Champions Remembered.* Brattleboro, Vermont: The Stephen Greene Press, 1982.

Fleischer, Nat. *All-Time Ring Record Book.* Norwalk, Connecticut: O'Brian Suburban Press, 1944.

——————. *Black Dynamite: The Story of the Negro in the Prize Ring from 1782 to 1938.* New York: *Ring* magazine, 1947.

——————. *All-Time Ring Record Book.* Norwalk, Connecticut: O'Brian Suburban Press, 1947.

Fletcher, Marvin E. *The Black Soldier Athlete in the United States Army 1890–1916.* Athens, Ohio: 1973.

Flood, Kurt. *The Way It Is.* New York: Trident Press, 1971.

Foner, Philip S. *Paul Robeson Speaks: Writings, Speeches and Interviews.* London: Quartette Books, 1978.

Foreman, Thomas Elton. *"Discrimination Against the Negro in American Athletics* (a monograph). Fresno, California: Fresno State College, 1957.

Fox, Larry. *Willis Reed: Take Charge Man of the Knicks.* New York: Grosset and Dunlap, 1970.

Franklin, John Hope. *The Free Negro in North Carolina 1790–1860.* New York: W. W. Norton and Company, 1969.

Frazier, Walt, and Berkow, Ira. *Rockin' Steady.* Englewood Cliffs, New Jersey: Prentice Hall Inc., 1974.

Frazier, Walt, and Jares, Joe. *The Walt Frazier Story: Clyde.* New York: Grosset and Dunlap, 1970.

Frommer, Harvey. *Rickey and Robinson: The Men Who Broke Baseball's Color Barrier.* New York: Macmillan Publishing Company, 1982.

The Fulani of Northern Nigeria. Lagos, Nigeria: Government Printing Office, 1945.

Gallagher, Robert C. *Ernie Davis: The Elmira Express.* Silver Spring, Maryland: Bartleby Press, 1983.

Gary, Lawrence E. *Black Men.* Beverly Hills, California: Sage Publications, 1981.

Gayle, Addison, Jr. *The Black Aesthetic.* Garden City, New York: Anchor Books, 1972.

Genovese, Eugene D. *Roll Jordan Roll: The World the Slaves Made.* New York: Random House, 1974.

Gewecke, Cliff. *Advantage Ashe.* New York: Coward McCann, 1965.

Gibson, Althea. *I Always Wanted to Be Somebody.* New York: Harper and Brothers, 1958.

Gibson, Bob. *From Ghetto to Glory: The Story of Bob Gibson.* Englewood, New Jersey: Prentice Hall Inc., 1968.

Goldstein, Allan. *A Fistful of Sugar.* New York: Coward, McCann and Geoghegan, 1981.

Graffis, Herb. *PGA: Official History of the PGA of America.* New York: Thomas Y. Crowell Publishers, 1975.

Griffin, Archie. *Archie: The Archie Griffin Story.* Garden City, New York: Doubleday and Company, 1977.

Grun, Bernard. *The Timetables of History.* New York: Simon and Schuster, 1979.

Halberstam, David. *The Breaks of the Game.* New York: Alfred A. Knopf, 1981.

Hamilton, Virginia. *Paul Robeson: The Life and Times of a Free Black Man.* New York: Harper and Row, 1974.

Harris, Merv. *On Court with the Superstars of the NBA.* New York: The Viking Press, 1973.

Haskins, James. *Sugar Ray Leonard.* New York: Lothrop, Lee and Shepard, 1982.

Hayes, Elvin, and Gilbert, Bill. *They Call Me "The Big E."* Englewood Cliffs, New Jersey: Prentice Hall, 1978.

Heller, Peter. *In This Corner: Forty World Champions Tell Their Stories.* New York: Simon and Schuster, 1973.

Henderson, Edwin B. *The Negro in Sports.* Washington, D.C.: Associated Publishers Inc., 1949.

Henderson, Edwin B., and *Sport* magazine. *The Black Athlete: Emergence and Arrival.* Cornwell Heights, Pennsylvania: Pennsylvania Publishers Company Inc., 1968.

Henderson, James H. M., and Henderson, Betty F. *Molder of Men: Portrait of a "Grand Old Man"— Edwin Bancroft Henderson.* New York: Vantage Press, 1985.

Hirschberg, Al. *Henry Aaron: Quiet Superstar.* New York: G. P. Putnam's Sons, 1974.

Hollander, Zander. *Great American Athletes of the Twentieth Century.* New York: Random House, 1966.

Holmes, Dwight Oliver Wendell. *The Evolution of the Negro College.* New York: Arno Press, 1969.

Holway, John B. *"Bullet Joe and the Monarchs"* (a monograph). Washington, D.C.: Capitol Press, 1984.

Isaac, Stan. *Jim Brown: The Golden Year 1964.* Englewood Cliffs, New Jersey: Prentice Hall Inc., 1970.

Isaacs, Neil D. *All the Moves: A History of College Basketball.* New York: Harper and Row, 1984.

Jackson, Reggie. *Reggie.* New York: Ballantine Books, 1984.

——————. *Reggie: A Season with a Superstar.* Chicago: Playboy Press Books, 1975.

James, C. L. R. *Beyond a Boundary.* New York: Pantheon Books, 1983.

Jares, Joe. *Basketball: The American Game.* Chicago: Follett Publishing Company, 1971.

"The Jesse Owens Dossier." Obtained from the Federal Bureau of Investigation Under the Freedom of Information Act.

Johnson, Arthur T., and Frey, James H. *Government and Sport: The Public Policy Issues.* Totowa, New Jersey: Rowman and Allanheld, 1985.

Johnson, Charles S. *Patterns of Negro Segregation.* New York: Harper and Brothers, 1943.

Johnson, Earvin "Magic," and Levin, Richard. *Magic.* New York: The Viking Press, 1983.

Johnson, Jack. *Jack Johnson Is a Dandy: An Autobiography.* New York: New American Library, 1969.

——————. *Jack Johnson: In the Ring and Out.* Chicago: National Sports Publishing Company, 1927.

Johnson, James Weldon. *Black Manhattan.* New York: Atheneum Press, 1977.

Jones, Cleon. *Cleon.* New York: Coward-McCann, Inc., 1970.

Jones, Wally, and Washington, Jim. *Black Champions Challenge American Sports.* New York: David McKay Company, Inc., 1972.

Jones, William H. *Recreation and Amusement Among Negros in Washington.* Westport, Connecticut: Negro Universities Press, 1970.

Jordan, Pat. *Black Coach.* New York: Dodd, Mead and Company, 1971.

Kaletsky, Richard. *Ali and Me: Through the Ropes.* Bethany, Connecticut: Andrienne Publications, 1982.

Katz, William Loren. *The Black West.* Garden City, New York: Anchor Books, 1973.

Keeneland Association Library. *Thoroughbred Record.* Lexington, Kentucky: Keeneland Association Library.

Kountze, Mabe "Doc." *Fifty Sport Years Along Memory Lane.* Medford, Massachusetts: Mystic Valley Press, 1979.

Kowet, Don. *Vida Blue: Coming Up Again.* New York: G. P. Putnam's Sons, 1974.

Lapchick, Richard Edward. *The Politics of Race and International Sport: The Case of South Africa.* Westport, Connecticut: Greenwood Press, 1975.

Leach, George B. *Kentucky Derby Diamond Jubilee.* New York: Gibbs Inman Publishers, 1949.

LeFlore, Ron. *Break Out: From Prison to the Big Leagues.* New York: New York. Harper and Row, 1978.

Lewis, David Levering. *When Harlem Was in Vogue.* New York: Alfred A. Knopf, 1981.

Lewis, Dwight, and Thomas, Susan. *A Will to Win.* Mount Juliet, Tennessee: Cumberland Press, 1983.

Lewis, William H. *"How to Play Football"* (a monograph). Boston: 1903.

Libby, Bill, and Haywood, Spencer. *Stand Up for Something: The Spencer Haywood Story.* New York: Grosset and Dunlap, 1972.

Libby, Bill *Goliath: The Wilt Chamberlain Story.* New York: Dodd, Mead and Company, 1977.

Lipman, David, and Wilks, Ed. *Bob Gibson: Pitching Ace.* New York: G. P. Putnam's Sons, 1975.

Lipsyte, Robert. *Free to Be Muhammad Ali.* New York: Harper and Row, 1978.

——————. *Sports World: An American Dreamland.* New York: Quadrangle Books, 1975.

Louis, Joe. *Joe Louis: My Life.* New York: Harcourt Brace Jovanovich, 1978.

Louis, Joe. *My Life Story.* New York: Duell, Sloan and Pearce, 1947.

Lyle, Sparky, and Golenbock, Peter. *The Bronx Zoo.* New York: Crown Publishers Inc., 1979.

Mackler, Bernard. *Black Superstars: Getting Ahead in Today's America.* New York: *Conch* magazine Limited Publishers, 1977.

Mailer, Norman. *The Fight.* Boston: Little, Brown and Company, 1975.

Major, Gerri. *Black Society.* Chicago: Johnson Publishing Company, Inc., 1976.

Matthews, Vincent. *My Race Be Won.* New York: Charter House Publishers, 1974.

Mays, Willie, and Einstein, Charles. *Willie Mays: My Life in and Out of Baseball.* New York: E. P. Dutton and Company, 1966.

McAdoo, Harriett Pipes, and McAdoo, John Lewis. *Black Children: Social, Educational, and Parental Environments.* Beverly Hills, California: Sage Publications, 1985.

McCallum, John D. *The World Heavyweight Boxing Championship: A History.* Radnor, Pennsylvania: Chilton Book Company, 1974.

McPhee, John. *A Sense of Where You Are: A Profile of William Warren Bradley.* New York City: New York. Farrar, Straus and Giroux, 1965.

McPhee, John. *Levels of the Game.* New York: Farrar, Straus and Giroux, 1969.

Michelson, Herb. *Almost a Famous Person.* New York: Harcourt Brace Jovanovich, 1980.

Michener, James A. *Sports in America.* New York: Fawcett Crest, 1976.

Miller, Margery. *Joe Louis: American.* New York: Hill and Wang, 1945.

Moore, Archie, and Pearl, Leonard B. *Any Boy Can: The Archie Moore Story.* Englewood Cliffs, New Jersey: Prentice Hall, Inc., 1971.

Morris, Willie. *The Courting of Marcus Dupree.* Garden City, New York: Doubleday and Company, 1983.

Movius, Geoffrey H. *The Second Book of Harvard Athletics, 1923–1963.* Cambridge, Massachusetts: The Harvard Varsity Club, 1964.

Murray, Florence. *The Negro Handbook, 1944.* New York: Current Reference Publications, 1944.

Nazel, Joseph. *Jackie Robinson: A Biography.* Los Angeles: Holloway House Publishing Company, 1982.

Neft, David S., Cohen, Richard M., and Deutsch, Jordan A. *The Sports Encyclopedia: Pro Football the Modern Era, 1960 to Present.* New York: Simon and Schuster, 1982.

Neft, David S., Cohen, Richard M., and Deutsch, Jordan A. *Pro-Football: The Early Years, 1895–1959.* Ridgefield, Connecticut: Sports Products, Inc., 1978.

Negro Population in the United States, 1790–1915. New York: Arno Press, 1968.

Newcombe, Jack. *Floyd Patterson: Heavyweight King.* New York: Bartholomew House Inc., 1961.

Noll, Roger G. *Government and the Sports Business.* Washington, D.C.: The Brookings Institution, 1974.

Norback, Craig, and Norback, Peter. *The New American Guide to Athletics, Sports, and Recreation.* New York: The New American Library, 1979.

Norman, Gardner L. *Athletics of the Ancient World.* Chicago: Associated Publishers, 1930.

O'Connor, Dick. *Reggie Jackson: Yankee Superstar.* New York: Scholastic Book Services, 1978.

The Official 1985 National Football League Record and Fact Book. New York: National Football League, 1986.

Olsen, Jack. *Black Is Best: The Riddle of Cassius Clay.* New York: G. P. Putnam's Sons, 1967.

Orr, Jack. *The Black Athlete: His Story in American History.* New York: Lion Books Publishing, 1969.

Owens, Jesse. *Blackthink: My Life as Black Man and White Man.* New York: William Morrow and Company, 1970.

————. *I Have Changed.* New York: William Morrow and Company, 1972.

————. *Jesse: The Man Who Outran Hitler.* New York: Fawcett Gold Medal Books, 1978.

Pachter, Mark. *Champions of American Sport.* New York: National Portrait Gallery, Smithsonian Institute, 1981.

Parker, Inez Moore, and Callison, Helen Vassy. *The Biddle Johnson C. Smith University Story.* Charlotte, North Carolina: Charlotte Publishing Company, 1975.

Palmer, Charles B. *For Gold and Glory: The Story of Thoroughbred Racing in America.* New York: Karrick and Evans Inc., 1939.

Patterson, Floyd, and Gross, Milton. *Victory Over Myself.* New York: Bernard Geis Associates and Random House, 1962.

Paul Robeson Archives. *Paul Robeson Tribute and Selected Writings.* New York: Paul Robeson Archives, 1976.

Payton, Walter. *Sweetness.* Chicago: Contemporary Books, Inc., 1978.

Pepe, Phil. *Stand Tall: The Lew Alcindor Story.* New York: Grosset and Dunlap, 1970.

Peterson, James A. *Slater of Iowa.* Chicago: Hinkley and Schmitt, 1958.

Peterson, Robert. *Only the Ball Was White*. Englewood Cliffs, New Jersey: Prentice Hall Inc., 1970.

Phillips, Ulrich Bonnell. *American Negro Slavery*. Baton Rouge, Louisiana: Louisiana State University Press, 1966.

Picott, J. Rupert. *"Selected Black Sports Immortals"* (a monograph). Washington, D.C.: Association for the Study of Afro-American Life and History, Inc., 1981.

Plimpton, George. *Sports!* New York: Abbeville Press/Harry N. Abrams, 1978.

Plosky, Harry A., and Brown, Roscoe C., Jr. *The Negro Almanac*. New York: Bellwhether Publishing Company, 1967.

Puckett, Newbell N. *The Magic and Folk Beliefs of the Southern Negro*. New York: Dover Publications, 1969.

Rader, Benjamin G. *American Sports*. Englewood Cliffs, New Jersey: Prentice Hall, 1983.

Randolph, Jack. *"Tom Molineux: America's 'Almost' Champion"* (a monograph).

Randolph, Wilma. *Wilma*. New York: New American Library, 1977.

Reed, Willis. *A View from the Rim: Willis Reed on Basketball*. Philadelphia: J. B. Lippincott, 1971.

Reichler, Joseph L. *The Baseball Encyclopedia*. New York: Macmillan Publishing Company, Inc., 1985.

Reidenbaugh, Lowell. *The Sporting News First Hundred Years, 1886–1986*. St. Louis: Sporting News Publishing Company, 1985.

Reuter, Edward Byron. *The Mulatto in the United States*. New York: Negro Universities Press, 1969.

Ritter, Lawrence, and Honig, Donald. *The 100 Greatest Baseball Players of All Time*. New York: Crown Publishers, 1981.

Roberts, Randy. *Papa Jack: Jack Johnson and the Era of White Hopes*. New York: The Free Press, 1983.

Robertson, Lawson. *College Athletics*. New York: American Sports Publishing Company, 1923.

Robeson, Susan. *The Whole World in His Hands: A Pictorial Biography of Paul Robeson*. Secaucus, New Jersey: Citadel Press, 1981.

Robinson, Frank. *Frank: The First Year*. New York: Holt, Rinehart and Winston, 1976.

Robinson, Frank. *My Life in Baseball*. Garden City, New York: Doubleday and Company, 1968.

Robinson, Jackie. *I Never Had It Made*. Greenwich, Connecticut: Fawcett Publications, 1972.

——————. *Jackie Robinson: My Own Story*. New York: Greenberg Publishers, 1948.

Robinson, Louie, Jr. *Arthur Ashe: Tennis Champion*. Garden City, New York: Doubleday and Company Inc., 1967.

Rogosin, Don. *Invisible Men: Life in Baseball's Negro Leagues*. New York: Atheneum Publishers, 1983.

Ross, Frank Alexander, and Kennedy, Louise Benable. *A Bibliography of Negro Migration*. New York: Columbia University Press, 1934.

Ruck, Ron. *Sandlot Seasons: Sport in Black Pittsburgh*. Urbana, Illinois: University of Illinois Press, 1987.

Russell, Bill, and Branch, Taylor. *Second Win: The Memoirs of an Opinionated Man*. New York: Random House, 1979.

Russell, Cazzie L., Jr. *Me, Cazzie Russell*. Westwood, New Jersey: Fleming H. Revell, 1967.

Russell, John A. *The Free Negro in Virginia: 1619–1865*. New York: Negro Universities Press, 1969.

Rust, Art, Jr. *"Get That Nigger Off the Field!"* New York: Delacorte Press, 1976.

Rust, Art, Jr., and Rust, Edna. *Recollections of a Baseball Junkie*. New York: William Morrow and Company, 1985.

Rust, Edna, and Rust, Art, Jr. *Art Rust's Illustrated History of the Black Athlete*. Garden City, New York. Doubleday and Company Inc., 1985.

Sample, Johnny. *Confessions of a Dirty Ball Player*. New York: The Dial Press, 1970.

Savin, Francine. *Women Who Win*. New York: Dell Publishing Company, 1975.

Saxon, Walt. *Darryl Strawberry*. New York: Dell Books, 1985.

Schapp, Dick. *The Perfect Jump*. New York: New American Library, 1976.

——————. *Sport*. New York: Arbor House, 1975.

Schneider, Russell, Jr. *Frank Robinson: The Making of a Manager*. New York: Coward, McCann and Geoghegan, 1976.

Schoolcraft, M. H. *"Letters on the Condition of the African Race in the United States by a Southern Lady"* (a monograph). Philadelphia: T. K. and P. G. Collins, 1852.

Schoor, Gene. *Dave Winfield: The 23 Million Dollar Man.* Briarcliff Manor, New York: Stein and Day Publishers, 1982.

——————. *Willie Mays: Modest Champion.* New York: G. P. Putnam's Sons, 1960.

Schubert, Frank N. "The Black Regular Army Regiments in Wyoming, 1885–1912" (a thesis). Laramie, Wyoming: University of Wyoming, 1970.

Scott, Jack. *The Athletic Revolution.* New York: The Free Press, 1971.

Silvermen, Al. *Best from Sport: An Anthology of Fifteen Years of Sport Magazine.* New York: Bartholomew House, Inc., 1961.

——————. *I Am Third: Gale Sayers.* New York: Viking Press, 1970.

Simpson, O. J. *O.J. : The Education of a Rich Rookie.* New York: The Macmillan Company, 1970.

Sims, Mary S. *The Natural History of a Social Institution—YMCA.* New York: Association Press, 1929.

Smith, Harry Worcester. *Life and Sport in Aiken.* Aiken, South Carolina: Derrydale Press, 1935.

"Softball Hall of Famers" (a monograph). Oklahoma City: Amateur Softball Association.

Sowell, Thomas. *Ethnic America: A History.* New York: Basic Books Inc., 1981.

Spalding's Athletic Library. *Interscholastic Athletic Association Guide Book for 1910, 1911, and 1913.* New York: American Sports Publishing Company.

Spink, J. G. Taylor. *Judge Landis and Twenty-Five Years of Baseball.* New York: Thomas Y. Crowell Publishers, 1947.

Spradling, Mary Mace. *In Black and White.* Detroit: Gale Research Company, 1980.

Stagg, Amos Alonzo, and Williams, H. C. "A Scientific and Practical Treatise on American Football for Schools and Colleges" (a monograph). Chicago: University of Chicago, 1893.

Staples, Robert. *Black Masculinity: The Black Male's Role in American Society.* San Francisco: The Black Scholar Press, 1982.

Stargell, Willie, and Bird, Tom. *Willie Stargell: An Autobiography.* New York: Harper and Row Publishers, 1984.

Stern, Robert. *They Were Number One: A History of the NCAA Basketball Tournament.* New York: Leisure Press, 1983.

Stingley, Darryl. *Darryl Stingley: Happy to be Alive.* New York: Beaufort Books Inc., 1983.

Sugar, Bert Randolph, and *Ring* magazine. *The Great Fights.* New York: Rutledge Press, 1981.

Super, Paul. *Formative Ideas in the YMCA.* New York: Association Press, 1929.

Tatum, Jack. *They Call Me Assassin.* New York: Everest House Publishers, 1979.

Taylor, Marshall W. "Major." *The Fastest Bicycle Rider in the World.* Worcester, Massachusetts: Wormley Publishing Company, 1928.

The Annals of America. Chicago: Encyclopedia Britannica Inc., 1976.

The Horizon History of Africa. New York: American Heritage Publishing Company, 1971.

The International Amateur Athletic Association Federation Statistics Handbook. Los Angeles: International Amateur Athletic Federation, 1984.

The Official Results of the 1984 Olympic Games. Los Angeles: Los Angeles Olympic Committee, 1984.

The Ring Record Book and Boxing Encyclopedia. New York: Atheneum Publishers, 1987.

The *Sporting Life's* Official Baseball Guide: 1890.

The Sporting News Official NBA Guide: 1984–1985. St. Louis: The Sporting News, 1985.

Trengove, Allan. *The Story of the Davis Cup.* London: Stanley Paul Publishers, 1985.

Truehart, William Elton. "The Consequences of Federal and State Resource Allocation and Development Policies for Traditionally Black Land-Grant Institutions: 1862–1954" (a thesis). Cambridge, Massachusetts: Doctoral Thesis for Graduate School of Education, Harvard University, 1979.

Tygiel, Jules. *Baseball's Great Experiment: Jackie Robinson and His Legacy.* New York: Oxford University Press, 1983.

United States Tennis Association. *The Official USTA Year Book and Tennis Guide.* Lynn, Massachusetts: H. O. Zimman Inc., 1986.

Wallechinsky, David. *The Complete Book of the Olympics.* New York: Penguin Books, 1984.

White, Solomon. *Sol White's Official Baseball Guide.* Philadelphia: Camden House, Inc., 1984.

Who's Who Among Black Americans. *Who's Who Among Black Americans, 1975-76.* Northbrook, Illinois: 1976.

Wills, Maury, and Gardner, Steve. *It Pays to Steal.* Englewood Cliffs, New Jersey: Prentice Hall Inc., 1963.

Winters, Manque. *Professional Sports: The Community College Connection.* Inglewood, California: Winnor Press, 1982.

Woodward, Bob, and Armstrong, Scott. *The Brethren: Inside the Supreme Court.* New York: Simon and Schuster, 1979.

Works Projects Administration. *Houston, Texas: A History and Guide.* Houston: Anson Jones Press, 1945.

Yannakis, Andrew; McIntrye, Thomas D.; Melnick, Merrill J.; and Hart, Dale P. *Sport Sociology: Contemporary Themes.* Dubuque, Iowa: Kendall/Hunt Publishing Company, 1976.

Young, A. S. "Doc." *Great Negro Baseball Stars.* New York: Barnes and Company, 1953.

——————. *Negro Firsts in Sports.* Chicago: Johnson Publishing Company, 1963.

Zinkoff, Dave. *Go, Man, Go!: Around the World with the Harlem Globetrotters.* New York: Pyramid Books, 1958.

NEWSPAPERS

The Aftro-American Newspaper (New York, New York)

The Atlanta Constitution (Atlanta, Georgia)

The Atlanta Independent (Atlanta, Georgia)

The Atlanta Daily World (Atlanta, Georgia)

The Birmingham Reporter (Birmingham, Alabama)

The Boston Chronicle (Boston, Massachusetts)

The Boston Globe (Boston, Massachusetts)

The Boston Guardian (Boston, Massachusetts)

The Brooklyn Daily Union (Brooklyn, New York)

The Brooklyn Times (Brooklyn, New York)

The California Eagle (Los Angeles, California)

The Cape May Star and Wave (Cape May, New Jersey)

The Cedar Rapids Republican (Cedar Rapids, Iowa)

The Chicago Bee (Chicago, Illinois)

The Chicago Defender (Chicago, Illinois)

The Chicago Tribune (Chicago, Illinois)

The City Sun (Brooklyn, New York)

The Cleveland Advocate (Cleveland, Ohio)

The Cleveland Call & Post (Cleveland, Ohio)

The Cleveland Gazette (Cleveland, Ohio)

The Daily Houston Telegraph (Houston, Texas)

The Daily Worker (New York, New York)

The Dallas Times Herald (Dallas, Texas)

The Detroit Free Press (Detroit, Michigan)

The Detroit Plain Dealer (Detroit, Michigan)

The East Tennessee News (Johnson City, Tennessee)

The Galesburg Register (Galesburg, Illinois)

The Harvard Crimson (Harvard University)

The Indianapolis Freeman (Indianapolis, Indiana)

The Interstate Tattler (New York, New York)

The Irish Times (Dublin, Ireland)

The Jamestown Evening Journal (Jamestown, New York)

The London Times (London, England)

The Los Angeles Sentinel (Los Angeles, California)

The Los Angeles Times (Los Angeles, California)

The Louisville Courier Journal (Louisville, Kentucky)

The Macon Telegram (Macon, Georgia)

The Miami Herald (Miami, Florida)

The Minnesota Journal (Mahtomedi, Minnesota)

The Montgomery Advertiser (Montgomery, Alabama)

The Morning Telegraph (New York, New York)

The Morning Transcript (Lexington, Kentucky)

The Nashville Tennessee Banner (Nashville, Tennessee)

The Newark Call (Newark, New Jersey)

The Newark Evening News (Newark, New Jersey)

The New Orleans Daily-Picayune (New Orleans, Louisiana)

The New Orleans Pelican (New Orleans, Louisiana)

The New Orleans Times (New Orleans, Louisiana)

The New Orleans Times-Democrat (New Orleans, Louisiana)

The New Orleans Weekly Louisianian (New Orleans, Louisiana)

The New York Age (New York, New York)

The New York American (New York, New York)

The New York Amsterdam News (New York, New York)

The New York City Illustrated News (New York, New York)

The New York Herald (New York, New York)

The New York Herald-Tribune (New York, New York)

The New York News (New York, New York)

The New York Post (New York, New York)

The New York Sun (New York, New York)

The New York World (New York, New York)

The Norfolk Journal and Guide (Norfolk, Virginia)

The Philadelphia Public Ledger (Philadelphia, Pennsylvania)

The Philadelphia Tribune (Philadelphia, Pennsylvania)

The Pittsburgh American (Pittsburgh, Pennsylvania)

The Pittsburgh Courier (Pittsburgh, Pennsylvania)

The Police Gazette (Ne.v York, New York)

The Record and Sun (Pennsylvania)

The Richmond News Leader (Richmond, Virginia)

The Richmond Planet (Richmond, Virginia)

The Richmond Times-Dispatch (Richmond, Virginia)

The Rochester Democrat and Chronicle (Rochester, New York)

The Rocky Mount Telegram (Rocky Mount, North Carolina)

The Rocky Mountain News (Denver, Colorado)

The Rome Tribune-Herald (Rome, Georgia)

The South Side Signal (Long Island, New York)

The Spirit of the Times

The Sporting Life (Philadelphia, Pennsylvania)

The St. Louis Argus (St. Louis, Missouri)

The St. Louis Post-Dispatch (St. Louis, Missouri)

The St. Louis Star (St. Louis, Missouri)

The Syracuse Standard (Syracuse, New York)

The Times Plain Dealer

The Washington Post (Washington, D.C.)

Tombstone Epitaph (Tombstone, Arizona)

MAGAZINES AND MAGAZINE ARTICLES

Abbotts Monthly

Backstretch

Black Enterprise (New York)

Black Sports (New York)

Black Tennis (Houston, Texas)

Boxing Scene (Palisades, New York)

Lowe, Albert S. "Camp Life of The Tenth U.S. Cavalry." *The Colored American* (Boston, Massachusetts), Volume 7, Number 3, 1904.

Collier's

Commonwealth (Charlottesville, Virginia)

Crisis

Ebony

Edwards, Harry. "Black Athletes and Sports in America." *The Western Journal of Black Studies,* Volume 6, Number 3, Fall 1982.

Esquire

Garvey, Edward R. "From Chattel to Employee: The Athlete's Quest for Freedom And Dignity." *Annals of the American Academy of Political and Social Science*. Vol. 445, September 1979.

Harper's Weekly

Hewetson, W. T. "The Social Life of the Southern Negro." *Chautauquan Magazine,* Volume 26, page 295, October 1897–March 1898.

Inside Sports

Lapchick, Richard E. "South Africa: Sport and Apartheid Politics." *Annals of the American Academy of Political and Social Science,* September 1979.

Lowe, Albert S. "Camp Life of The Tenth U.S. Cavalry." *The Colored American* (Boston, Massachusetts), Volume 7, Number 3, 1904.

New Directions: The Howard University Magazine (Washington, D.C.)

New York Times Sunday Magazine

Newsweek

Opportunity

Racquet Quarterly (New York)

Reach's Official Baseball Guide

Roberts, Milton. "50 Years of the Best in Black College Football." *Black Sports,* June 1976.

——————. "First Black Pro Gridder." *Black Sports,* November 1975.

Spivey, Donald, "The Black Athlete in Big-Time Intercollegiate Sports, 1941–1968." *Phylon,* Volume 44, pages 116–25, June 1983.

Sport

Sports Illustrated

Stumpf, Florence, and Cozens, Fred. "Some Aspects of the Role of Games, Sports and Recreational Activites in the Culture of Modern Primitive Peoples." *Research Quarterly,* 1949.

Tennis (Trumbull; Connecticut)

The Black Scholar (San Francisco)

The Negro History Bulletin

Time

Wiggins, David K. "The Play of Slave Children in the Plantation Communities of the Old South,

1820–1860. *"Journal of Sport History,* Volume 7, Number 2.

——————. "Sport and Popular Pastimes: Shadow of the Slave Quarter." *Canadian Journal of History of Sport and Physical Education,* Vol. 11, May 1980.

ORGANIZATIONS, FOUNDATIONS, AND INSTITUTIONS

The Carter G. Woodson Institute for Afro-American and African Studies, University of Virginia, Charlottesville, Virginia

The Jackie Robinson Foundation

The Jesse Owens Foundation

Moorland Spingarn Research Library, Howard University

Norfolk, Virginia, Public Library

Northern University: Center for the Study of Sport in Society

Schomburg Library for Research in Black Culture

Tuskegee University Archives

Index

Abbott, Cleveland, 108–109
Achebe, Chinua, 7
Acme Colored Giants, 77
African-American AAU National Champions,
    through 1919, 135
African-American Stars on White College Basketball
    Teams, through 1919, 175
African-American Stars on White College Teams,
    through 1919, 136
African-American Jockeys, 125–126
African-American Olympic Medalists, 1904 and
    1908, 135
African-American World Boxing Champions,
    113–124
African-American World Record Holders, through
    1919, 136
Aikens, 97
Akron Indians, 99
Albion Cycle Club, 55
Alcinous, 3
Alexander, A. A., 93
Algona Brownies, 83
Ali, Muhammad, 36, 57
Allen, Dudley, 51
Almeida, Rafael, 85
Alpha Physical Culture Club, 105, 106
Amalinze the Cat, 7
Amateur Athletic Union (AAU), 60, 104
Amenophis II, 3, 58
American Association of Baseball Clubs, 70, 71, 74
American College Baseball Association, 79
American Cycle Racing Association, 56
American Professional Football Association (APFA),
    103
American Racing Cyclists' Union, 57
Anderson, Robert, 105
Anderson, Spider, 49
Anglo-Africans, 21–28
Anson, Adrian "Cap," 71, 74
Apperious, Sam, 78
Apreece, Sir Thomas, 20
Arcaro, Eddie, 48
Aristocles, 4
Aristotle, 4

Armstrong, Bob, 36
Armstrong, Frank, 78
Arthur, Chester A., 72
Atlanta Deppens, 83
Austin, Dan, 50
Austin, Mary, 32
Austin, Sam, 22

Baker, 106
Baker, Charles "Doc," 99
Baker, Henry, 68
Baker, William J., 3, 68
Baldwin, E. J. "Lucky," 47, 51
Baltimore Orioles, 72, 82
Barbot, Jean, 6
Barco, Henry E., 98
Barnard, Robert, 105
Barnes, Shelby "Pike," 49
Barries, Frank, Jr., 48
Barry, Jim, 30
Barton, Sherman, 81
Bass, Tom, 52
Beart, Charles, 58
Becker, W. E., 56
Bell brothers, 107
Bennett, James Gordon, 62
Berenson, Senda, 104
Berger, Sam, 35
Betts, William "Big Greasy," 107
Binga, William, 81
Bird, William "Bill," 51
Bishop, Sylvia, 53
Blackburn, Charles Henry "Jack," 30
Black Codes, 9
Black Football Players at White Colleges,
    1889–1919, 173–174
Blake, Tom, 20
Blassingame, John, 68
Bonner, C., 50
Booker, Pete, 85
Boston Resolutes, 74
Boyd, Ben, 72, 73
Boyle, John, 74
Breland, Wilbert, 52

Bright, J. M., 75, 76
British Empire Games, 59
Britt, Jimmy, 29
Britton, Tom, 49, 51
Brodie, Steve, 31
Brooklyn Atlantics, 72
Brooklyn Royal Giants, 86, 87
Brooks, Frederick, 52
Brooks, Nott, 52
Brotherhood of Professional Baseball Players, 74
Broughton, Jack, 18
Brown, Aaron "Dixie Kid," 25, 30
Brown, Aaron L., 118–119
Brown, Al, 53
Brown, Ed, 51
Brown, Edward "Brown Dick," 51
Brown, Elzy, 52
Brown, Harry, 105, 106
Brown, Henry E., 12
Brown, Joseph, 98
Brown, Morris, 79
Brown, Nathaniel, 93
Brown, Oscar, 79
Brown, Walter, 74
Bryant, James, 79
Buckner, Harry, 81
Buckner, William, 52
Bullock, Matthew, 61, 93, 97
Burke, Thomas E., 63
Burleigh, G. C. H., 63
Burns, 81
Burns, "Professor," 36
Burns, Tommy, 33, 34, 36
Burrows, Jack, 20
Bush, Sam, 52
Bustil, Maria Louisa, 100
Butler, Edward Solomon, 66, 67
Butler, Sol, 109

Cable, Theodore "Ted," 64
Calvin, John, 8
Cameron, Lucille, 38, 41
Camp, Walter, 60, 90, 91, 97, 100, 101, 102
Canton Bulldogs, 99
Carpenter, George, 39
Carpenter, J. C., 64
Carr, Arthur D., 92
Cartwright, Alexander, 68
Caruthers, R. L., 74
Carver, Robin, 11
Cary, Tom, 41
Castiglione, Baldassare, 8
Ceasar, George E., 94
Central Intercollegiate Athletic Association (CIAA), 97
Chadwell, George, 92
Chadwick, Henry, 69
Chalk, Ocania, 78
Charles, 89

Charles, Duke of Orleans, 5
Charles II, 9
Charles V, 5
Charlton, George E., 18
Chestnut, J. L., 105
Chicago American Giants, 84, 86, 87
Chicago Columbia Giants, 82
Chicago Cubs, 84
Chicago Leland Giants, 84
Chicago Union Giants, 82–83, 83, 84
Chicago Unions, 77
Chicago White Sox, 82, 86
Choynsky, Joe, 32, 36
Cincinnati Crowns, 74
Cincinnati Reds, 71–72
Cincinnati Red Stockings, 70, 85
Circus Maximus, 4
Clark, 106
Clark, M. Lewis, 46
Clayton, Abe, 49
Clayton, Alonzo, 49
Clelland, John M., 97
Clement of Rome, 5, 17
Cleveland Panthers, 99
Clifford, Maurice, 105
Cobb, Ty, 85
Coffroth, Jimmy, 35
Cole, Dora, 106
Collins, Eugene, 93
Collins, Fred, 85
Collins, Henry, 97
Colored Intercollegiate Athletic Association (CIAA), 61, 80, 97
Colosseum, 5
Colston, Raleigh, 47, 51
Columbus Buckeyes, 71
Comiskey, Charles, 82
Company E, 106
Conley, Jess, 50
Conway, William, 29
Cook, Charles C., 92, 95
Cook, Victor, 96
Cook, Walter, 73
Cooper, Albert, 51
Corbett, James J., 23, 26, 27, 33, 35, 36, 37
Corella, Frank, 32
Cortés, Hernando, 9
Cotton, George "Kid," 36
Craig, Frank "The Harlem Coffee Cooler," 30
Craig, Ralph, 65
Craighead, William, 92
Crawford, D. D., 79
Crescent Athletic Club, 105
Cribb, Tom, 18–19, 20, 21, 26, 30
Croker, Richard, 49
Crowhurst, E., 50
Cuban Giants, 72, 73, 74, 75, 76
Cuban Stars, 83
Cuban X-Giants, 77, 83, 84

Cumbert, Charles W., 79
Cummings, F. H., 94
Curley, Jack, 40, 41
Curtis, Arthur, 105
Curtis, Harry, 77

Dabney, Milton, 72
Dale, Thomas, 9
Dana, Charles A., 27
Danville (Illinois) Unions, 83
Davenport, Charlie, 10
Davis, A., 76
Davis, Sullivan, 53
Day, Guy, 72
Decater, W. A., 14
Delaney, Billy, 36
Dickerson, Denver, 36, 41
Dickerson, Spencer, 63
Dishmon, C., 50
Dishmon, M., 50
Dismond, Henry Binga, 65
Dixie Kid, 118–119
Dixon, George, 22, 23, 24, 27, 30, 56, 121–124
Dobbs, Bobby, 28, 30
Donaldson, John, 86
Dorsey, 106
Dougherty, Charles, 85
Douglass, Frederick, 10, 21, 59
Drew, Howard Porter, 64–65, 67, 84
Driscoll, Paddy, 101
DuBois, W. E. B., 16, 40, 59
Duffey, Arthur, 65
Duluth Eskimos, 99
Duncan, Frank, 85
Dunlop, John Boyd, 54
Dupree, Jimmy, 52
Durham, 14
Durousseau, Louis, 53
Duryea, Etta, 35, 38
Dwyer, Michael F., 49

Eastern Interstate League, 76
Eato, E. V. C., 12
Edward III, 5, 89
Edward VII, 33
Egan, Pierce, 21
Eggleston, William, 72
Ellerson, L. B., 94
Ellis, William W., 89
Elyiot, Sir Thomas, 8
Epps, J. R., 79
Erberstein, Charles, 39
Erne, Frank, 28
Estees, Mr., 95
Everett, Deborah, 52

Ferguson, J., 66
Figg, James, 17
Fisher, John "Jack," 51
Fisk, 96, 97

Fitzpatrick, Sam, 24, 33, 34
Fitzsimmons, Robert, 27, 38
Flanagan, Tom, 39
Flannigan, Tom, 36
Fleischer, Nat, 22, 25, 41
Flippin, George A., 91
Flynn, Jim, 38
Foley, Larry, 25
Follis, Charles W., 98, 99
Fort Waco (Texas) Yellow Jackets, 84
Foster, Andrew "Rube," 39, 83, 84, 85, 86
Foster, Georgeanna, 53
Fowler, Bud (née John W. Jackson), 70, 71, 77
Francis, James, 77–78
Franklin, John Hope, 10, 68
Franklin, Lester, 52
Frazier, Joe, 36
French Lick (Indiana) Plutos, 83
Frye, Jack, 73, 76
Funderbunk, Bright, 94
Furey, Barney "Doc," 36

Gans, Joe, 16, 25, 28, 57, 119–121
Gardner, Arthur, 56
Garland, C. N., 94
George I, 18
George III, 22
Gilbert, Private, 66
Gillette, James C., 36
Gleason, Jack, 35
Gleason, W. E., 74
Godbald, Hector, 10
Godfrey, George, 25
Goines, Leon J., 52
Gordon, Samuel Simon, 92
Goss, 97
Gould, Alan J., 65
Govern, S. K., 73
Graney, Ed, 29, 35
Granger, W. Randolph, 66
Grant, Charles, 81, 82
Grant, Frank, 75, 76
Grant, Ulysses S., 95
Gray, Edward B., 97, 105
Green, Pete, 52
Gregg, Charlie, 50
Gregory, Eugene, 78
Griffith, D. W., 99
Grillo, J. Ed, 34
Grivat, W. C., 55
Groves, Alfred, 105
Gulick, Luther, Jr., 12

Hadley, Arthur, 92
Haig, W. H., 94
Halas, George, 101
Hall, 106
Halswelle, Wyndham, 64
Hamilton, Andrew, 49

Hamilton, William, 9
Hamilton-Brown, G., 7
Hamlin, Robert, 92
Hampton, Wade, 94
Hampton Institute, 60
Hardy, Arthur, 86
Harper, Frank, 45
Harris, Frank, 72
Harris, Joe, 51
Harris, Nate, 85
Harrison, Abe, 73, 82
Hart, Frank, 59
Hart, Marvin, 32
Hart, Sig, 35, 36
Hartack, William, 50
Haughton, Percy D., 94
Havana Stars, 83
Hawkins, Abe, 46
Henderson, Edwin B., 14, 61, 62, 96, 97, 105
Henderson, Erskine, 49
Henry, Richard, 52
Hereford, Al, 28
Herodotus, 6, 58
Hewlett, Abraham Molineaux, 11, 12
Hicks, J., 50
Hicks, Willie, 50
Higgins, Robert, 76
Highland Games, 59
Hill, Pete, 85
Hill, Preston, 85
Hillman, Harry, 64
Hitchcock, Tommy, 52
Holmes, Ben, 72, 73
Holmes, W. C., 64
Holt, George, 51
Homestead Grays, 107
Hot Springs (Arkansas) Majestic White Sox, 83
Howard, 78
Howe, Irving T., 66
Hubbard, George W., 98
Hubert, Benjamin, 93
Hudgins, Johnny, 50
Hunton, Mrs. Addie, 12
Hunton, William, 12
Hurd, Babe, 49
Hutton, J. H., 94

Ignatius, 5, 17
Incorporators, 106, 107
Indianapolis ABC's, 83, 86, 87
Indianapolis Hoosiers, 72
International League of Independent Professional
    Baseball Clubs (ILIPBC), 83
Intercollegiate Amateur Athletic Association of
    America, 63
Intercollegiate Athletic Association (CIAA), 92–93,
    107
Intercollegiate Conference of Faculty
    Representatives, 91–92

International League, 22
Interscholastic Athletic Association (ISAA), 13–14,
    61, 105
Isthmian Games, 4

Jackson, Alexander Louis, 64
Jackson, Andrew, 44, 45
Jackson, Peter, 25, 26, 27, 28, 30, 33
Jackson, Sherman, 90, 91
Jackson, William Henry Lewis, 63
Jackson, William Tecumseh Sherman, 63, 66
Jacksonville (Florida) Young Receivers, 84
James, Ronald, 52
James I, 9
Jeanette, Joe, 30, 32
Jefferson, Thomas, 44
Jeffries, Edward, 85
Jeffries, Jim, 34, 35, 36, 37, 38
Jersey City YMCA, 105
Jeweth, George, 91
Jockey Club, 50
Jockey Hall of Fame at Pimlico, 50
Johns, Island, 97
Johnson, Ben, 66, 85
Johnson, Byron Bancroft, 85
Johnson, Fred, 22
Johnson, George "Chappie," 81
Johnson, Grant "Home Run," 77, 81, 85, 86
Johnson, Jack, 30, 67, 84, 99, 113–115
Johnson, John Arthur, 30, 34, 35, 36, 37, 38, 39, 40,
    42
Johnson, Junior, 81
Johnson, Lewis S., 105
Johnson, Lucy, 31
Johnson, Robert, 93
Johnson, Walter, 86
Johnson, Wickware, 86
Johnson, William, 10, 21, 59
Johnson, William Arthur, 91
Johnson, William N., 92
Joiner, W. A., 14
Jones, Alfred D., 79
Jones, Tom, 40
Joyner, Bill, 82

Kansas City Blue Diamonds, 106
Kansas City Giants, 83, 86
Kansas City Royal Giants, 83
Kelly, Tommy, 22
Kentucky Derby, 22
Kerr, Clara, 32, 34
Ketchel, Stanley, 36
Key Races Stakes Won by African-American
    Jockeys, 127–130
Kindle, William, 93, 94, 108
King, Charles, 74
Knickerbockers, 68, 69

Lamar, E. B., 77
Landis, Kennesaw Mountain, 39

Lang, John L., 73
Langford, Sam, 30, 36
Langston, John, 90
Lashley, Joe, 21
Lathram, W. A., 74
Lattimore, George, 105
Lattimore, Robert, 105
Lavigne, George "Kid," 24
Law, Horton, 25
Law, Lewis, 25, 35
Lazzareff, Michael, 50
League of American Wheelmen (LAW), 55
League of Colored Baseball Clubs (LCBC), 74
Le Carré, John, 39
Leckie, William E., 14
Lee, Howard J., 92
Lee, Jimmy, 49, 126
Leeds, Tom, 25
Leland, Frank C., 83, 84
Leland Giants, 86
Leroy, Paul, 100
Levis, Henry, 94
Lew, Gerald, 93
Lewis, Cecil, 66
Lewis, George, 49
Lewis, Oliver, 46, 49
Lewis, Walter, 31
Lewis, William H., 22, 97
Lewis, William Henry, 90, 91
Lilly, Marshall, 52, 53
Lincoln, Abraham, 11
Lincoln Giants, 87
Little, George, 35, 36
Livingston, Odell, 52
Lloyd, John, 84, 85, 86
Lloyd, John Henry, 84, 85
Loendi Big Five, 107, 108
London, Jack, 34
Loudon, Henry, 52
Louis, Joe, 30, 41
Louisville Eclipses, 71
Louisville Fall Citys, 74, 83
Louis X, 5

MacArthur, Douglas, 78
Mack, Connie, 86
Madden, Will, 106
Maddox, Ethel Posey, 79
Maddox, George, 18
Mahoney, 106
Mailer, Norman, 36
Mann Act, 39
Marathone Athletic Club, 105
Marsans, Armando, 85
Marshall, Ernie, 92
Marshall, Napoleon Bonaparte, 63
Marshall, Robert "Bobby," 93, 99
Martin, "Denver" Ed, 32
Martin, Howard, 66

Mason, Johnny, 52
Massillon Tigers, 98
Matthews, William Clarence, 78, 92, 95
Mattingly, R. N., 14
McCarthy, Cal, 22
McCarthy, Molly, 45
McCary, Tom, 35
McClay, Hattie, 35
McClelland, Dan, 83, 85
McCurdy, Robert, 53
McDonald, Henry, 99
McDowell, 50
McGinnis, Paul, 52
McGovern, Terry, 24, 28
McGrath, H. Price, 45, 46
McGraw, John, 85
McGraw, John J., 82
McGraw, Muggsy, 82
McIntosh, Hugh "Huge Deal," 33, 34, 35
McMahon, Jess, 86
McVey, Sam, 30
Mears, Charles M., 56
Mellody, Billy "Honey," 25
Memphis Tigers, 83
Mendoza, David, 18
Menocal, Mario, 40
Meredith, James E., 66
Meredith, Ted, 66
Meridian (Mississippi) Southern Giants, 83
Metz, W. L., 94
Middle States League, 76
Miller, 81
Miller, G. Smith, 90
Miller, George, 52
Mills, Dave, 36
Milwaukee Athletic Club, 64
Minnesota Marines, 99
Mitchell, Charles, 27
Mitchell, Willie, 52
Molineaux, Algernon, 19, 20, 21
Molineaux, Tom, 17, 19, 26, 124
Monticello Delaney Rifles, 106, 107
Moore, Chester, 105
Moore, George "Docky," 18
Moore, Harry, 85
Moran, Frank, 40
Morrill Act of 1890, 13, 92
Morrow, Will, 94
Motin, R., 72
Muldrow, H. H., 94
Munger, Louis "Birdie," 54
Murphy, Green, 47
Murphy, Isaac, 47, 48, 51, 53, 57, 71, 125–126
Murphy, Lucy, 47, 48
Murphy, Michael C., 63, 65
Murphy, Mr., 94–95
Muscular Christianity Movement, 12
Myer, A. T., 65

Nabrit, James, Jr., 79–80
Nabrit, James M., 79
Naismith, James, 104
National Association for the Advancement of
    Colored People (NAACP), 40, 86
National Association of Baseball Players (NABBP),
    69
National Association of Colored Baseball Clubs of
    America and Cuba, 83
National Association of Professional Baseball
    Players (NAPBBP), 70
National Basketball League (NBL), 104
National Collegiate Athletic Association (NCAA), 93
National Colored Professional Baseball League, 83
National Cycling Association (NCA), 56
National Football League (NFL), 98, 103
National League of Professional Baseball Clubs
    (NLPBBC), 70, 71, 74
Nemean Games, 4
New England Colored League, 84
New York Athletic Club (NYAC), 59
New York Gorhams, 72, 74, 75
New York Lincoln Giants, 86
New York Metropolitans, 71, 72
Nicholls, Richard, 44
Nichols, Charles, 72
Nielson, Oscar M. "Battling Nelson," 29
Nix, Bill, 59
Nixon, Henry T., 105
Nolan, Billy, 29
Norfolk (Virginia) Red Stockings, 74, 75, 83
Norris, 107
Norton, Charles, 71

Odd Fellows, 60
Oliver, 97
Oliver, Hudson J., 105
Olympia Club, 22
Olympian Athletic League, 105
Olympic Games, 4, 5, 64, 104
Oneida Football Club, 90
O'Neill, J. E., 74
O'Neill, James, 74
O'Rourke, John, 83
O'Rourke, Tom, 22, 24, 25
Overton, Monk, 49
Owens, James Cleveland "Jesse," 67
Owings, Richard, 47
Oxford Pros, 99

P. B. S. Pinchbacks, 74
Page Fence Giants, 77
Parego, George, 72
Parker, Hale, 93
Park Owners Association (POA), 84
Parmer, Charles, 43, 50
Parrot, Harold, 78
Patrick, Charles H., 94
Patterson, John "Pat," 81
Patton, George, 52

Payne, Andrew, 85
Penn Relay Carnival, 60
Pensacola Giants, 83
Percy, Hugh, 18
Perkins, James "Soup," 49
Perkins, William, 51
Perrossier, Arthur, 52
Perry, Alex, 51
Peterson, H. L., 94
Petway, Bruce, 85
Phidippides, 58
Philadelphia Athletics, 72
Philadelphia Giants, 83, 84
Philadelphia Phillies, 86
Philadelphia Professionals, 83
Philadelphia Pythians, 74
Phillips, James, 92
Pickens, Wil, 38
Pinder, Norman, 36
Pineau, Irene Marie, 41
Pinkett, John, 93
Pittsburgh Alleghenys, 72
Pittsburgh Keystones, 74, 75
Plair, S. M., 94
Plato, 4
Poage, George, 64
Pocahontas, 9
Poles, Spot, 86
Police Athletic Leagues (PALs), 62
Pollard, Frederick Douglass "Fritz," 100, 101, 102,
    103
Pollard, Leslie, 93, 97, 102
Posey, Cumberland, 79, 106, 107, 108
Posey, Seward, 106
Prather, M., 94
Price, Ap Rhys, 20
Prosser, Gabriel, 19
Public Schools Athletic League (PSAL), 62
Pythian Games, 4

Quaker Giants, 83
Quinn, Pat, 64

Rader, Benjamin G., 59
Radford, Calvin, 94
Rainwater, W. E., 79
Randolph, John, 95
Ransom, Samuel, 92, 97, 108
Ravenelle, Jim, 66
Raymond, H. E., 55
Redding, "Cannonball" Dick, 86
Red Stockings, 71
Reed, Clarence, 50
Reed, Harry, 49
Register of African-American Managers, 1872–1919,
    137–170
Register of African-American Officials, 1872–1919,
    137–170
Register of African-American Players, 1872–1919,
    137–170

Register of African-American Umpires, 1872–1919, 137–170
Rencher, R. J., 94
Reynolds, 81
Rhodes, Gus, 38
Richardson, Hosea Lee, 53
Richmond, 107
Richmond, Bill, 124
Richmond, William, 17, 20, 21, 30
Richmond Virginians, 72
Rickard, George Lewis "Tex," 29, 35, 36, 37
Rickey, Branch, 78, 98
Ricks, James "Pappy," 107
Riverton-Palmyra Athletics, 83
Robbins, W. C., 64
Roberts, 98
Roberts, Anthony, 29
Rooberts, Charles E., 92
Roberts, Milton, 97
Roberts, Milton, All-Time Black College Squad, 171–173
Robeson, Paul, 66, 100, 101
Robeson, William Drew, 100
Robinson, Howard, 79
Robinson, Jackie, 78, 101
Robinson, Merton P., 77
Robinson, Sam, 21
Robinson, W. H., 74
Rochester Jeffersons, 99
Rock Island Independents, 99
Rogers, Dewey, 63
Rogers, Will, 52
Roosevelt, Theodore, 15, 57, 92
Ross, Chester, 53
Ross, Clinton, 93–94
Rousseau, Jean-Jacques, 8
Rowan, Carl T., 101

St. Christopher Athletic Club, 105
St. Christopher Five, 106
St. Cyprian Athletic Club, 105
St. Louis Browns, 71
Sande, Earle, 48
Santop, Luis, 86
Schiffer, Frank C., 98
Schlicter, Walter, 83
Schorling, John, 86
Schrieber, Belle, 35, 39
Scott, Angus, 52
Scott, Clifford, 52
Scott, Emmett J., 39
Scrotton, Charles, 105
See-Saw Circle Club, 55
Selden, William, 76
Sessoms, James "Stretch," 107
Sheehan, Jack, 24
Shelby Athletic Association, 98
Shelton, Tom, 21
Shipley, Hugh, 94

Shute, C. H., 94
Siler, George, 29
Silk League, 80
Simm, Willie, 126
Simms, A., 52
Simms, Willie, 49
Simon, "Monkey," 44, 45
Simpson, R., 50
Sitgraves, Carl, 52
Skelly, Jack, 23, 56
Slater, Fred "Duke," 66
Slaughter, Fred M., 97
Slaughter, John H., 26
Smart, Matthew, 52
Smart Set Club, 62, 105, 106
Smith, Billy, 24
Smith, Francis, 11, 59
Smith, Gideon E., 99
Smith, Harry, 83
Smith, Howard, 63
Smith, Jim, 26
Smith, John, 9
Smith, Solly, 24
Smoot, Charlie, 52
Somers, Dale, 73
Southern Intercollegiate Association, 91
Southern Intercollegiate Athletic Conference (SIAC), 107
Southern League of Colored Base Ballists, 73
Spencer, Herbert, 15
Stagg, Amos Alonzo, 65, 91
Staples, Fred, 95
Stentonworth Athletic Club, 105
Stephenson, Joseph, 21
Stevens, John Cox, 11
Stewart, Colston R., 61
Stewart, Henry "The St. Louis Flyer," 55
Stoval, John, 49, 51
Stovey, George, 73, 74
Strong, Nat, 85
Strothers, 92
Sullivan, Dave, 24
Sullivan, John L., 23, 26, 27, 31, 34, 36
Sullivan, Mike, 29
Sutton, Frank, 36

Talladega, 96
Tanner, David, 47
Tarlton, L. P., 48
Tattersol, Jack, 98
Taylor, Edward, 56
Taylor, Frank, 51
Taylor, Gilbert, 54
Taylor, J. J., 94
Taylor, John Baxter "Doc," 63, 64, 65–66, 84
Taylor, Marshall, 31, 33
Taylor, Marshall "Major," 54, 56, 57, 84
    Bicycle Racing Record, 1891–1908, 131–135
Tecumseh, William, 90

Tennessee Rats, 86
Terry, Floyd Wellman "Terrible," 96
Tertullian, 5
Thomas, Arthur, 73, 76
Thomas, Charles Lee, 78
Thomas, Henry, 92
Thompkins, Sim, 30
Thompson, Bob, 31
Thompson, Frank, 72, 73
Thorpe, Jim, 99
Titus, Fred, 56
Tokahama, Charlie, 82
Toledo Mudhens, 71
Topeka Giants, 83
Treadwell, Fred, 52
Trent, William T., 94, 95
Trice, George, 105
Trigg, Joseph, 93, 102
Trusty, Shep, 73
Tuskegee Institute, 13, 60
Tyler, Frank, 52

Union Athletic Club, 22

Veal, T. R., 94
Villa, Pancho, 40
Villard, J. R., 94
Von der Ahe, Chris, 74
Vulcan Athletic Club (VAL), 62, 64

Wagner, Honus, 84
Walcott, Joe, 24, 25, 30, 32, 116–118
Walker, Moses Fleetwood, 70, 71, 74, 76, 77
Walker, "Silver," 51
Walker, Weldy, 71, 75
Walker, William "Billy," 45, 49, 51
Wallace, Felix, 85
Wallace, Lew, 92
Wallace, Nunc, 22
Ward, Andy, 65
Ward, Drew, 65
Ward, Joe, 20
Ward, John M., 74
Warner, 97
Warrne, Earl, Jr., 53
Washington, Booker T., 16, 39, 78, 79, 99
Washington, George, 66
Washington, James B., 13, 60
Washington, William, 92

Washington Capitol Citys, 74
Washington Mutuals, 70
Washington Nationals, 72
Watkins, Fenwich H., 79, 93, 108
Welch, Curt, 74
Welch, Jack, 40
West, Ed, 49
West, Tommy, 24
West Balden Sprugels, 83
Whaler, J. W., 94
Wheeler, H. H., 92
White, Billy, 73, 76
White, Johnny, 28
White, Raymond, 52
White, Solomon, 73, 76, 81, 82, 83
White, William Allen, 13
Whitney, Caspar, 60
Wickware, Frank, 86
Wiggins, David K., 10
Wilkinson, G. C., 14
Willard, Jess, 40
Williams, 102
Williams, Atkin, 50
Williams, Clarence, 73
Williams, George, 73, 76
Williams, George Walter, 78
Williams, H. C., 91
Williams, James, 51
Williams, James T., 47
Williams, Leroy, 50
Williams, Robert "Tiny," 49
Williams, Schley C., 66
Williams, "Smokey Joe," 86
Williams, William H., 92
Wilmington Giants, 83
Wilson, George, 81
Winkfield, Jimmy, 49, 50, 51, 57, 126
Winterwood, Charles, 92
Wissahickon School Club, 105, 106
Withers, George, 49
Wood, Wilbur, 108
Wooster Athletic Association, 98
Wright, George, 22

Yelverton, J. B. A., 94
Young, Ray, 92
Young, William T., 107
Young Men's Christian Association (YMCA), 12–13, 59